ANTI-APARTHEID

Studies in Human Rights
Series Editor: *George W. Shepherd, Jr.*

The Politics of Race and International Sport: The Case of South Africa
Richard Edward Lapchick

White Wealth and Black Poverty: American Investments in Southern Africa
Barbara Rogers

ANTI-APARTHEID

Transnational Conflict and Western Policy in the Liberation of South Africa

GEORGE W. SHEPHERD, Jr.

Graduate School of International Studies
Center on International Race Relations, University of Denver

Studies in Human Rights, Number 3

GREENWOOD PRESS
Westport, Connecticut • London, England

Library of Congress Cataloging in Publication Data

Shepherd, George W
  Anti-apartheid.

  (Studies in human rights ; no. 3)
  Includes bibliographical references and index.
  1. South Africa—Race relations. I. Title. II. Series.
DT763.S39   301.45'1'0968   77-71868
ISBN 0-8371-9537-3

Copyright © 1977 by Center on International Race Relations

Library of Congress Catalog Card Number: 77 71868
ISBN: 0-8371-9537-3
ISSN: 0146-3586

First published in 1977

Greenwood Press, Inc.
51 Riverside Avenue, Westport, Connecticut 06880

Printed in the United States of America

*To Clara Sargent Shepherd
and George W. Shepherd*

CONTENTS

PREFACE

Anti-apartheid is much more than a slogan or a movement; it is an idea which captures the essence of the human-rights concern of this era—decolonization and liberation of the majority of the human race from Western racial-economic domination. While the struggle against forms of racism is universal in its sources of support, this study attempts to analyze and understand only one part of the worldwide movement against apartheid. But it is concerned with "the belly of the beast"—the very center of the problem—namely, structural support for apartheid in the United States and the United Kingdom and American and British nongovernmental opposition to it.

The material for this study stems from over twenty years of involvement, research, and organizational activity, during which I have functioned as a participant-observer. In a subject where there is no neutral ground, the best research is by those who declare their own biases and try to stand outside themselves with as much objectivity as possible.

Innumerable opportunities and much assistance have been given to me for this work by a variety of organizations, educational institutes, and individuals. The Graduate School of International Studies and, in particular, the Center for International Race Relations have provided me with leaves and financial aid of critical importance, as well as editing and secretarial help. However, the major institution to whom credit is due is UNITAR of the United Nations, which, under Dr. Davidson Nichol's direction, first saw clearly the importance of this subject and granted me a fellowship to undertake it. Through two panels of intensive discussion of preliminary papers, United Nations and NGO representatives criticized and helped to shape the early stages. UNITAR has kindly given permission for the publication of several of the papers in revised form here. Several individuals at the United Nations, including Oscar Schacter, Berhanykun Andemicael, Robert Jordan E. S. Reddy, Sean MacBride, and several delegation representatives from Europe, Africa, as well as the United States and the United Kingdom, were very helpful, even when they disagreed and their policies were subjected to criticism. Several groups and institutes (better left anonymous) in South Africa have also been helpful. Should this study find its way to them through the censor's ban, I express my gratitude and debt to them and their activities and research and salute their courage. To my alma mater, the London School of Economics, and their fine library, as well as the British press, where courtesy and interest was shown me, I express thanks I can never repay.

The NGOs who cooperated with me in this study have all been cited and given credit. Their cooperation is especially appreciated since they gave time and thought to a study which seemed far removed from the daily problems of decision making, funding, and keeping going, which test the mettle and objectives of these men and women too numerous to mention here. I hope this study will reassure them and in some way help their important work, which we scholars greatly respect and frequently envy.

Finally, to those in the Ford Foundation who were willing to fund controversial research, I express my sincere thanks. The final result is my full responsibility. I only hope those who took the time and helped pay the costs will find the result worthy of their confidence.

GEORGE W. SHEPHERD, JR.

FREQUENTLY USED NGO ABBREVIATIONS

AAI	African American Institute
AAM	Anti-Apartheid Movement (U.S., Britain, Europe)
ACOA	American Committee on Africa
AHSA	African Heritage Studies Association (U.S.)
AI	Amnesty International (U.S., Britain)
AMSAC	African American Society for African Culture (U.S.)
ANC	African National Congress (of South Africa)
ASA	African Studies Association (U.S.)
BCC	British Council of Churches
BPC	Black Peoples Convention (South Africa)
CARD	Campaign Against Racial Discrimination (U.S.)
CBC	Congressional Black Caucus (U.S.)
CCI	Committee on Corporate Information (U.S.)
CCSA	Council for Christian Social Action (U.S.) also: Christians Concerned About South Africa (Britain)
CI	Christian Institute (South Africa)
CORE	Congress on Racial Equity (U.S)
CSC	Christian Student Movement (Britain)
FNLA	Front for the National Liberation of Angola
FRELIMO	Front for the Liberation of Mozambique
ICFTU	International Confederation of Trade Unions
ICJ	International Commission of Jurists (Geneva)
IDAF	International Defense and Aid Fund
IFCO	Interreligious Foundation for Community Organization (U.S.)

IRR	Institute of Race Relations (London) also: Institute of Race Relations (South Africa)
IUEF	International University Exchange Fund
LSM	Liberation Support Movement (U.S.)
LWF	Lutheran World Federation
MPLA	Popular Movement for the Liberation of Angola
NAACP	National Association for the Advancement of Colored People
NCC	National Council of Churches
NUSAS	National Union of South African Students
OPEC	Organization of Petroleum Exporting Countries
PAC	Pan African Congress (South Africa)
PAIGC	African Party for the Independence of Guinea and Cape Verde
PLAN	Peoples Liberation Army of Namibia
PRP	Progressive Reform Party (South Africa)
SAC	Southern Africa Committee (U.S.)
SAN-ROC	South African Non-Racial Olympic Committee
SASO	South African Student Organization
SNCC	Student Nonviolent Coordinating Council (U.S.)
SPROCAS	Study Project on Christianity in Apartheid Society
SWANU	South West African National Union
SWAPO	South West African Peoples Organization
UCC	United Church of Christ (U.S.)
UNDP	United Nations Development Program
UNITA	National Union for Total Independence of Angola
UNITAR	United Nations Institute for Training and Research
USSALEP	United States South Africa Leadership Exchange Program
WCC	World Council of Churches
WFTU	World Federation of Trade Unions
ZANU	Zambian African National Union
ZAPU	Zambian African Peoples Union

ANTI-APARTHEID

chapter 1

TRANSNATIONAL REVOLUTION AGAINST APARTHEID

In a century filled with conflicts between nations and races, the struggle against apartheid, as a form of human bondage, has become a central issue for the world. South African racism, as the final focal point of white Western power in Africa, has been under attack by nationalist and revolutionary movements for more than sixty years.

Western interests in Africa are centered in South Africa, despite the official rejection of her racial way of life, and, in the name of "peaceful change" and resistance to "Communist expansion," the Western powers provide the means for resistance to African rule.

Apartheid

Apartheid is the concept coined by the Afrikaners in the early 1940s to claim the inevitability of white dominance in this region of Southern Africa, whose northern and western boundary is the Cunene River and whose eastern boundary is the Zambezi.[1]

Dr. D. F. Malan, leader of the Nationalist opposition party, in his first use of the term *apartheid* in Parliament, June 24, 1944, spoke of a policy "to ensure the safety of the white race and of Christian civilization by the honest maintenance of the principles of apartheid and guardianship."[2] Later, in 1947, a Nationalist Party commission equated such a policy with separate development: "The policy of our country should encourage total apartheid as the ultimate goal of a national process of separate development.''[3] Thus, the concepts are interchangeable and both mean supremacy, although Nationalist Party spokesmen have attempted in recent years to use *separate development* rather than *apartheid* when speaking to external audiences because *apartheid* has become synonymous with *racism.*

Not all whites in South Africa support apartheid either in theory or in practice. Many are part of the anti-apartheid movement; yet most believe they are gradually reforming and need time to achieve a change from apartheid to a more equitable social system. The United Party, the official opposition party, has its own way of defining the necessity for white leadership, and even the Progressive Reform Party, while denouncing apartheid, is an exclusively white party as required by law.[4]

In a similar vein, the Rhodesian whites, although they have ridiculed the theory of apartheid, have insisted upon white rule and have proclaimed its necessity for the next one thousand years.[5] Thus, apartheid is not simply a racial theory but a way of life that perpetuates settler rule in Southern Africa and has lifeline links overseas within the Atlantic world.

African nationalists have denounced and opposed this doctrine both peacefully and violently. Also, through liberation movements, Southern Africans, internally and externally, have resisted the continuation of white supremacist rule in their countries, which they now call Zimbabwe, Namibia, and Azania (South Africa). These liberation movements have found not only pan-African support but also considerable moral and material backing throughout the world from anti-apartheid movements. Thus, a major conflict is under way among these interests, groups, races, and nations, in which the central issue is white supremacy and its dependency upon Western power versus the populist and equalitarian African nationalists, supported by the anti-apartheid movement and the socialist states. It is not only a national struggle but is increasingly an international class and racial conflict.

Racial Revolution

The South African conflict is a racial revolution with a class base, which has grown gradually into an international war. Therefore, its resolution depends upon measures relevant to a conflict of war and revolution. The kind of reconciliation possible after the violence has run its course depends upon the recognition of the true nature of the conflict by the various parties concerned.

This conflict is already an international conflict. The resolution of the apartheid issue is central to the continued maintenance of world order and all the related interests of peace. It cannot be brushed aside as an African problem or a domestic issue for the South Africans to work out for themselves.

The revolution is primarily racial because in South Africa, as Van den Berghe and Adam have demonstrated, race predetermines class.[6] Yet the class structure of capitalism in South Africa is built upon race and dependent for its continuance on migratory, cheap, segregated labor. It is true that a small middle-class African elite has emerged in South Africa, with privileges and interests different from the migratory laboring class, but in contrast to their counterparts elsewhere in Africa, their identification with the underclass is assured by the racial system of apartheid, which prevents assimilation. Thus, many middle-class Africans are revolutionaries, especially after the Soweto riots in June 1976.[7]

Elsewhere in Africa, this elite is characterized by high consumption and an antirevolutionary attitude stemming from its control of the local political system. The attempt of progressive capitalists to form an alliance with this African elite is at the root of the various white reform movements in South Africa, Rhodesia, and Namibia. They have been frustrated to date by the racial fears of the whites, who refuse to grant any real power to blacks. The Transkei pseudo-state is sovereign in name only, as financial and military authority have not been transferred, and most of the remaining Bantustan leaders oppose the government's policy and have indicated unwillingness to move toward such pseudo independence.[8]

Revolutionary warfare has broken out with greater intensity in Rhodesia and Namibia, where the settler interest is weaker. To counter this, South Africa has sought, through "détente," to facilitate alliances between the African elite and settler interests forged in these marginal areas. The economic dependence of these groups on South African financial, industrial, and communications facilities will make it impossible—South Africa hopes—for Africans to threaten the center of white supremacy, provided the moderate African elite takes over, rather than the "Marxist" liberation leaders.

Anti-Apartheid

The anti-apartheid movement is a part of this racial class revolution. It, of course, has several component parts: the exiled and imprisoned leaders of all races; the internal opposition to apartheid; the various groups, classes, parties, organizations in the "homelands"; as well as the external movements, intellectuals, organizations (essentially nongovernmental) which are the focus of this study. Many governments from various parts of the world are also a part of the anti-apartheid movement. Their activities tend to cluster around the United Nations and its related organizations.

Who is anti-apartheid and who is not is not easily determined since, outside of Southern Africa, it is a broad-based cause. Many governments and groups present their policies as opposed to South Africa's apartheid when, in fact, the reverse is true. However, one of the important objectives of this study is to differentiate between those policies which support the transnational revolution and those which in reality help sustain the system of white rule.

The understanding of this distinction begins with the conception of the nature of the conflict.

Social science has not been very accurate or useful in assessing these questions, because of its predisposition to the status quo or to gradual-and-peaceful-change alternatives. Only a theoretical framework that is able to encompass revolution and liberation struggles is suitable to the study of anti-apartheid. This view must take into account the more fundamental revolutionary forces of populist consciousness and class in Western civilization, as especially operative over the last 150 years. Most contemporary social science, with its amoral, pseudoscientific pretensions and especially its Western status-quo bias, has shed very little light on the subject.

Antislavery

Emancipation, with all its significant yet limited results, was achieved by the nineteenth-century abolition movement. Today, the abolition of apartheid remains the goal of the twentieth-century liberation and decolonization movement. Many have long considered apartheid a form of slavery (forced labor). Thus the attack upon apartheid is a continuation of the abolition movement. The attorney general of Alabama, in 1974, took action against the importation of coal from South Africa on the ground that the coal was produced by slave labor or indentured labor under penal sanctions.[9]

The dynamic of revolutionary change against forms of human oppression over the past 150 years from abolition to anti-apartheid is fundamentally an equalitarian drive of the human spirit, developing a universal equalitarian consciousness as basic as the laws of thermodynamics. As Teilhard de Chardin has stated: "Driven by the forces of love, the fragments of the world seek each other so that the world may come to being." This universal consciousness has become a populist force, challenging inequalities based on race, class, or caste, and all ideologies, religions, classes, and nations which sustain the systems of racial inequality.[10]. Thus, conflict stems from the transnational revolutionary spirit which aims at the leveling of all stratification barriers of groups, from state to class. Both classical liberal democracy, and modern Marxism have provided useful concepts for understanding this struggle for the realization of human rights. The idea of the inevitability of the success of the powerless against the oppressive forms of bondage in our age has been called Utopian, because its ideals are far from realized; yet, it remains a primary motivational force.[11] And "realists" who discount it have generally wound up on the counterrevolutionary side.

The original vision has deep roots in various civilizations and received new impetus in the Renaissance around a new concept of human dignity implicit in the Judaic-Christian heritage of the West. However, to limit its source to the West would be absurd in this era of Third World revolution. Gandhi, Mao, Luthuli, and Nyerere are all major leaders from non-Western societies whose revolutionary spirits have made major contributions to the spread of "the leveling spirit" in the twentieth century. Marxist and Socialist revolutions are branches of this populist, human-rights movement. The democratic revolutions in England, France, and America are earlier manifestations corrupted by virtue of their success and prosperity.

Class struggle is a modern manifestation of the equalitarian spirit, based upon new economic needs created by capitalism and industrialization and the modern major dependency systems of multinational corporations and state capitalism. Rivalry between the democratic and socialist revolutions should be seen as the hatred of brothers. Marx, after all, gave a modern "scientific" rationale for the early communalism preached by the Christian Church, which was lost in the avarice of the church-become-state and buried by the worship of private property by the Protestants of the Industrial Revolution.

The "powerless" today are not only those who are oppressed but also those who identify with them, share their suffering, feel their aspirations, and struggle for the transformation and overthrow of the social structures and ideas which perpetuate racial and other forms of inequality. They are generally without conventional power in the sense of wealth or military or political position. They are the opposition and underground in South Africa. They are the exiles, the African liberation forces, the black groups, civil-rights organizations, ecumenical churches, and left-wing groups, who support freedom for South Africa. Their strategies range from moderate to radical and revolutionary, but all are caught up in the varied manifestations of the leveling, populist, anti-apartheid movement. Rivalries over ideology and strategy should not obscure the breadth of the movement, which has many martyrs of all races, and has seen much suffering from loss of livelihood to death of guerrilla fighters. But the powerless continue to exist and are supported by a growing ethos of world sympathy, which has no clearly articulated belief system or organizational form. Ben Bella, a revolutionary Algerian leader, once compared the guerrillas to the fish who swim in the sea. In this case, the broad equalitarian consciousness of people is the sea that sustains the anti-apartheid movement.

During the nineteenth century, in those countries which still maintained slavery despite growing international outrage, there emerged transnational movements opposed to the inhuman system, where governments continued to defend it. The process was one of intellectual and economic interaction across national boundaries, frequently in conflict with powerful interests and officials. There was little international organization at that time, but there was international law and morality. The British Empire, for its own interests, banned the international slave trade and attempted enforcement with wide influence particularly in Africa and the New World. The United States was in the same position as South Africa today, in that she sought to maintain her system of bondage, despite the transnational and international revolutionary pressures, and finally plunged into Civil War over an issue that could not be resolved by nonviolent means. Many Southerners who deplored the system were unable to give up a way of life based on exploitation. After the bloodiest war of that era, emancipation, though by no means complete freedom, was achieved for American blacks. Many nineteenth-century antislavery activists were paternalistic do-gooders, who failed to appreciate the full dignity of the Negro person and his culture and the economic class bases of servitude. Similarly, many modern anti-apartheid advocates often have failed to understand the depths of racial, economic and social discrimination. Like his predecessors, the apartheid abolitionist is a product of the times, caught up in a struggle all the implications of which he does not fully understand, yet who is directed through all the confusion and conflict by an awareness of the universal leveling law of equality, manifested in the racial class struggle.

The old debate over humanitarian versus economic determinants in the abolition of slavery continues today in relation to the modern apartheid issue. Economic determinists saw the end of slavery primarily as a necessary industrial change to "wage slavery," while humanists stressed the value changes.[12] Obviously, both influences were at work on the slavery issue as they are today with apartheid.

The entrenched interests opposing the anti-apartheid groups— military, corporate, and racial—have important parallels with the abolition period, as well. This structural support for apartheid is not limited to South Africa but pervades the culture and elitism of the Atlantic world.

There is clearly a direct line of descent from the emancipation ideas of the eighteenth and nineteenth centuries and contemporary self-determination ideas of freedom for colonial people, and the anti-apartheid movement. An African political scientist has pointed out how this world movement must not be minimized or limited to an African phenomenon:

It would be a mistake to focus upon the domestic African response as the main factor in the formation of world attitudes. For one thing, it was not so much the opposition within South Africa to apartheid but the worldwide revolt against colonialism in the post war period especially that not only encouraged hopes and militancy on the part of South African blacks themselves, but also dramatized the world-wide rejection of the imperialist order then passing, of which South Africa was both a remnant and a potent symbol.[13]

One of the most important differences from the past is the scope of the threat to world peace. The danger of racial war in southern Africa escalating into a major war is very real.[14] Raw materials essential to the Great Powers are mined in this area, and it is surrounded by strategic oceans they seek to dominate. While the initial issue of the American Civil War was not slavery but protectionism, the human issue soon inflamed the conflict to the point where the original differences were forgotten. Bloodshed, ethnic kinship, historic relationships, and appeals to patriotism, have a way of taking hold and turning the most rational of us into unyielding partisans.

Under the modernizing impact of technology, the influences of nongovernmental organizations across national lines are far greater today than ever before. The most obvious example of this is the multinational corporation, which frequently maintains technical staffs and budgets in smaller countries greater than that of the governments concerned. In addition, numerous education and culture groups, as well as political organizations, have a pattern of interaction internationally which has existed previously only within national boundaries.[15]

Finally, the self-liberation of the victims of apartheid is far more significant than the way in which the slaves were freed—by paternalistic abolition. Few slave revolts outside of Haiti succeeded for long. Abolition was essentially a conflict between dominant white groups, whereas liberation today is under the primary impetus of the oppressed, with abolitionists playing an auxiliary role, as FRELIMO,

PAIGC, and MPLA in former Portuguese Africa demonstrated in their anticolonial revolution.

Concepts

Several concepts are employed in this study. These need explanation:

The Atlantic System

The Atlantic system is a concept drawn from regional and dependency theory.[16] It is used to indicate the interdependence of the Western industrialized core powers and the dependency of South Africa in that system.[17] The Atlantic core system is in varying stages of conflict with other regional systems of the world, such as commodity cartels, OPEC, and communist regional systems, as well as the OAU, over white minority rule. Major countries in the Atlantic system and the Sino-Soviet systems are competitors, as Galtung has observed, for the transitional peripheral areas. Only in a broad sense does the North-South split describe the world dependency system. The real conflict is core regional systems competing for the Third World periphery, which systems increasingly assert their independence and raise the price and terms of continuing trade and association through OPEC, CAP, the UNCTAD negotiations, and numerous world forums.

Within this Atlantic system there are core powers, semiperipheral range powers and peripheral areas. South Africa is seen as a semiperipheral power of the system which has a high degree of dependency upon the core powers (the United States, the United Kingdom, Germany, and France) while providing essential services to them. South Africa also acts as a subsidiary of Atlantic capitalist powers to penetrate economically the rest of the Southern African periphery. This dependency relationship of South Africa upon Western powers is defined in numerous ways, but particularly in cultural, military, technological, and corporate terms. Much confusion has been caused by the failure to perceive South Africa's role as essentially an extension of the Atlantic world in Africa.

The Transnational Actors

The transnational actors within the Atlantic system are part of the interdependent network of relationships which integrate the system and at the same time provide the basis for conflict within the system. As defined by Nye and Keohane,[19] transnational actors are nongovernmental groups based on interests, ethnicity, race, ideology, and class. They cut across state boundaries, influencing cultural, racial, and political decisions within the system. Some are in close association with the existing governmental policies, while others are in direct conflict. It is this latter group—the conflict-oriented transnational human-rights actors working against apartheid—who are the major focus of this study.

Several of the transnational human-rights nongovernmental organizations (NGOs) are nonviolent in conviction and strategy. The liberation movements are also transnational actors and have both a revolutionary and a nonviolent dimension, reinforcing each other. The distinction made here between human-rights NGOs and the interest groups has been stressed by younger scholars, such as Laurie Wiseberg, who has developed several case studies of human-rights NGOs.[20] UNITAR has begun a major study of the role of NGOs as transnational actors under Dr. Berhanykun Andemicael's direction.

The Human Rights NGOs

The term *NGOs* covers thousands of organizations in United Nations terminology but only a small percentage of these are concerned directly with the subject matter of this study. Many NGOs have no official affiliation but exert great influence.[21] Most important to this thesis are the *human-rights NGOs* opposed to the apartheid system. As we have stated, these NGOs cover a broad spectrum, with educational, relief, activist-lobbying, and interest-group origins. Some have been in existence for a long time, such as the Anti-Slavery Society; others are very ephemeral. A few have large budgets, like churches and labor organizations, but most are poor, with primarily voluntary staffs. Business and professional groups are not included because they tend not to play an anti-apartheid role directly. Some NGOs, of course, oppose the anti-apartheid movement and are directly allied with the South African government, such as the South African Foundation, which has several branches in Western European states.

This study does not seek to identify all the anti-apartheid NGOs or to give an organizational typology of their characteristics, although the most effective ones are described. This would have required time and resources far beyond those available to this author. Such information is currently included in the UNITAR study project on NGOs. It is also a part of the agenda of the International Studies Association Internet on Human Rights.

The effectiveness of human rights NGOs is assessed here in terms of their role in legitimizing liberation from apartheid within the developing transnational debate and the domestic politics of the United States and Great Britain, as well as their impact on South African conflicts. The multinational corporations are, in the main, a pro-apartheid transnational force. Most multinational corporations protest they are neutral, but recent studies of the effect of their activities raise much evidence to the contrary, as this study will demonstrate.

The major test of anti-apartheid applied here is the extent to which NGOs contribute to the growth of transnational abolition pressures on apartheid—through education, support, aid, and strength of the liberation and majority movements. The focus is upon the policy results rather than on the organizations themselves.

A thesis tested here is the proposition that nongovernmental actors, especially human-rights NGOs, play a formative role in world politics, occasionally more determinative than that of major powers.

That the end of apartheid will not come about peacefully but through widening conflict in a revolutionary war already underway is one of the assumptions. The relevant major issue remaining is this: What kind of a reconciliation can be ultimately achieved out of the contending forces and groups? The anti-apartheid movement, after the ordeal of abolishing apartheid throughout the societies of Southern Africa, could be a major instrument for bridging the gulf between Africans and the West, provided it has not grown too wide.

Notes

1. Brian Bunting notes the first use of the term *apartheid* by *Die Burger* on 26 March 1943. "The Origins of Apartheid," in Alex La Guma, *Apartheid* (New York: International Publishers, 1971), p. 23.

2. Ibid., p. 24.

3. Ibid., p. 25.

4. See David Welsh, "The Politics of White Supremacy," in Leonard Thompson and Jeffrey Butler, *Change in Contemporary South Africa* (Berkeley: University of California Press, 1976), p. 73.

5. See Reginald Austin, *Racism and Apartheid in Southern Africa: Rhodesia* (Paris: UNESCO Press, 1975), pp. 67-74.

6. In South Africa it is clear that apartheid has developed along with capitalism and industrialism; yet it is racial separation that has enabled the cheap labor system to develop. Race has predetermined the class status of Africans and economic growth has not changed this. Pierre Van den Berghe, *South Africa: A Study of Conflict* (Middletown, Conn.: Wesleyan University Press, 1965).

Heribert Adam in *Modernizing Racial Domination* (Berkeley: University of California Press, 1971), pp. 110-111, while stressing the castelike status of blacks, argues that an African middle class, which aligns with white interests, is emerging. Thus, he argues, class is becoming determinative in a more classical Marxian sense, and the real revolution is suppressed, "government is able increasingly to replace coercion with built-in self-policies, self-regulating . . . institutional controls, by steadily increasing the numbers of non-whites with a vested interest in the maintenance of the system."

7. John F. Burns, *The New York Times,* 7 July 1976.

8. Burns, *The New York Times,* 12 July 1976.

9. *The Star Weekly,* Johannesburg, 9 November 1974.

10. Pierre Teilhard de Chardin provides the "cosmo-genesis" philosophical basis of this assertion in his *The Phenomenon of Man* (London: Collins, 1959).

11. John Bennett, *The Radical Imperative* (Philadelphia: Westminster Press, 1975), p. 14, maintains there is a "divine partiality" which creates this process, because "God's love for all persons implies a strategic concentration on the victims of society."

12. There are two contrasting views: Eric Williams, *Capitalism and Slavery* (Chapel Hill: University of North Carolina Press, 1944) and Arthur Zilver-Smit, *The First Emancipation: The Abolition of Slavery in the North* (Chicago: University of Chicago Press, 1967).

13. Sam Nolutshungu, "The Impact of External Opposition," in Thompson and Butler, op. cit. p. 396.

14. *The Manchester Guardian* said, 22 February 1976, that the world was on the brink of plunging into a racial conflagration in Southern Africa.

15. "The U.S. owned and managed corporations have transcended their own country in interest, outlook, and strategy," Richard Barnet and Ronald E. Muller, *Global Reach: The Power of Multi-National Corporations* p. 27.

16. The ideas of A. Gundar Frank and John Galtung are particularly employed in dependency theory along with the regionalism of Louis Cantori and Steven Spiegel, *The International Politics of Regions* (Englewood Cliffs, N.J.: Prentice Hall, 1970).

17. South Africa is not generally regarded as being a dependency of the Western powers but is regarded as having a regional system of her own. See Kenneth Grundy, *Confrontation and Accommodation in Southern Africa* (Berkeley: University of California Press, 1975), Chapter I.

18. John Galtung, "A Structural Theory of Imperialism," *Journal of Peace Research,* Vol. VIII, No. 2 (1971).

19. Robert O. Keohane and Joseph S. Nye, eds., *Transnational Relations and World Politics* (Cambridge, Mass.: Harvard University Press, 1973). They describe transnational relations as "contacts, coalitions, and interactions across state boundaries that are not controlled by the central foreign policy organs of government," p. xi.

20. Harry Scoble and Laurie Wiseberg, "Human Rights NGOs: Notes Toward Comparative Analysis," *Human Rights Journal,* September, 1976.

21. See David Weissbrodt, "The Role of International Non-governmental Organizations in the Implementation of Human Rights," forthcoming in J. Buergenthal and F. Newman, eds., *Implementation of International Human Rights.*

chapter 2 ═══════════

UNITED NATIONS LEGITIMIZATION OF LIBERATION

Although there is now a revolution well under way against apartheid, there is much debate over its extent and legitimacy. Indeed, one of the principle weapons of counterrevolutionary warfare is refusal even to recognize that the conflict is based upon significant and valid grounds, and to discount the representative character of its leaders and supporters. This is what the South African government has attempted to do in relation to the anti-apartheid revolution, by describing the nationalist leadership as "terrorist" and generating the belief that change is taking place through gradual, peaceful means under white leadership. This view is widely accepted in the Atlantic world, for most analyses of the apartheid conflict do not admit the fact that a revolution exists—or is likely to exist—because of the immense power of the South Africans to contain it.[1]

Deliberations in the United Nations, however, have become a major legitimizing process for national revolutions over the thirty years of its existence. The legitimizing process has been described by Thomas Trout as "the continuing effort to provide the necessary quality of toughness to a society's presiding institutions and to their actions."[2] Thus the process of moving from illegitimacy to legitimacy is a psychological one of acceptance as opposed to rejection, the emergence of an internationally accepted reality which governments interact with and recognize as a political authority.

The United Nations Legitimization Process

Several scholars have noted the important role played by the United Nations since 1945 in this process of legitimization for African liberation movements, notably Yassin El-Aouty, who stated, in 1972:

> The legitimization of African national liberation movements by the UN system has given rise to a view of the revolutionary organisms in South Africa as legitimate recipients of international aid and as authentic representatives of their populations . . . in terms of international conferences, these quasi-sovereign entities are competitors for international recognition with the "established regimes" in Southern Africa. This is the crux of the political revolution which the UN system, although based on state membership, has undergone since 1945.[3]

Most of this process has been rejected, discounted, and attacked throughout the period of decolonization by the Western nations concerned: the Dutch in Indonesia; the French in Algeria; the British in many parts of Africa; and the United States in Indo-China. Yet the United Nations has played the role of both catalyst and legitimizer in the historic revolution of many former colonial peoples. Later attempts by the colonial powers to co-opt the nationalist movements by neocolonial devices are the result of change. Legitimization has generally begun with vague support resolutions, moved frequently to measures of active intervention through various committees and agencies of the international organization, and finally, when the independence struggle has been completed, United Nations membership has become the major facilitator for full diplomatic recognition. This is the important legitimizing process of the transnational revolution of the "powerless," which moves forward despite the opposition of dominant governments of the area toward a culmination in final recognition and acceptance by virtually all nation-states.

Not all revolutions attain this level of international recognition, but in most cases in the history of the United Nations, when this level of the legitimizing process has been reached, the process has usually culminated in the de-facto if not de-jure acceptance of the revolution. This is not to say that United Nations legitimization has been decisive in successful decolonization nor has it been simply a barometer of change. The United Nations role in most cases has been essentially that of a facilitator. This fact in itself has given immense prestige and significance to the transnational legitimizing process. Most of Africa has moved through this process with differing degrees of violence and speed of acceptance. The Portuguese territories had the most protracted conflict. Rhodesia, through the United Nations-sponsored sanctions campaign combined with the liberation struggle, may well prove to be the classic case. South Africa has, since 1960, been a major subject of gradual expanding legitimization of revolution—a campaign of anti-apartheid pressures, boycotts, embargoes, and aid to liberation movements.

Thus, the United Nations legitimizing process has become an important aspect of the transformation from outlaw to quasi-sovereignty and the generation of support for the liberation movements.

The implication of this is not that the world has produced some marvelous moral sanctifying device in the form of the United Nations majority, as some naive interpretations imply. The United Nations majority has not only been misguided at times but also on occasion quite wrong, as, for example, the 1975 resolution "racism and zionism," which oversimplified the issue. Nevertheless, there has developed a process of information gathering, assessment, recognition, resolution, and implementation of support of a pacific nature, which has become of great importance to the revolutionary groups. This process has been described in different ways by various authorities. Some look upon it as an integral part of the United Nations structure from its beginning, placing emphasis upon the Declaration of Human Rights and the trusteeship system.[4] Others see the process developed especially through the special committees, like the Committee of Twenty-Four and the Committee on Apartheid.[5] The major committee has been the Special Committee on the Situation with Regard to the Implementation of the Declaration on the Granting of Independence to Colonial Countries and Peoples, which was created in 1961, following the adoption in 1960 of Resolution G.A. 1514. Later, with an expanded membership, it came to be known as the Committee of twenty-four. Largely under African state leadership, this committee in the 1960s swept aside all attempts of colonial powers to keep colonial matters under the domestic jurisdiction section of the U.N. Charter, Article 2, Section 7. James Mittelman has described the legitimizing techniques of the Committee of twenty-four:

The Special committee dispatches visiting groups and receives petitions, serves as a channel for communication among global international organization, regional organizations, and liberation movements, gathers information on the economic, social, and political development of non-self-governing territories, monitors the activities of the specialized activities as regards decolonization; and grants observer status to designated liberation movements.[6]

The process has been very important in the development of certain nongovernmental organizations, for these groups have in themselves played a role in the transnational revolution by serving as sources of information for international organization, as support for the liberation leaders, and as public education and political pressure on their own power centers and governments. Though frequently weak and small themselves, these NGOs have found within the United Nations process itself their self-validation and direction for policies. As nongovernmental actors, they have been dependent upon a central organizing purpose and process in order to have direction and effect. Thus, in the United Nations, in all its collective decolonization process of committees and agencies, the NGOs have found a way to activate the process of legitimization on behalf of the powerless. They have influenced the identification of these liberation movements, the recognition of their real grievances, and which types of assistance and recognition to be given to them within the United Nations system and their own countries. Representatives of NGOs have frequently been the first to visit a liberated territory and to bring back evidence of success.

It would be easy to exaggerate this process. Yet it has worked, despite the opposition of the Western powers who have frequently placed the more activist NGOs in the same category of subversion with the liberation movements.[7] Conflicts between governments and NGOs over the legitimacy of the FLN in France, the Viet Cong in the United States, and the southern African liberation movements in Portugal and England have, at times, reached the level of massive demonstrations and riots.

At the central nerve point of the world, the United Nations decolonization process of legitimizing revolution has moved forward because, despite all its shortcomings and failures, it has managed to continue to create points of contact and dialogue over the vast differences among the conflicting actors and has provided a fairly rational way of accepting substantial changes.[8]

There are no agreed criteria by which one revolution or movement is considered to be legitimate and another is not. There are, however, certain basic characteristics of those movements which have emerged in this legitimization process. First, they are colonial in character, reacting against the imperialism of the West, by documenting extensive grievances and injustice. Generally, they have been suppressed by the colonial power or a racist state. There has been evidence that they have a large following. A racial character has existed; where the oppressive power has been white and Western, the movements have almost always been nonwhite and ethnically non-Western. The movements have demonstrated a capacity to exist despite repression and, in several cases, have held territory against the repeated attempts of the colonial powers to dislodge them. Increased international support has been a prime indicator of growing strength.

The legitimization of the South African revolution has proceeded to the point where the liberation movements are recognized by the United Nations and given quasi-sovereign status at the United Nations sessions and the various agencies of the United Nations have taken direct action to assist them.[9] All of this has created a confrontation with South Africa and her Atlantic core partners, who are overwhelmingly outvoted and forced increasingly to resort to the veto.[10]

The liberation movements of South Africa have come to be regarded by the vast majority in the United Nations as possessing these characteristics and have therefore been inducted into the legitimizing process despite the protests of South Africa about domestic jurisdiction and the active resort to the veto by the major Western powers.

When the United Nations accepts a liberation movement as legitimate, the debate focuses around what kind of assistance should be rendered and what sorts of sanctions applied. Because of the powerful position of the Western states, the capacity of the United Nations to undertake any direct action, especially under Chapter 7 of the Charter, has been curbed. These debates are, in themselves, significant indicators of the gradual progression of the legitimizing process. They move from recognition of the conflict to recognition of movements involved, to pacific forms of assistance such as arms embargoes, to economic sanctions and direct assistance. The more severe measures—sanctions for intervention and support for liberation groups—are the most bitterly contested forms of transnational assistance. At this point, the non-governmental actors have played a very significant role in support of United Nations programs, especially in the area of humanitarian assistance to liberation movements. Some are ready to provide information and general recognition while a few NGOs are fully revolutionary.

United Nations Liberation Process and Apartheid

The United Nations began to establish a broad liberation approach to apartheid in the early 1960s. This position on apartheid has been defined primarily by the General Assembly and, to a lesser extent, by the other agencies and instruments of the Special Committee on Apartheid, the Committee of twenty-four, Council for Namibia, and sympathetic specialized agencies such as the ILO, UNESCO, and FAO. The majority liberation position, as set forth by the General Assembly, must be distinguished from the position of the Security Council, which has not been able to take a similar line toward South Africa because of the opposition role played by the United States, the United Kingdom, and France, as permanent members possessed of the veto. General Assembly resolutions have established the basic majority position, while it has been modified by other agencies, particularly the Security Council, which has been granted under the Charter the prerogative of taking enforcement action. This is not simply a legal question, because the Western powers are the principal economic and security partners of South Africa, and their readiness to cooperate with a resolution of the Security Council is highly determinative of its success.[11]

United Nations legitimization of revolution against apartheid began with general resolutions regarding the independence of Namibia, rights of the African and nonwhite majority, and requests for diplomatic disengagement, arms embargo, aid for liberation movements, and economic sanctions to enforce these measures. In the seventies this has moved to far more active support through special committees, funds, and agencies.

Transnational legitimization of anti-apartheid in South Africa dates from the Sharpeville Massacre, March 1960. Prior to this mass killing of unarmed Africans, the internal racial policies of South Africa were regarded essentially as "domestic jurisdiction," though they were deplored. After the South African government demonstrated its determination to crush the growing nonviolent African rights movement by force,[12] opinion in Western government circles began to shift, and a Security Council resolution was adopted. This called for "the Republic of South Africa to cease forthwith its continued imposition of discriminatory and repressive measures . . . to liberate all persons imprisoned, interned, or subjected to other restrictions for having opposed the policy of apartheid . . . all states to cease forthwith the sale and shipment of equipment and materials for the manufacture and maintenance of arms."[13]

Western powers have wavered in their support of an arms embargo, and France has been the most open violator[14] of the generally accepted ban on the sale of weapons to South Africa. The British and American governments have supported voluntary military embargo since 1963. However, the attempt to implement this embargo has failed, as we shall see, and the Security Council has balked at a compulsory arms embargo.

The major point of difference between the majority position, which has asked for economic sanctions on trade, investment, and industry in South Africa, and the major Western powers is that the latter have consistently opposed economic sanctions and liberation support.[15] With some modifications, this is also true of the smaller Western powers and Japan (although the latter maintains a ban on investment). However, smaller Western states have contributed from the beginning to the victims of apartheid through the United Nations Special Fund for South Africa and gradually have showed support for the United Nations process of legitimizing revolution against apartheid.

The United Nations majority has called for a reduction in diplomatic ties and a ban on cultural and sports relations as long as South Africa continues its discrimination against black freedom of movement and participation in society. Here there emerges a significant difference between the great Western powers and the smaller Western states, with the latter increasingly supporting such expressions of opposition as a sports ban on South Africa and a reduction in diplomatic ties. With changes of government in 1972 in Australia and New Zealand, this gradual shift of policy against apartheid became pronounced.[16]

The major driving spirit and agency at the United Nations behind the legitimizing of liberation in South Africa has been the Special U.N. Committee on Apartheid, established in 1962, by resolution of the General Assembly, to keep under review measures recommended by the General Assembly, such as diplomatic and economic sanctions.[17] The committee was enlarged from eleven to seventeen members in December 1965. The Western powers, who initially supported the Committee of twenty-four until 1970, opposed and ignored the activities of the new committee, because this Committee on Apartheid encouraged support for liberation movements and advocated economic sanctions.

The conflict between the Organization of African Unity (OAU) position on support for liberation movements and the United States-United Kingdom position of opposition to the use of violence was brought to a head in the debate over the Programme of Action, developed in consultation with the OAU and submitted to the United Nations through the Special Committee of twenty-four, in the twenty-fifth Session as G.A. Resolution 2621 1970.[18] The United States and the United Kingdom opposed liberation support through an alternative resolution of Italy, Norway, the United Kingdom, and the United States, which requested all parties to seek peaceful nonviolent settlement. When the request for support of liberation was adopted, the United States and the United Kingdom withdrew from the Special Committee of twenty-four, because, they concluded, "the future activities of the United Nations on the adopted programme would be unconstructive."[19]

Recommendations from the United Nations-OAU Oslo Conference on Southern Africa (9-14 April 1973) regarding the implementation of resolutions of support by all United Nations specialized agencies have brought the issue to the forefront in United Nations activity. This culminated in the acceptance of the liberation movements of Southern Africa as the "authentic representatives" of their people.[20] The movements in the Portuguese territories have completed the process of legitimization except for the delay in Angola's United Nations membership caused by the United States veto. The others in Zimbabwe, Namibia, and South Africa (Azania) are still in process. At the Twenty-Ninth Session of the General Assembly, it was decided to invite as observers on a regular basis representatives of the liberation movements recognized by the OAU, in the relevant work of the Assembly and its related agencies, with the United Nations Secretariat providing facilities.[21] Western opposition to this recognition has been weakened by the transformation of former liberation movements in the Portuguese quasi-territories into governments and by OAU insistence upon quasi-diplomatic status for the remaining movements in Southern Africa.

This study does not take up in any detail the South African liberation movements themselves, as this has been done elsewhere.[22] Supported by the African states, the NGOs and the liberation parties are the auxiliaries and the attack force of the abolitionists on apartheid within the Atlantic system.

The Role of the Western NGO

In this legitimizing process of liberation in South Africa and anti-apartheid, the Western NGOs have played an indispensable role. There are hundreds of human-rights groups, largely based in the Western world, who represent church, civil, ethnic, racial, economic, and humanitarian concerns. They range from small yet influential groups like the International League for the Rights of Man to large labor unions and ecumenical religious movements.[23] They are termed "the powerless" here, in contrast to their own governments, as they generally lack wealth, prestige, and military might. Their strength is in their ideals and commitment to extending human rights. Nor have they been unable, as Ernest H. Haas points out, to see the implications for their own domestic scene, or afraid, as Harlan Cleveland argues, "to have the UN turn its attention to the mote in our own eye."[24]

The term *NGO* is used here in a different context from the way it is generally used at the United Nations and as defined by the ECOSOC categories.[25] Some are recognized for direct association with certain agencies; others have observer status only, which gives them access to the offices and meetings of the United Nations. There are thousands of these, most of which are professional or trade associations, who play no role in the process of legitimizing liberation or opposing it.[26] The NGOs included in this study are actively concerned about human rights. They may or may not be officially registered with the United Nations or its specialized agencies but are clearly nongovernmental in origin and independent in financial support and policy. In this age of covert as well as overt government use of organizations, this is not always a clear characteristic. However, this study focuses on those Western NGOs and INGOs which actively oppose apartheid and other racial policies of the South African government over a broad range of strategies, at home and abroad.

The role of the human-rights NGOs has been to assist the United Nations process of identifying injustice and recognizing the legitimate representatives of the powerless people by gathering evidence, presenting petitions, assisting petitioners, and lobbying member governments and agencies. They have also provided direct assistance to the victims of apartheid and assisted their representatives in gaining a hearing before the United Nations.

These NGOs have gone through various phases of development and change themselves as a result of success and failures of their activities. These were occasionally produced by a change in government policy, but more generally there has been a tendency for those who began with moderate reformist policies to shift toward stronger liberation positions. This has led to considerable conflict among them, as in the era of slavery. A gradualist group seeking primarily reform and peaceful change comprises the largest set of actors, while an abolitionist group demanding total structural revolutionary change has increasingly pressed its demand in Western countries.

The role that many of these organizations play within their own societies in influencing the general direction of policy has received increasing attention. But the transnational role of reaching beyond national policies to assist in major struggles going on overseas and at the United Nations is, in all probability, of greater importance in the long run. This has laid the groundwork, as we shall see, for the final conflict of "the powerless" with the Atlantic apartheid system, as a result of the rising cost of conflict and major shifts in economic relations and priorities between the industrial core states and their peripheral areas. The decolonization process has been a major forerunner of the abolition of the apartheid movement, both in the creation of a political forum in the world in which liberation movements could be legitimized and assisted and, at the same time, producing major new bargaining relationships between the dominant wealthy powers and the new states, assisted by the communist world. Peaceful change and reconciliation can come, but only after a transnational revolution, which breaks down the structures of injustice and privileged power and enables new political relationships to emerge.

This case study particularly of the British and American NGOs is only a part of the total process of NGO legitimization of racial revolution in Southern Africa. It, however, provides the general basis for understanding the nature of the Western anti-apartheid and abolitionist movement. This study attempts to show how the seemingly hopeless impasse among governments is being bypassed by the transnational actors who assist into reality a process of revolutionary change. Winnie Mandela, the courageous wife of the imprisoned African National Congress leader, Nelson Mandela, stated in early 1976:

I can tell you that from my own personal experience over the past fifteen years when I was confined and restricted, that I got my inspiration from the very knowledge that one is not alone, the knowledge that the struggle is an international struggle for the dignity of man and that you are part of this family of man—this alone sustains you. In our particular struggle those outside groups have a tremendous psychological effect on the masses, on us as individuals just that knowledge alone that we belong to a family of man in a society where we have been completely rejected by a minority.[27]

Notes

1. See George Kennan, "Hazardous Courses in Southern Africa." *Foreign Affairs,* January 1971.

2. Thomas Trout, "Rhetoric Revisited: Political Legitimization and the Cold War," *International Studies Quarterly,* Vol. 19, No. 3 (September 1975), p. 253.

3. Yassim El-Ayouty, "Legitimization of National Liberation: The United Nations and Southern Africa," *Issue,* No. 4 (1972), p. 43.

4. See Martinus Nijhoff, *The United Nations and Decolonization: The Role of Afro-Asia* (The Hague: Martinus Nijhoff, 1971), or Robert W. Cox and Harold R. Jacobson (eds.), *The Anatomy of Influence: Decision-Making in International Organization* (New Haven: Yale University Press, 1973).

5. James Mittelman, "Collective Decolonization and the UN Committee of 24," unpublished paper for the International Studies Association, 19-22 February 1975, p. 9.

6. Ibid.

7. A series of vetoes was registered by the United States, France, and Britain over the South African expulsion resolutions of October 1974 and the Namibia question in September 1975.

8. I do not agree with those who denigrate the decolonization process by pointing to the continuing reality of neocolonialism. Dependency is not eliminated with the decolonization stage, but as Cabral and Nkrumah before him have argued, political independence is a necessary first step in what is a continuing revolution for peoples of the Third World who now emphasize economic inequities.

9. From its inception, the U.N. Special Committee has given de-facto recognition to liberation movements, and in the twentieth General Assembly in 1965, the Assembly requested "all states to provide material and moral assistance to the national liberation movements in colonial territories." Resolution G.A. 2105 (xx). Later, this was made more specific with the decision to invite liberation movement representatives on a regular basis and to provide them with assistance in appearing. Resolution G.A. 3280 (xxix).

10. On 6 June 1975, a triple veto was made by the United States, the United Kingdom, and France, on the question of sanctions over Namibia, Resolution S.C. 1713, put forward by Guyana, Iraq, Mauritania, and Tanzania.

11. Japan is included among the major trading partners of South Africa. Her industrial dependence on South African iron ore and uranium has grown phenomenally, as have her auto sales to South Africa. See Yoko Kitazawa, *From Tokyo to Johannesburg, A Study of Japan's Growing*

Economic Links with the Republic of South Africa (New York: Inter Faith Center on Corporate Responsibility, 1975).

12. See Bishop Richard Ambrose Reeves, *The Shooting at Sharpeville* (London: Gollancz, 1960).

13. The Security Council by a vote of 9-0 declared the situation on South Africa, if continued, "might endanger international peace and security," Resolution S.C. 182, 4 December 1963.

14. France supported Resolution S.C. 182 in 1963 but has not observed the arms embargo since that time, as will be discussed more fully later.

15. See "The Report of the UN Committee of Experts" in February 1965 on these differences.

16. *The New York Times,* 23 May 1973, and 24 January 1973; also Bruce Brown, a study of political relations in *New Zealand Listener,* 10 October 1969. With the election of Conservative governments in New Zealand and Australia, a return to the norm has taken place.

17. Resolution G.A. 1761, 6 November 1962. The vote was 67 for and 16 against, with 23 abstentions.

18. See Resolution G.A. 2054 A, December 1965, for an indication of how support of the Committee on Apartheid has grown. Small Western states did not serve on the committee but they frequently supported its proposals.

19. See Berhanykun Andemicael, *The OAU and the UN: Relations Between the Organization of African Unity and the United Nations,* a UNITAR Regional Study (New York: Africana Publishing Co., 1976), for an excellent discussion of this issue.

20. The Special Committee of twenty-four of the United Nations 4th Committee first invited liberation leaders to participate as observers. At the Twenty-Seventh Session of the General Assembly, a resolution on Portuguese territories recognized that the liberation movements "are the authentic representatives of the true aspirations of the peoples of those territories" (Resolution G.A. 2918). They requested all governments, specialized organizations, to deal with them on those terms.

This was extended to Zimbabwe and Namibia in the Twenty-Eighth Session of the General Assembly (Resolution G.A. 3115) and (Resolution G.S. 3111).

21. Resolution G.A. 3280 in the Twenty-Ninth Session.

22. A large and growing literature exists:

C. P. and Dale R. Potholme (eds.), *Southern Africa in Perspective* (New York: The Free Press, 1976).

Kenneth Grundy, *Guerrilla Struggle in Africa* (New York: Grossman, 1971).

G. W. Shepherd, *Non-Aligned Black Africa* (Cambridge, Mass.: Lexington-Heath, 1970).

Nelson Mandela, *No Easy Walk to Freedom* (New York: Basic Books, 1965).

Edward Feit, *African Opposition in South Africa* (Stanford, Calif.: The Hoover Institution on War, Revolution, and Peace, 1967).

Martin Legassick, *Class Nationalism and South African Protest: The South African Communist Party and the Native Republic, 1928-34* (Syracuse, N.Y.: Maxwell School, 1973).

Peter Walshe, *The Rise of African Nationalism in South Africa: The African National Congress* (Berkeley: University of California Press, 1973).

Andreas Shipanga, *Namibia, SWAPO* (Victoria, B.C.: I.S.M. Information Center, 1973).

Alfred Nzo, *South African National Congress* (Victoria, B.C.: I.S.M. Information Center, 1972).

Mathew Nkoana, *Crisis in the Revolution* (London: Mafube Publications, 1968).

J. Karis, G. Carter, *From Protest to Challenge,* 2 vols. (Stanford, Calif.: Hoder Inst. Press, 1973).

Kees Maxey, *The Fight for Zimbabwe* (London: Rex Collings, 1975; New York: Africana, 1975).

23. Ernest H. Haas in *Tangle of Hopes* (Englewood Cliffs, N.J.: Prentice-Hall, 1969), pp. 186-189, discusses the NGO role in the broad area of protection of human rights symbolized by the adoption of the Universal Declaration of Human Rights. "Between 1945 and 1955 one or more civic, religious, business, child welfare, women's, technical, legal, medical, criminology, professional, informational and labor groups pressed vigorously for machinery to handle human rights communications and petitions for the right of complaint by individuals or organizations." Haas points out how the attempt to extend this role of the United Nations was repeatedly rebutted by the Great Powers, including the Soviet Union. This independence from official Great Power authority and desire to extend human rights through national and global action is their distinctive quality.

24. Harlan Cleveland, "The Evolution of Rising Responsibility," *International Organization,* Summer 1965, p. 832.

25. ECOSOC Resolution 1296 and Article 71 U.N. Charter.

26. A comprehensive study of a much wider spectrum of NGOs is found in Werner Held, *Non-Governmental Forces and World Politics: A Study of Business, Labor, and Political Groups* (New York: Praeger, 1972).

27. *SANA* (Southern African News Agency), an irregular newsletter from the underground, February-March 1976, Capetown, pp. 10-11.

chapter 3 ═══════════

FROM PROTEST TO ACTION: THE COMING OF AGE FOR HUMAN-RIGHTS NGOs

The era of international organization in the twentieth century has seen the emergence of numerous human-rights organizations with transnational connections. American and British societies have been among the most fruitful sources for such organizations because of their long historical concern for human rights and their connection with the immediate problems of decolonization as major Atlantic core powers. A comparative study of the origins and changing activities of these Anglo-American NGOs can help to clarify the motivations and effectiveness of the anti-apartheid movement, domestically and transnationally.

Since the founding of the United Nations, there has been a steady growth of many organizations which support human rights as a primary purpose. Their development can be analyzed in terms of three periods, each reflecting the character and influence of certain predominant ideas and the major nongovernmental organizations (NGOs) active at the time. These periods can be defined as an initial protest period of legalistic focus on reform of law and constitutional relations, followed by a period of direct action and of populist growth, later developing into one of direct support. The first period corresponded roughly with the decade of the forties and extended well into the fifties. As the conflict deepened in the settled regions of southern Africa, populist participation (in the United States and the United Kingdom) developed increasingly a transnational consciousness and a gradual shift from moderate-reform proposals to action and support of liberation. This coincided with a growth in power and legitimization of the liberation movements.

Liberal Internationalism

The interwar period laid the basis for human-rights concerns in the United States and the United Kingdom, when the ideas behind the League of Nations—self-determination and gradual preparation for self-rule of colonial peoples under the mandate system—were first developed. These grew out of the reformist creed of the day, described as "liberal internationalism,"[1] which regarded international government as a device for settling the clashes of national claims and in particular, the narrowly defined mandate system as a sacred trust by which the former German territories were to be prepared for self-rule.[2] Rival interests in the expansion of empire were to be curbed by international law, arbitration, disarmament, and sanctions against the aggressor rather than by the arms race and conquest by superior force.

Criticism of this concept of international settlement existed, for many people did not view the League as an instrument of international justice. International socialists of all shades believed that only the overthrow of capitalism could open the way for decolonization. The isolationists tried to develop a myth of noninvolvement in order to avoid the reality of rival imperialisms and to enjoy the fruits of the continuation of colonial subjection, without taking responsibility for removal of the system.

A more perceptive criticism was provided by E. H. Carr, who in the midst of the Second World War wrote:

The crisis of national self-determination is parallel to the crisis of democracy. Self-determination, like democracy, has fallen on evil days because we have been content to keep it in the nineteenth century setting of political rights. We have failed to adapt it to the twentieth century context of military and economic problems.[3]

In the United States and Great Britain, the first period of organizational concern for international action on human rights was dominated by individuals and groups which reflected the liberal internationalism of the interwar period. This internationalism was perpetuated in the structure of the United Nations, especially in the Trusteeship Council and the Universal Declaration of Human Rights. This period was legalistic and unrealistic about military and economic power. Men like Ralph Bunche and Roger Baldwin in the United States and Leonard Woolf and Arthur Creech Jones in England saw the implementation of the Charter in terms of gradual decolonization and growing pressure for organized condemnation of racism. Baldwin and his International League for the Rights of Man were far more impatient than the others and thoroughly condemned the reluctance of Western powers to implement decolonization. Yet, the pace he and others accepted was "the inevitability of gradualism" which also characterized the Fabian Colonial Bureau in this period.[4] In relation to apartheid, this legalistic view was prepared to condemn the racism of the system, but Fabians were not anxious to undertake international action against its military and economic structure, especially where such action, they believed, would be contrary to prevailing Western economic and security interests. The liberal notion that industrial change in the colonies, and with this the racial systems of Southern Africa, would bring about new conditions of modernization and precipitate reform from within was a prevailing hope in human-rights groups as well as Western governments.[5] This gradualism provided a sophisticated rationalization of the interests of Atlantic core powers and was vulnerable to attack from the colonial peoples, newly independent states, and the emerging NGO human-rights groups.

In the late forties and early fifties, Asian states were only beginning to be recognized, no new African state had emerged, and the Cold War had begun to make anticolonial criticism suspect in the eyes of dominant elites. Thus change came slowly. In the United States, black groups were oriented toward legalistic and moderate internal goals and paid little attention to world affairs. In England, Nkrumah, Kenyatta, and Padmore helped create in 1948 the Congress of Peoples Against Imperialism, headed by Fenner Brockway, who was an Independent Labour party M.P. They had begun their active postwar campaigns for colonial freedom in Africa with the Pan-African Congress in Manchester (1945). Brockway understood the economic and military realities of class, race, and empire, and had long been a major leader of the left wing in the Labour Party, critical of the gradualism of Liberals and Fabians. A comparable group to the Congress of Peoples Against Imperialism emerged in postwar American politics, headed initially by Max Yergan and then Paul Robeson. The Council on African Affairs provided an early socialist critique of liberal internationalism, which was dismissed as subversive by the foreign-policy establishment.

The emergence of the Afrikaners to power in South Africa in 1948 and the establishment of the official doctrine of apartheid was the precipitating event of change for the fifties, leading to a pacific-action period. Pacific action sought to evoke immediate acceptance of independence for African states and nonviolent collective action against apartheid. The organized representation of pacific activism began with several new personalities and organizations, which entered the field in the early 1950s. These groups sought to use transnational machinery for decolonization. They were largely motivated by a concern for human rights and were led by liberal pacifists who dissented sharply from the prevailing gradualism of government policy. Both the Africa Bureau and Christian Action have roots back into the Anti-Slavery Society, which was founded in 1906 and in turn emerged out of earlier antislavery groups.[6] In the United States, the American Committee on Africa grew out of Americans for South African Resistance, which had been created by George Houser to support the South African National Congress, then connected with the pacifist Fellowship of Reconciliation (FOR). In all of these groups, the major leadership was predominantly Protestant, pacifist and white. There were, however, black and African participants who later were to emerge as major leaders. In England, Kwame Nkrumah had organized the Pan-Africa Manchester Congress and returned to the Gold Coast to head up the Gold Coast National Convention, and Dr. Hastings Banda and George Padmore were active in the new NGOs. In the United States, Bayard Rustin, Bill Sutherland, and Robert Browne were among the early black organizers of the American Committee on Africa. The African American Institute, founded in 1953 in Washington, D.C., by former missionaries and government officials, had from its inception a semiofficial character, as it derived much of its funding from United States government sources.

These organizations were among the first to request unequivocal intervention by the United Nations and other international agencies against what was viewed at that stage more as a violation of human dignity than a threat to peace. Michael Scott, an Anglican clergyman, was the first Western spokesman on behalf of the Herero people of South West Africa. He succeeded in establishing the right of petition for peoples of the Trust Territories directly before the Trusteeship Council.[7] George Houser and a group including Peter Weiss, Bayard Rustin, A. J. Muste, Donald Harrington, and others, including this author, many of them connected with the Fellowship of Reconciliation, supported Scott's plea for justice for Africans caught in the apartheid system.[8] Canon John Collins was another pioneer in England. He, like A. J. Muste in the United States, was a nonconformist pacifist Christian and advocated social justice and nonviolent action to achieve these goals.

At the time these activist organizations were created, nonviolence was the creed of South African nationalists as well as a majority of African nationalist movements throughout Africa, as the Accra Conference of the All Africa Peoples Conference in 1958 showed in proposing nonviolence.[9] In the 1950s the ANC of South Africa was still practicing nonviolent resistance. Therefore, the issue of revolutionary struggle and warfare was not divisive at this point for either the American Committee on Africa, Defence and Aid, or the Africa Bureau. They found the ideas of pacific action wholly consistent with support for freedom movements in Africa.

These pacific, human-rights groups were transnationalist in the sense of utilizing international structures to intercede actively on behalf of the rights of Africans in South Africa, with, of course, varying interpretations of the appropriate measures and tactics to be used. They stressed the moral and legal authority of the United Nations in these matters as against the domestic jurisdiction view of government officials and their gradualist supporters, supported by reference to Article 7 Section 2 of the Charter.

Pacific activists were undoubtedly influenced by the thought of African nationalists with whom they worked. However, their programs were derived from the broad populist principles which had created the pacific settlement procedures of the United Nations. They rejected the narrow legalism which constituted the Western government views of the period about "domestic jurisdictions" concerning colonial and South African racial policies. They demanded that representatives of the nationalists be heard and issues debated. Their expectations concerning the speed of revolutionary change in South Africa were that rapid adoption of majority rule in South Africa must come and would lead to the complete abolition of separate development of the races, within a decade or two at the most.

Houser, Scott, and Collins, in the 1950s, developed an attack on the economic and military core system of support for apartheid. Sharp debate developed not only with Western officials but with other opponents of United Nations intervention, among them the South African academic emigrees, Professor Charles Manning, former professor of International Relations at the London School of Economics,[10] and C. W. De Kiewiet, former president of Rochester University.[11] The prevailing academic and political climate in both Britain and the United States tended to oppose the internationalization of the apartheid issue.

The NGO attack on this gradualism became centered in the ACOA in America and in the Africa Bureau in England, as the movements of change in the decolonization era began.

The statement of purpose of the Africa Bureau, formed in 1952, represented in England the concrete concern of "the men and women of the three main political parties" that steps be taken:

> (a) to inform people in Britain and elsewhere about African problems and African opinions thereon, and to convey to Africa accurate reports on events and attitudes in Britain that concern them;
> (b) to help peoples in Africa in opposing unfair discrimination and inequality of opportunity and to foster cooperation between races. . . .[12]

Later more specific purposes were added "to oppose racial tyrannies in Africa . . . [and] to promote the achievement of nondiscriminatory majority rule in Africa."[13]

The Africa Bureau from the beginning was a small group centered around the activities of the ascetic and dedicated Reverend Michael Scott, an expelled missionary of the Church of England in South Africa. Concern for honesty and accuracy characterized the style of the group of intellectuals and politicians it represented.[14] During the decade of African Independence, 1956-1965, the Africa Bureau thought and activity penetrated English policy with wide influence at the United Nations. As the pacific movement radicalized and broadened and Africans sent their own representation to London, the bureau played the quieter role of elder statesman and an advocate of nonviolent change in South Africa.[15] Michael Scott has consistently opposed proposals for the use of force by the United Nations against South Africa.

The American Committee on Africa reflected similar ideas in its early history. The major difference lay in the more radical style of the ACOA precipitated by the significant participation of black leaders like Robert Browne, who became more prominent in the organization over the years.

In the 1950s, the ACOA was primarily concerned with the independence of African states. Its approach to apartheid was to call for United Nations investigation, as in September 1955 it requested the United States to support "the reestablishment of the United Nations Commission on the Racial Situation in the Union of South Africa," which Western powers had opposed because it interfered with domestic jurisdiction. ACOA, at this stage in its activities, requested United Nations technical assistance be extended to South Africa as well as other African states.[16] Concern over growing investments in racist South Africa was expressed in the first activist steps against the bank loans to that country, but the intense boycott and disinvestment campaigns arose later. The ACOA in the United States raised funds directly for the defense of African political leaders in the famous treason trials and other legal challenges, as did the Defence and Aid group in England. Because of its predominantly radical orientation, the pacific leadership of the ACOA made the transition from nonviolent pacific action to support for liberation with comparatively little strain.[17]

The Turn to Liberation

The 1960s began a new period, inaugurated ominously by the Sharpeville massacre. The pacific activists, frustrated by the intransigence of apartheid (supported by rising Western financial investment and continued military complicity), turned from nonviolence to liberation tactics in support of armed struggle.

The emergence of direct support for liberation groups in Southern Africa arose out of the increased conflict in that area, especially in the Portuguese territories, and the growing conviction that Western governmental support for the military efforts of Portugal and South Africa must be ended by an arms embargo and other concrete actions rather than by mere verbal pledges from governments. In South Africa, the growing use of force and violence to suppress nationalist movements such as the African National Congress, the Pan-Africanist Congress, and the South African Council of Trade Unions, all of whom had employed nonviolent tactics during the fifties, led to exile and resort to armed insurrection by the Africans.

This caused a reconsideration of nonviolence as a philosophy and effective means by many groups, particularly those formed out of a pacific core. The fact that British and American governments opposed any resort to force against apartheid or other Southern African regimes only aggravated the tensions.

Direct action through mass marches and campaigns became the new tactic. Large new groups, not committed to religious pacifist ideas, began to enter the movements against apartheid. In England these consisted of members of the Campaign for Nuclear Disarmament, which represented universities, trade unions, large numbers of youth, and the radical wing of the Labour Party, Communist Party, and assorted Marxist groups. The campaign against arms to South Africa resonated with the antinuclear war ideas propounded by Bertrand Russell, and new voices, like Judith Hart and Ronald Segal, attacked the connection between Western preparation for war against communism and government use of South Africa as an ally.

Thus, the Anti-Apartheid Movement (AAM), formed in 1959 out of these elements in England, became very quickly the central coordinating agency for direct action campaigns, which brought continuous pressure against British policy and gave support to the majority United Nations position.[18] The overall ideological concept was still pacific action, but the younger, more radical groups brought in ideas of "liberation" such as boycotts, demonstrations, strikes, and even civil disobedience.[19] These in turn gave rise to mass actions such as the demonstrations against arms in the early 1960s in England and again in 1970 and the widely spread action against racism in sport, which resulted in the Stop the Seventy Tour campaign sparked by young liberals like Peter Hain and vastly enlarged by the anti-apartheid network.

The leadership of the Anti-Apartheid Movement has frequently been characterized as white South African exiles.[20] The principal nonwhite among these exiles is Abdul Minty, an Indian exile from South Africa and resident in the United Kingdom since 1957.[21] While the liberation movements play an active role in the work of the AAM, "those with offices in London" have a seat and voice in the 150-person national committee, yet they do not have a vote. Some of the African liberation people would like a greater role, although they accept the present dominance of whites as justified by the need to appeal to an overwhelmingly white electorate. The limited participation by British blacks stems as much from a paternalistic atmosphere of English racial politics as from immigrant fears, and will be discussed more fully.[22]

Despite the importance of ex-South Africans like Ethel de Keyser, Ronald Segal, Ruth First, and Abdul Minty in the running of the AAM, they would have been impotent without the substantial representation of British churchmen, including bishops, trade unions, academics, and Labour and Liberal M.P.s in the active work of the movement. Their presence represents the spreading politicization of the apartheid issue in British society.[23]

A group closely associated with the Anti-Apartheid Movement is the International Defence and Aid Fund, which is the primary agency for raising money for liberation groups, especially those working against apartheid. This group, founded by Canon John Collins in 1952 as an outgrowth of Christian Action, has as its prime objective the raising of funds to assist with the legal defense of people of all races on trial for treason. Needy members of their families are assisted too.[24] The fund has broadened its support in recent years to educational work among South African refugees, and has channeled some funds into South Africa, despite its ban against this, and has provided assistance for political prisoners in Rhodesia. A South African exile group operates the fund. Phyllis Altman, a former South African, is director, assisted by Hugh Lewin, who was imprisoned in South Africa, and Allen Brooks, who edited their research survey. Dennis Brutus, a Coloured South African connected with the ANC, was active while resident in Britain and later joined the Northwestern African Studies Program. Canon

Collins, the founder, maintained a firm grip on direction, while running St. Paul's Cathedral and Christian Action. His social action, and "justification by works," a major movement in the ecumenical church, represents the spirit of Defence and Aid. Unlike Hewlett Johnson, the "Red Dean of Canterbury," who accepted the Communist Manifesto, Collins holds to a Christian pacifist conception of evil as implicit in the undemocratic state. The presence of exiled South African Communists in active roles in both the fund and the AAM does not bother him, although it has been a prime point in the criticism of such groups by the gradualists and those who oppose revolutionary intervention.

The radical Christians are not anticommunist. Generally, they find more in common with the Marxists than liberals, since Marxists seek revolutionary change and are the allies of the radicals against an establishment supported by liberal gradualists. To them communism in South Africa is quite different from communism in England, as the conditions of social change are different. Members of the South African Communist Party have seldom functioned as revolutionaries in English society. With the collapse of the "foreign conspiracy" fears, which have governed so much of Western thought and public opinion, and the legitimization of liberation, South African Marxists are exercising prominent roles in anti-apartheid.

The penetration of the thinking of the AAM into other larger more establishment-related groups—such as the Labour and Liberal Parties, the press, Anglican, and Catholic churches—is the most effective part of its work. Many prominent people in these areas of British life are influenced by the AAM, although they would not want to be directly associated with it, either because they do not share all of its views, or because it carries a "radical image." Several prominent Labour and Liberal M.P.s respect the work of the AAM—such men as Dennis Healey, a labour government figure,[25] and Richard Wainwright, chairman of the Liberal Party.

The British press is sensitive to apartheid issues and very quick to dramatize them, although the point of view of the press, even the liberal papers, is gradualist, ready to denounce racism but not in favor of liberation action. However, press visibility has extended the influence of AAM into levels of British society not yet touched by counterpart groups in the United States.[26]

The AAM has coalesced and cooperated readily with other groups.

Individuals with special interests—for example, the Portuguese Territories, the Friends of Namibia, and the numerous university campaign groups—have served on its national committee while carrying out their own work. In addition, during the 1960s, there was a steady growth of AAM regional affiliates (numbering forty-five) in all major areas of the United Kingdom and Ireland.[26] An informal international coordinating network, which has been useful in terms of information as well as universalizing pressures, has emerged among Western European committees and Scandinavia.

In the United States, the era of the 1960s was also marked by a populist expansion and the use of direct-action tactics to support liberation in Africa. This direction, which became marked only in the latter part of this decade, was slowed by the all-encompassing priority given to the Vietnam issue by the left in American society, plus the uneasiness created by the initial impact of black-power ideas. With the demise of the Vietnam War, the anti-apartheid groups in the United States have felt the same influx of new elements as the Campaign for Nuclear Disarmament produced in England. In the United States these new elements have consisted principally of recruits from the peace movement, church, and youth groups, with some involvement of the universities and labor unions. The press coverage of Southern Africa has been poor, with little attention paid to apartheid and Southern African issues. Only when a major conflict like Algeria or Angola has broken out has the American press become significantly involved.

The black-white issue of control caused some tension among human-rights groups, especially among the gradualists who were not prepared to take an abolitionist stand on apartheid. The ACOA expanded its activities during this period. Its liberation-support programs reflected the populist drives of the blacks, radical young churchmen, and academics. Prexy Nesbitt opened a Chicago office as did Gary Gappert and later Charles Hightower in Washington, D.C. *Africa Today,* founded by the ACOA, moved to the University of Denver under the guidance of a multiracial editorial board of associated scholars. Early in 1972, Edgar Lockwood undertook the running of the Washington Office on Africa, with the help of the ACOA and church groups. The African American Institute developed educational programs in Africa and provided fellowships.

The difficulties of the African Studies Association illustrated the tensions many organizations faced over the issue of white paternalism, as blacks turned to black power. This surfaced particularly during several annual sessions of the ASA, culminating in the confrontation between black and white in Montreal in 1969. A parity formula basis for compromise won a slim majority at Montreal but was later repudiated in a referendum of the ASA membership.[28] The issue was a complex one, but it basically reflected the differences between blacks and whites over whether an academic organization should take an activist stand on issues, and the question of whether blacks, which included Africans, had any primacy of interest in organized African affairs. White academics, who had long presumed that scholarly prestige governed such relations, not race, were incensed by the accusations of blacks that they were practicing racial paternalism if they refused to grant parity to blacks in the control of the organization and its access to research funds. Although a majority of whites in Montreal sided with the black opinions of spokesmen like John Henry Clarke, who urged that the convention doors be opened to wider black participation on the basis of nonacademic criteria, a referendum showed the majority clearly preferred the status quo.

This confrontation reflected the wider issue in American race relations of the day, which was greater black participation in areas that concerned them. The decision resulted in secession of most blacks, although not most African members, from the ASA.

Other organizations dealing with Southern Africa, which because of their charter or ideological limitations could not meet black-participation demands, were damaged by this breakdown in race relations. The liberal church organizations were the first to feel this pressure and met it by constituting related but black-operated agencies to develop programs and receive funding in support of liberation. Much of this added to the broadening stream of Southern Africa action. The demands of James Foreman helped to launch the Committee of Black Churchmen and the Inter Religious Foundation for Community Organization, which under Lucius Walker developed both pacific action and liberation support.

Other American organizations attempted to deal with Southern Africa from a nonactivist and educational perspective. This produced, from 1962 on, a number of scholarships for southern Africans from the African American Institute, but the establishment image of these agencies, which depended on government funds, was difficult to shed. Those dependent upon corporate funding came under even greater criticism of their South African connections. The United States and South African Leadership Exchange Program (USSALEP), headed by business and foundation leaders, supported human rights in principle but did not favor liberation intervention.[29] USSALEP in particular developed a gradualist change rationale for apartheid, directly contrary to the opinions of those arguing for increased transnational revolutionary pressures. Heavily subsidized by industry, banking, and foundations, the USSALEP has concentrated on trying to influence South African whites regarding the need for moderate racial reform and, in turn, to persuade the American elite that South African whites should be understood, not pressured. A number of prominent and influential people such as George Kennan have been converted to this modern version of "the white man's burden."[30]

This contrasts with the emergence in the late sixties of young radical groups led by younger scholars and Peace Corps returnees, who turned in the direction of support for liberation movements. Their orientation was anti-imperialist and incorporated significant Marxian influence derived from overseas experience and the days of student-radical politics. The Africa Research Group (ARG) based in Cambridge, Massachusetts, produced a series of studies of African problems focusing particularly on Southern Africa.[31] The Southern Africa Committee came out of a widespread student concern for research on imperialism and racial problems and led to the identification of the importance of American corporations in United States' relations with the Third World.[32] This committee, initially based in New York, produced *Southern Africa,* a radically oriented monthly news digest, and later, a radio Africa News Service, now expanded to a press service as well. Closely associated with the latter is a group of young Christian radicals who spawned a variety of organizations like the Committee for a Free Mozambique and the Gulf Oil boycott campaign. Most of these groups supported the liberation tendency within the ACOA. The research of these groups and the ACOA had the effect of triggering the economic controversies of the 1970s concerning withdrawal of investments from

South Africa. They emerged in the late 1960s as a part of the widening attack in the churches and colleges on imperialism and, in particular, on the core-power support of apartheid.

Southern African liberation movements, with assistance from African and socialist states and Western NGOs, had already made substantial headway by the early seventies. The Portuguese revolution in 1974 gave them tremendous impetus, and movements within the other settler regimes took on new life.

Thus, by the seventies a third stage had been inaugurated in which Western NGOs established a clear working alliance with African liberation movements, and provided a common ground for black and white Americans to work closely again.

It also marked the emergence of a serious split within the anti-apartheid movement. One group of individuals saw prospects for real peaceful change in South Africa resulting from judicious pacific external pressures, while those described above saw change coming only through revolution and liberation pressures.

The reformists see change coming about in South Africa primarily as a result of industrial growth and new skilled labor demands. External pressures are considered secondary at best and counterproductive at worst. Although they strongly denounce support of apartheid and favor pacific international action, their strategy is sometimes difficult to distinguish from the pronouncements of their governments and is regarded by abolitionists as frequently counter-revolutionary.[33]

The success of the liberation movements in Vietnam and in the Portuguese territories and now in Rhodesia has added to the abolitionist idea that such undertakings are not "futile acts of martyrdom" but real revolutionary developments.[34] FRELIMO and other liberation movements in Portuguese territories have succeeded more quickly than their Western supporters thought possible. The differences in South Africa in terms of relative strengths are very great indeed when the ANC and PAC guerrilla and civil-disobedience potential is compared to the South African army and its lines of support in the Western world. However, the idea has gained wide credence beyond liberation circles in the United States and the United Kingdom that these groups can and will ultimately win.

Thus, there have emerged two different anti-apartheid strategies: one in the direction of domestic reforms with minimal external pressure and the other in favor of disengagement and support for liberation. The former stems from the gradualist, reformist ideas institutionally expressed through the AAI in the United States and the Africa Bureau and others in the United Kingdom, while the latter reflects the abolitionist pressures of the AAM, the ACOA, SAC, and particularly the American black activists. There is some organizational overlap and a few individuals and programs do not fit into one or the other, but the distinction is valid.

The Ecumenical NGOs

A radical Christian approach to liberation emerged on both sides of the Atlantic, signified by the historic actions of the World Council of Churches, beginning in September 1970, in establishing the Fund to Combat Racism, which provided grants to southern African liberation movements. These grants went to other groups as well, such as the Aborigines of Australia, but the focus was upon humanitarian assistance to movements "that align themselves with the victims of racial injustice,"[35] and more than half the allocation went to the southern African groups. Aiding liberation movements was quite a departure for established institutions of the church, which generally limited themselves to quietly aiding nationalist groups through education of refugees or humanitarian programs in southern Africa itself and complied in general with prevailing governmental policy. The courageous examples of those priests and bishops who had dared defy the Afrikaners, such as Scott, Huddleston, Reeves, Ffrench-Beytagh, and Winter were regarded by the official hierarchy of the Church of England as embarrassing yet worthy acts of martyrdom. Indeed, the Church of England, under the Archbishop of Canterbury's leadership, opposed the decision of the World Council and has steadfastly refused to contribute, as an institution, to the World Council's Programme to Combat Racism.[36] The free churches, particularly Methodist and United Reformed, have been active supporters. Catholic action has moved through other ecumenical channels. The major American denominations grouped in the National Council of Churches gave lip service to the program but very little financial assistance.[37] Although the liberation view is prevalent among many professional leaders of the churches, the general membership and those who control the funds are gradualists at best. The former stated clerk of the Presbyterian Church, U.S.A., Eugene Carson Blake, secretary general of the World Council of Churches, was deeply sensitive to racial issues. The role of black American churchmen was crucial in gaining the acceptance of this far-reaching liberation program, but apart from the United Methodists, as Adler shows, they failed to secure funds.

Opposition to this program of liberation emerged in the United States as well as in Europe and was reflected in two *Reader's Digest* articles which charged a Communist takeover of the WCC.[38] The impact of these articles on "lay opinion" was considerable and resulted in a low-profile approach to liberation on the part of many Western church leaders. British spokesmen were peeved by what they called "lack of consultation and arbitrary decision making" by the World Council.[39] Gradualists pointed to the harsh reaction of South Africa, where even the friends of the World Council, under enormous pressure, were forced to denounce this external action, and the Council of Churches of South Africa threatened to withdraw from the World Council.[40] The liberal British press, which is reformist also, had a negative reaction. *The Times* glowered in disapproval of church support for organizations which are "engaged in terror whatever their grievances."[41] The response of the American press was similar, echoing a gradualist caution against shutting off doors of contact within South Africa.

The Christian Century, in responding to the criticism of the World Council of Churches' action in extending humanitarian help to liberation, raised this question: "Must the body of Christ risk its own life in the sharing of burdens with those who have been exploited and humiliated and disinherited?"[42] They concluded that "the Church's long record of acquiescence in violence by white establishments" justified this step.

For pacifist Christians, the decision was most difficult to justify. However, David Harding, general secretary of the Fellowship of Reconciliation, wrote to the *London Times:*

Christian pacifists are against violence but not against justice. Therefore they are likely to support the World Council of Churches gift to liberation movements, explicitly given for non-violent means of realizing their just objective.[43]

Canon John Collins also wrote to the *Times* in a similar vein.

A major study commission report was issued by the British Council of Churches on the subject of violence in Southern Africa, which came to very similar conclusions:

For most of us, our social understanding of love has not taken us beyond an understanding of elementary justice. And this is not to be despised in a world of bitter injustice and inhumanity.[44]

The report called for "solidarity with the aims of the revolutionary struggle in Southern Africa," yet cautioned that resort to force was not the only means. And in a careful delineation of options, it distinguished between the morality of contributions to the Defence and Aid Fund and soliciting arms for the guerrillas. However, not all anti-apartheid activists agreed with this.

The most important debate took place around the effectiveness of certain means of revolutionary intervention. One wing of the British Council of Churches is still convinced that only nonviolent intervention can be effective as well as morally justified. They published their findings in *Non-Violent Action,* a report commissioned by the United Reformed Church.[45]

In the United States and in England, younger radical and ecumenical Christians created new groups to support liberation, such as the Committee for a Free Mozambique in the United States and the Committee on Freedom in Mozambique, Angola, and Guinea in the United Kingdom. The American Committee on Africa was a major force in persuading leading Catholic groups and Protestant denominations to declare their support for aid to the liberation movements.

The Corporate Debate

The younger liberation advocates raised a new issue by their hard-hitting charges of racism in American industry abroad and their activist tactics at corporate stockholders' meetings and in boycott campaigns against Gulf Oil and Polaroid.

In England, a similar anti-investment campaign has been undertaken by the AAM and Counter Information and supported by radical Christians. In the churches, especially in the United States, considerable discussion of disinvestment from South African-linked corporations preceded the Utrecht Statement of the WCC, which called for disinvestment through the sale of stocks.[46] However, to date activists have failed to persuade any major denomination to undertake anything more than token withdrawals and sales of stock. The British Council of Churches (BCC) issued a statement which simply reviewed the various positions of "economic growth," "reform," "disassociation," and "withdrawal."[47] The complex of arguments pro and con is set forth with no preference indicated.

The council and the major British denominations have consistently tabled motions for action on any disinvestment, pending further study. While the Church of England Board of Commissioners sold International Gold Field stock shortly after the Utrecht Statement, Elliot Kendall of the BCC maintained that this was due to other reasons, as was their skepticism over the Rio Tinto Zinc investments in northern Namibia, which simply violated "codes of human decency." Church leadership in England has welcomed corporate reform in South Africa but has refrained from recommending either church or national disinvestment.

American church leadership has been divided between gradualists and abolitionists. The National Council of Churches (NCC) favors disassociation and withdrawal, although it still studies the matter.[48] The controversy has become a very complex one, with churchmen debating the significance of corporate reform in South Africa, as well as what kinds of external pressures might have real impact on conditions of life for blacks. Various church committees have been established, such as the Corporate Information Center, related to the NCC, which researches the evidence, organizes proxy campaigns, and cooperates with nonchurch groups, such as the ACOA, AAI, and the Southern Africa Committee. University research interest has been aroused as well. The subject is not a new one. For years, the United Nations, ACOA, International Defence and Aid, and the AAM have published findings about racial discrimination in corporations in Southern Africa. Yet, it has become important, because it reflects the basic issue of the use of forceful nongovernmental action as against the gradualist and legal strategy of the establishment in the West. For the present, the gradualist bias of

churches and research groups has blunted the drive of the abolitionists and given the South African Foundation, and partisans of
South African paternalism, especially corporations, more time in
which to make their case. They have leaped to their own defense
and made skillful use of such opportunities as the House of Commons Select Committee Hearings on the South African investments
of British industry to justify themselves, claiming to have made
improvements of African working and living conditions.[49] By removing the discussion from the context of the total apartheid system
to a focus on wages and cost of living in South Africa, they have
managed to convey the impression of general beneficence of industry mixed with ultimate hope for improvement in the practices of
discrimination in South Africa. The gradualists have found their
lagging fortunes suddenly revived by this issue, as the British and
American foreign-policy establishments feel directly threatened by
the attack on corporations.[50]

Compromise

However, in both Britain and America a compromise between
the two poles has emerged as represented appropriately in their
United Nations Associations (UNA). In a document widely circulated in the American UNA, *Southern Africa: Proposals for
Americans,* a panel headed by Cyrus Vance called for restrictive
action on American corporations investing in Namibia and a mora-
torium on future investment in South Africa.[51] In its annual general
meeting, the British UNA pressed several measures, including the
exclusion of South Africa from "more favorable terms for the
export of her goods to the Community (EEC)," and "to work for
the suspending of South Africa from GATT." On investments,
there was only a request for further investigation of corporate policies, though the matter of the "contract labor system, reminiscent
of slavery" was raised.[52] Sympathy for liberation movements also
began to grow. Strong sentiment for limiting further investment in
South Africa and repealing favorable double taxation laws surfaced
in liberal political circles in both the United States and the United
Kingdom.[53] This was far from the goal of withdrawal held by the
World Council and the liberation movements. Yet it opened up for

consideration the extent to which the South African economy depended on the West and therefore the whole question of Western complicity in the crimes of apartheid.

The anti-apartheid movement had clearly come of age in the midseventies, despite the decline of radicalism on both sides of the Atlantic. The trend of events in Southern Africa showed that the foreign policy of communication and "tilt to the settlers" to bring gradual, peaceful change had been bypassed by the revolution. Events in Angola, with major Russian and Cuban intervention, brought this dramatically to the attention of the world. And the siege of Rhodesia by liberation forces threatened the whole basis of Western strategic economic interests. South African apartheid had to be abolished. The dilemma for the establishment remained: How? A study of the proposals of anti-apartheid over the years offers many alternatives.

Notes

1. See George W. Shepherd, Jr., "Liberal Internationalism in the British Labour Party (1900-1945)," Ph.D. thesis, London University, 1952.

2. E. H. Carr, *Conditions of Peace* (London: Macmillan and Co., 1942), p. 37.

3. Ibid., p. 38.

4. The phrase was coined by Sydney Webb in reference to Socialism but is applicable to self-determination as well. Webb served under MacDonald as Colonial Secretary and had been a civil servant in the India Office. Under Dr. Rita Hinden, the Fabian Colonial Bureau was far more outspoken on issues concerning Colonial Africa than on the issues of white supremacy.

5. Lord Hailey's work is most representative of this group and period. See his *An African Survey* (London: Royal Institute of International Affairs and Oxford University Press, 1938, 1956). It is an enormous collection of information within this liberal-legal framework of gradualism, which treats South Africa as a part of the colonial problem without recognizing how the racial conflict there creates an entirely different condition for change. Sir Andrew Cohen's writings and career represent the practical application of Fabian gradualism in which there is little recognition of the dangers of apartheid and conventional intervention in support of white supremacy or the necessity for international action against the system.

Sir Andrew Cohen, *British Policy in Changing Africa* (Evanston, Ill.: Northwestern University Press, 1959).

6. The Anti-Slavery Society for the Protection of Human Rights came out of a union in 1909 of the British and Foreign Anti-Slavery Society, founded in 1839, with the Aborigines Protection Society, founded in 1838.

7. Michael Scott, *A Time to Speak* (New York: Doubleday, 1958), pp. 239-266. Here, he describes this unusual accomplishment.

8. While the ACOA was founded in 1953 with the author as the first secretary, it did not get fully underway until 1955 when George Houser left the FOR to become the first full-time paid executive. See George W. Shepherd, Jr., *They Wait in Darkness* (New York: John Day, 1955), pp. 299-308. Also see George Houser, ''Meeting Africa's Challenge: The Story of the American Committee on Africa,'' *Issue,* vol. VI, no. 2/3, 1976.

9. Tom Mboya, *Freedom and After* (London: Andre Deutsch, 1973), p. 30.

10. Charles A. W. Manning is representative of a school of South African white liberal academics who have emigrated and vigorously defend their motherland from its foreign critics. They are critical of apartheid; but like their counterparts in South Africa in the United Party, they would maintain a white-dominance system of paternalistic guidance. Such academics have often achieved eminence in the Western world, where they have been regarded as spokesmen for enlightened South Africa. For example, the evidence given the World Court by Professor Manning and Dr. E. Von der Haag (professor of social philosophy at New York University) on behalf of South Africa's claim to South West Africa and her right to practice plural differentiation among peoples, was simply support for continued racial control.

11. C. W. De Kiewiet, *The Anatomy of South African Misery* (London: Oxford University Press, 1956), exemplified the gradualist white liberal view of South Africa.

12. ''The Constitution of the Africa Bureau,'' mimeographed. Africa Bureau, London, 1952.

13. ''AIMS,'' Africa Bureau, mimeographed. Africa Bureau, London, 1952.

14. Leading lights over the years have been Mary Benson, Jane Symonds, Sir Berhard de Bunsen, Lord Caradon, Nicholas Deacon, Guy Arnold (a former secretary), and Colin and Margaret Legum.

15. Sir Bernard de Bunsen, in an interview, 14 May 1973, stated that a majority of the board would probably not support violent change in South Africa.

16. ACOA Executive Committee Statement, September 1955.

17. Bayard Rustin's departure from ACOA in the early sixties exempli-

fied this difference over violence, which became a major issue between gradualists and abolitionists.

18. See *Annual Report,* Anti-Apartheid Movement, 19 September 1970-19 August 1971.

19. Ethel De Keyser, executive secretary of the AAM stated in an interview in June 1973 that the AAM does not officially endorse civil-disobedience campaigns but believes in demonstrations.

20. Jariretundu Kozanquizi in "The South African White Left and the Struggle for Liberation," *Race Today,* September 1969, sees the AAM as "firmly in the hands of South African whites" who he also maintains have a sense of mission "to maintain white liberalism and paternalism," p. 144.

21. The South Africans or British who have lived for many years in South Africa are frequently the most outspoken voices of the AAM, such as Ruth First and Ethel De Keyser. The former Anglican bishop of Johannesburg, the Right Reverend Ambrose Reeves, is honorary president of AAM.

22. John Ennals, chairman of the AAM, whose brother Martin ran the National Committee for Commonwealth Immigrants, spoke actively on behalf of the Commonwealth Immigrants' Amendment Act of 1968, which black and brown Britons in general strongly opposed. This did not help AAM relations with the immigrant communities.

23. In 1971, honorary sponsors were Lord Brockway, Lord Collison, Thomas Hodgkin, Jack Jones, Right Honorable Reg Prentice, M.P., David Steel, M.P., and Angus Wilson, which represents a broad spread in British society.

24. Aims of the fund are (a) to aid, defend, and rehabilitate the victims of unjust legislation and oppressive arbitrary procedures, (b) support their families and dependents, (c) keep the conscience of the world alive to the issues at stake.

The International Defence and Aid Fund stands for freedom and democracy and is in full accord with the Charter of the United Nations and with the Universal Declaration of Human Rights.

25. Interview by the author with Dennis Healey in October 1972.

26. AAM officials do not feel well treated by the press, although their campaigns are well covered, as both Abdul Minty and Ethel De Keyser told the author in interviews.

27. See *Anti-Apartheid News,* published monthly by the AAM, which carries many items on local activity.

28. The October-December 1969 issue of *Africa Today* (Vol. 16, Nos. 5 & 6) reviewed the various positions, and the further developments were reviewed in the January 1971 issue (Vol. 18, No. 1).

29. The United States-South African Leadership Program was launched

in the early 1960s to exchange people and ideas between the two countries and to enlighten policy. Many prominent liberal white South Africans and Verlichte Afrikaners joined, but the American side was weaker, consisting of a few American gradualists like Professor Edwin C. Munger, who had long opposed liberation action. No prominent black civil-rights leaders joined.

30. See George Kennan, "The Hazardous Courses in Southern Africa," *Foreign Affairs,* January 1971, which he wrote after a USSALEP-sponsored tour of South Africa.

31. See Alan Kellock et al., *Race to Power: The Struggle for Southern Africa* (Cambridge, Mass.: Africa Research Group, 1971).

32. The ARG disbanded in 1973 and turned their files and publication rights over to a black research and information group: African Information Services, based in Harlem and headed by Robert Van Lierop. Many ARG members became active with the Southern African Committee.

33. Numerous expositions of this reform view exist in both countries and in South Africa. It was presented in the United States in *Southern Africa and the United States,* edited by William Hance (New York: Columbia University Press, 1968), and more recently in England by *Change in Southern Africa* by Anthony Wilkinson, Merle Lipton and Jack Spence, edited by Godfrey Morrison (London: Miramoor Publications, Ltd., 1975, for *Africa Confidential*).

34. Davis M'Gabe, "The Reality of Guerrilla Warfare," *Africa Today,* Vol. 19, No. 1 (Winter 1972).

35. The criteria for support cited in a memo of 5-9 September 1971, a year later, were as follows: (a) the movement must be capable of aiding the racially oppressed; (b) its activities must be consistent with the general purposes of the WCC, (i.e., humanitarian activities), and (c) it must have control over its own funds. Document No. 25 A, World Council of Churches, Executive Committee.

36. Elizabeth Adler, *A Small Beginning,* an assessment of the first five years of the Programme to Combat Racism (Geneva, WCC Press, 1974) cites the grants made, p. 92.

37. Ibid.

38. C. W. Hall, "Must Our Churches Finance Revolutions?" *Reader's Digest,* October 1971, and "Which Way the World Council of Churches?" *Reader's Digest,* November 1971.

39. Confirmed in an interview with officials of the British Council of Churches, who claimed that one of the West Indian groups aided didn't even exist.

40. *Rand Daily Mail,* 12 September 1970.

41. *The Times* (London), 15 September 1970.

42. *Christian Century,* 23 September 1970.

43. *The Times* (London), 18 September 1970.

44. "Violence in Southern Africa: A Christian Assessment," p. 62. Mimeographed. Department of International Affairs, British Council of Churches, 1970. The commission was chaired by Philip Mason.

45. "It is doubtful whether one nation-state should intervene to overthrow the government of another: as long as nation-states remain, the precedents are dangerous."

This group preferred actions such as a "pre-emptive non-violent strike" and "non-violent invading forces." United Reformed Church, *Non-Violent Action* (London: SCM Press, 1973).

46. "Investments in Southern Africa," WCC Central Committee Meeting, Utrecht, a resolution mimeographed, 13-23 August 1972. This position requested all member churches "outside of Southern Africa to use all their influence including stockholder action and disinvestment to press corporations to withdraw investments from and cease trading with these countries," p. 1.

47. *Investment in Southern Africa,* Department of International Affairs of the British Council of Churches and the Conference of British Missionary Societies, 1973.

48. The Dallas statement of the NCC, January 1973, on southern Africa.

49. Verbatim reports of hearings of the Select Committee on Expenditure Trade and Industry Sub-Committee can be found in *The Guardian,* April-June 1973.

50. The withdrawal position of the AAM was outlined in "Memorandum to the House of Commons Select Committee on Expenditure Trade and Industry Sub-Committee," 13 June 1973, in which the history of the AAM opposition to the structure and character of the South African economy is reviewed. The document was drafted by Abdul Minty, Ruth First, Christabel Gurney, and others; mimeographed, AAM, 1973.

51. The panel included several businessmen such as George Lindsay, John R. Banting Jr., and Harvey Russell, as well as dissenter Hans Ries.

52. UNA twenty-eighth annual general meeting held at Weston-Super Mare, 13, 15 April 1973. Resolutions mimeographed, GC 73/20.

53. Both the Democratic Party in the United States and the Labour Party in Britain by 1972 had included anti-apartheid proposals in their platforms for the repeal of tax credits to corporations. By the mid-seventies prominent leaders sympathetic to liberation movements held key positions. The implications and consequences of this will be discussed in later chapters.

chapter 4

FROM ASSIMILATION TO CONFLICT AND COALITION: BLACK NONGOVERNMENTAL ORGANIZATION

The rediscovery of a common cultural heritage and an increasing consciousness of common victimization links blacks in the United States and the United Kingdom to blacks in Africa.[1] Although as Harold Cruse observed about American blacks, they may "have little in common with the foreign revolutionaries they have read about," many blacks, both moderate and militant, have come to regard their ultimate freedom as inseparable from the freedom of Africa.[2]

Blacks on both sides of the Atlantic have moved in this century through very similar phases of rejection of their heritage, recovery of it, and alignment with the transnational liberation struggle. The shift of the black movement from a preoccupation with middle-class, primarily domestic conflicts to a recognition of its role in the vanguard of transnational effort and a commitment to African liberation has been slow and difficult, but the struggle of liberation movements in Africa played a key role in the awakening of blacks in the Atlantic powers to the relationship between the ghettoes of the core states and the apartheid structure of the southern African periphery.

The forces and ideas bringing about change in the perception of black minorities of their role are similar to those that moved the human-rights NGOs toward active liberation struggle. The blacks first developed a passive-protest stance and a legalistic approach, and then moved on to activist and liberation-commitment phases. This has meant division in their ranks between gradualist and abolitionist protagonists, and a considerable conflict between assimilationist and liberationist elites. It is essential to understand the basis of these differences to appreciate fully the way racial transnational consciousness has created a new unity and a revolutionary force.

The names of W. E. B. Du Bois, Paul Robeson, Charles Garvey, Ralph Bunche, Martin Luther King, and Malcolm X all stand out in the annals of American black concern for Africa. They, and the movements they created, have influenced the radical shift in direction and attitude of blacks in the United States. In England, black leaders have always been, for the most part, exiles—liberation leaders—and students from Africa and the West Indies, and a number of them, such as Jomo Kenyatta, Kwame Nkrumah, and George Padmore played significant roles in the politics of the black world in the formative years of the anticolonial movements. Later leaders, such as Dipak Nandy, a brown Briton of the Runnymede Trust, or Michael X, a black-power leader, became well-known in English politics. During their student years, men like Kwame Nkrumah were highly successful organizers of anticolonial and freedom conferences. Some West Indians, such as Eric Williams, also contributed a great deal to an early and flourishing awareness of the need for transnational black consciousness and power. Their impact was especially significant through the pan-African congresses they organized in the early post-World War II years. In contrast, the African student or political leader in the United States had, until very recently, little impact, because as a black man, he was expected to work with and through the black community, where his status was very low, both as an alien and an African. In the United States he was perceived as a threat to the status quo by the white majority and to its tenuous position by the black community. In England, the African did not threaten the power structures directly. He had the status of a colonial or Commonwealth subject, which legitimized a low level of political participation in the policy-formulation process.[3]

A few Afro-Americans, like George Padmore, had careers which spanned both countries. Padmore, as a West Indian, played a minor role in the left-wing politics of Harlem, but when he moved to London, he became first an organizer of the International Communist Movement and later, after breaking with Moscow, an important link with the African leaders in London at the time—much like Kwame Nkrumah.[4] Padmore and other such noted Caribbeans as Marcus Garvey and the Harvard Ph.D., W. E. B. Du Bois, moved across continents, stirring inspired support for the pan-African ideal of unity of black peoples everywhere. These ideas were, of course, fundamental in the development of solidarity movements of varying size and importance, from the Versailles Conference of 1919 to the Manchester Conference of 1945 and the later pan-African congresses in Africa.

The end of World War II, when so many old values and structures had been shattered, marked the beginning of a new era in the black struggle. There were hard days ahead, but a rising wind from Africa was sweeping north and west, bearing seeds of change.

A New Spirit and New Directions

In the postwar era in the United States, there emerged a multi-racial, predominantly black-led civil-rights movement, which achieved limited reforms in education, employment, and housing.[5] However, the younger generation of blacks, often the sons and daughters of the new black middle-class, turned in the 1960s to new ways of expressing the demands of black consciousness—away from the multi-racialism of the older movements, whose efforts they derided, and toward an aggressive advocacy of resistance and liberation. This activity in the United States had three major phases: the legal actions of the NAACP in the 1950s; the direct-action strategy of SNCC, CORE, and the Southern Leadership Conference in the 1960s (an outgrowth of which was the advocacy of self-dependence by the Black Muslim and Black Panther militants); and the wave of the 1970s, which inaugurated black collective bargaining, coalition politics, class struggle, and the accelerated assimilation of a black elite.

As the civil-rights movement radicalized from the fifties through the sixties and into the seventies, it became less tolerant of white liberals, accusing them of betrayal, and more stringent in its demands for immediate and substantial benefits for blacks. For some, the new radicalism had the effect of moving African—especially southern African—affairs to the top of the agenda, but others continued to reject identification with Africa.

The rise of black power and the breakdown of multiracial cooperation is widely misunderstood and misrepresented in both the United States and England. Much initial black consciousness was a reaction against the definition of black problems by white liberals and those who controlled the finances of organization. As Hamilton and Carmichael noted:

Whenever a number of persons within a society have enjoyed for a considerable period of time certain opportunities of getting wealth, of exercising power and authority, and for successfully claiming prestige and social deference, there is a strong tendency for these people to feel that these benefits are theirs by "right." . . . Proposals to change the existing situation arouse the reactions of "moral indignation."[6]

Similar views were expressed in England by Chris Mallard, the leader of the Black House Community, who criticized the domination of research and policy in the race field by whites: "Up to now, the white race establishments, together with politicians, have initiated all policy, be it on immigration or race matters."[7] This acute perception of the fundamental paradox in black-white "cooperation" determined the subsequent phases of the development of the black movements.

The cultivation of a sense of Afro-American identity by leaders like Bobby Seale and Stokely Carmichael turned one section of the American movement back toward coalition building for the purposes of collective bargaining and black-power politics, and away from the self-destructive internecine strife that had weakened the militant black community.[8] With new self-confidence based on Afro-American identity, a new valuation of the African heritage, and a recognition of the gains made by an elite through the coalition politics of the 1960s, many American black leaders returned to the idea of coalitions with whites as a formula for preserving black independence while widening the capacity to use the power structure for black ends. Jesse Jackson's assessment of new found black strength expressed this pragmatic viewpoint:

We have more consciousness now. We are less likely to be put back into slavery. We are better equipped intellectually, emotionally, and technically to protect ourselves. We finally had to come to that independence to get to the next step.[9]

In both England and the United States, the direction of black power has settled into a pattern of self-determination, building black interest structures in which some groups are willing to work with whites on a class basis, while others accept a coalition basis for action. The influence of Marxist ideas on the nature of the class struggle has transformed some black leaders, like Amiri Imamu Baraka, into "new communism" advocates. This poet of the Black Renaissance stated that the struggle

is ultimately a struggle to destroy capitalism, the center of racism . . . [and] skin nationalism cannot do that. We need to gain a clear knowledge of socialist theory and unite with those who really want to build a new world. That is the only criteria: Black liberation is socialist revolution.[10]

Other black scholars and activists, however, such as Ron Walters of Howard University, continue to emphasize the primacy of the "black diaspora" in determining the direction and outcome of the struggle, while Charles Hamilton adds a further dimension to Baraka's view in maintaining that blacks are acutely conscious of class because "we are *all socialists now,* and differences over race are not that great."[11] In England, the recognition of the importance of class is reflected in the Institute of Race Relations, which transformed its journal, *Race,* to *Race and Class,* while maintaining on its editorial board such liberation-oriented whites as Thomas Hodgkins and Basil Davidson.

The class issue for blacks, despite its widely disparate ideological formulations, has inaugurated a new phase in which white liberals are castigated for maintaining bourgeois paternalism, while black elites are accused of opportunism.[12] Nevertheless, it has provided as well the basis of renewed collaboration between radicals and human-rights NGOs and blacks. At the same time, however, the ideological approach has led to rifts with a number of African leaders of new states who prefer to work with the Western powers and promote "dialogue" with South Africa. The Sixth Pan-African Congress in Dar es Salaam in 1974 demonstrated that most African governments are much less ideologically committed to race and class concepts and are very wary of the effect ideological debate can have on their own parties and intellectuals.[13]

In short, although there is a wide range of disparate viewpoints and strategies among black movements in the United States and the United Kingdom—from pragmatic coalition politics to purist separatism to revolutionary Socialism—there is a clearly defined new direction toward transnational alignment for liberation and a new spirit of unity of Western and African blacks.

The Black Struggle in the United States

The movement of Africa to the foreground of black group thinking has taken place as a result of the growing populism, militancy, and romanticism widespread throughout both England and the United States. African identification is far more marked on the American scene, however, because the pace and quality of *change,* from moderate, passive protest to radical activism for liberation, has been more dramatic. Black organizational roles can be analyzed in terms of the era in civil-rights history in which they emerged— periods of regression, consolidation, or revolution in American social philosophy.

The Phelps-Stokes Fund and the NAACP had a long history of involvement in human-rights concerns predating the United Nations. The fund was established to advance African education. Initially the NAACP was actively involved in African colonial affairs through the pan-African views of Dr. Du Bois. Both organizations, together with related, moderate, middle-class Negro organizations, contributed ideas to the human-rights and trusteeship structure of the United Nations as representatives to the founding San Francisco Conference.[14] The Phelps-Stokes Fund, under Dr. Emory Ross and Dr. Patterson, produced a document, "The Atlantic Charter and Africa," proposing African decolonization within a moderate, legalistic framework and mildly criticizing South African racial policies.[15]

However, apart from Du Bois and Paul Robeson, very few American black leaders in these organizations either knew much about African (especially southern African) matters or were prepared to make an issue out of racism. Preoccupied as they were with effecting legal and material gains within the white establishment in the United States, they were reluctant to jeopardize limited, practical benefits for the sake of transnational, humanitarian abstractions. Africa had a low priority for them. The Urban League was even more typical of this provincialism, since it was founded primarily to assist Negroes in breaking through the barriers of opportunity in the cities and industries of the United States. Only much later did such individuals as Whitney Young begin to change this insular image, and indeed, it was individuals rather than groups who led the fight for a larger, human-rights consciousness among American blacks. Dr. Ralph Bunche, an early NAACP leader and later Associate Secretary-General of the United Nations, was devoted to the problems of southern Africans, and President Mordecai Johnson of Howard University was highly influential in human rights. Professor Rayford Logan and Professor John Davis are two among many black scholars whose work over several decades on African human rights had an important impact on the black movement. The list of concerned individual black Americans is a long one. In terms of groups, one short-lived but important exception to the organization pattern of according secondary status to African concern deserves special mention.

The Council on African Affairs

In the 1940s and 1950s when the prevailing attitude toward African affairs among American black moderates was, at best, indifference, the Council on African Affairs was two decades ahead of its time in working for African liberation in the black community. The council was embroiled in the McCarthyism of the fifties, which divided and destroyed it, but not before this significant NGO made a major contribution to the growing postwar concern of American liberals, radicals, and blacks with Africa.[16] Max Yergan, who as a YMCA worker spent several years working with Africans in South

Africa where the African National Congress helped to radicalize his thinking, returned to the United States and formed the International Committee on African Affairs in 1937. In 1941, when Paul Robeson and his wife, Eslanda, joined the group, it became the Council on African Affairs with Robeson as chairman. From the outset, the council was committed to the political liberation of Africans; it sought to develop direct contacts and aid toward that end, and to educate the American public.

Many distinguished American blacks, such as Dr. Mordecai Johnson, Ralph Bunche, and W. E. B. Du Bois played a role in the council, together with such activists and Africanists as Raymond Leslie Buell of Harvard and Norman McKenzie of Toronto University. Max Yergan and Paul Robeson worked in harmony during the war years, and the organization played a minor role in the creation of the United Nations, which was seen as an instrument for decolonization. With the onset of the Cold War, the council was subjected to harassment in the anticommunist "witch hunts" of the era, which resulted in a split over how to answer the charges. Max Yergan sought compromise, although he was then considered a fellow traveler; Robeson, a forthright Marxist, favored confrontation. Yergan lost out to Robeson and Du Bois; Dr. W. Alphaeus Hunter took over as director, continuing the publication of *New Africa* and the council's activities at the United Nations. The adverse publicity caused a number of prominent members to drop out, however, and Yergan increasingly engaged in right-wing attacks on the council, which diminished its slim financial resources. The American black Africanist and church sources of support for African concerns were clearly disturbed by the alleged communist connections of the organization, which took a very strong anti-imperialist line and had a number of openly avowed Marxist intellectuals on its governing board, and their loss was critical.

Whether the council was or was not a "front for the Communist Party of the U.S.A." is not the major historical issue, and certainly not a matter the House Un-American Activities Committee was capable of settling. The council was the first major expression of American NGO—and especially militant black NGO—concern for African human rights in the postwar era. Needless to say, this counted for nothing in the atmosphere of the times. The U.S. Department of Justice pressed charges in an attempt to force the council to register with the Subversive Activities Control Board as a "communist front" organization. The charges were never proved, but the council's support dwindled away, and it fell a victim to the anti-communist hysteria of the period when it disbanded in 1955—one of the many victims of McCarthyism—and American NGO activity suffered a major setback. The intimidation reinforced the tendency of American blacks not to press for reform of American foreign policy or to try to raise the level of human-rights consciousness and transnational concern for Africa.

Diverse Problems, Differing Voices

As the rising streams of awareness and confrontation, black consciousness and black power flowed toward their convergence, the floodtide of the 1960s, a wide variety of groups and individuals responded to the new problems, perceptions, and constraints that rose to the surface in the 1950s.

Self-interest contributed to the general black indifference to southern African problems during the fifties. Bayard Rustin, whose career spanned the period, from his work with the Fellowship of Reconciliation to that with the A. Philip Randolph Institute, viewed this diffidence in a typical light when he said, "The immediate problems of Negroes' lives are so vast as to allow them very little time or energy to focus on a large scale upon international crises."[17] Nevertheless, it was the international crises of war and decolonization that changed the outlook of many American blacks, including Rustin himself.

The rise and demise of two related organizations in the late fifties and early sixties illustrate the difficulty that black leaders experienced in organizing the interest and financial support necessary for a major effort for African human rights, despite their own repeated avowals of concern. An academic group, founded by and limited to black intellectuals, with money from an Irish philanthropist, the African American Society on African Culture (AMSAC) was organized in 1956, with close ties to the journal *Presence Africaine* in Paris, and began an impressive series of conferences and an academic journal. AMSAC was primarily concerned with the emergence of new African states, however, and paid little attention (with the exception of one conference in 1963 at Howard University, Washington, D.C., which produced a number of papers) to the problems of Southern Africa.[18] Unable to obtain adequate funding, apparently, and in striking contrast with the Council on African Affairs, AMSAC took funds from a CIA conduit foundation, which was a fatal mistake in the developing ethos of the black politics of the 1960s.[19] Once again, a predominantly black NGO fell afoul of the United States establishment's desire and determination to control. AMSAC did serve, however, as a launching pad for a number of black ambassadorships under the Kennedy Administration, and provided the basis for generating intellectual contact and cultural interaction with Africa in response to the growing interest of middle-class blacks in their heritage.

A related organization of the early 1960s, the American Negro Leadership Congress on Africa, brought together, under A. Philip Randolph's chairmanship, representatives of the NAACP, AMSAC, CORE, the Southern Leadership Conference, trade unions, and churches. It flowered briefly in the euphoric early Kennedy days, when the U.S. State Department was looking for black support under the civil-rights activist leadership of G. Mennen Williams, Assistant Secretary of State for Africa. This black NGO, too, withered on the vine, more from lack of funding than from government interventions, again reflecting the low priority of Africa among black American organizations. Although black movements were enjoying a period of unprecedentedly strong financial support, from members as well as foundations and government subsidies, little money or attention was divered from domestic concerns to African problems.

Even with the advent of younger leadership and new groups, such as CORE and SNCC, which had well-educated student leadership—including James Farmer and Stokely Carmichael—the situation did not change quickly. After Farmer made a trip to Africa, he urged his fellow blacks to "take a definite position in support of the aspirations of the African liberation movement. . . ."[20] Africa only became top priority for Carmichael after his departure from SNCC and his long period of tutelage under Kwame Nkrumah, most of it in Conakry during Nkrumah's exile. On Carmichael's return to the United States in 1972, he started his all-black political party with the ideology of pan-Africanism. His dual citizenship symbolized his commitment from that time on. "I am a citizen of Guinea," he stated, "and I would urge all blacks to become citizens of an African country and have dual citizenship."[21]

Most important of all in the current of change, however, was the influence of Martin Luther King, one of the most universal of all black American leaders. King derived much of his inspiration from Gandhi, and Chief Luthuli's philosophy. Nonviolent action campaigns in South Africa had great influence on the American leader's adoption of the passive-resistance-direct-action doctrine and technique.[22] Another powerful guiding spirit of the "new" blacks in the United States was Malcolm X. While Malcolm X and Martin Luther King may have differed in their philosophy of violence and non-violence, they shared a deep identification with the struggles of cololnial peoples and Africans under white oppression in Africa. True religious spirits, one from Islam, the other from Christianity, they each had a stronger sense of the universal human values than most men. Unfortunately, the nationalism of their followers, who were caught up in the competition for the rewards of politics, proved incapable of sustaining the larger view for long. This was illustrated when King brought the civil-rights movement into the Vietnam War protest because he so strongly believed that racism and oppression had to be combated, in all its forms and everywhere in the world as well as at home, especially when one's own government is the oppressor. King was vehemently attacked for this action by other civil-rights leaders, who did not wish to compromise the gains made under the Johnson Administration by attacking American foreign policy. Even one of his closest lieutenants, Bayard Rustin, joined Hubert Humphrey in chiding King for his involvement in protesting the war.[23]

Throughout the 1960s, King, Malcolm X, and black-power advocates Bobby Seale, Eldridge Cleaver, and Stokely Carmichael created in American black politics a new African liberation consciousness, which, in turn, influenced the middle class in such established organizations as the NAACP to give greater attention to the human-rights crisis in Southern Africa. A resolution passed by the NAACP annual meeting showed black support for economic disengagement:

"We call upon the United States Government to prevent further investment by American companies in the economy of minority-dominated governments."[24] Still, middle-class black American leaders tended to echo the conventional establishment wisdom concerning developments in Southern Africa. It was therefore not surprising that when Roy Wilkins visited South Africa in 1972, he returned with the suggestion that American industry should continue to invest in the land of apartheid to promote its "reform." This promptly raised a storm of protest from the advocates of disinvestment, who had believed, on the basis of its earlier statements, that the NAACP favored economic sanctions. Wilkins later explained that he did not believe industrial growth in South Africa would necessarily cure the cancer of apartheid, but the episode clearly revealed that business-minded black Americans are as prone to think paternalistically about the advantages of investment abroad as their white counterparts, even when their profits depend on what has been called a slavery system.[25] Given the prevailing values of the American system, the color of a man's skin does not necessarily determine his attitude toward accommodation of apartheid, as more than one black ambassador demonstrated in the 1960s.

Liberation Nongovernmental Organizations

The black-consciousness phenomenon of the 1960s and early 1970s has irrevocably changed the basic trends on Africa in the black community in the United States. The basic demand that assimilation and white dominance end has inspired the recovery of African traditions and the establishment of solidarity links with liberation groups, as well as with the new African states. While the black movement continues to flow in diverse streams, these streams increasingly converge in African consciousness and identification. Even the NAACP, its elderly leadership replaced by a younger, more Africa-conscious elite, is responding to the racial-linkage theme. The breakdown of the strategy of cooperation with white leaders and dependence on establishment resources led such black nationalists as Stokely Carmichael toward coalition building. Other black-power leaders opposed total disassociation from the white society and continued to work with liberal organizations they considered dedicated and useful to the black cause. After the break of the black scholarly community with the African Studies Association in 1968, however, the black-consciousness thesis was more succinctly stated and more readily implemented than ever before. When the black Africanists who left the ASA formed the African Heritage Studies Association (AHSA) in the same year, its first president, Professor John Henry Clarke, addressing the almost entirely black membership, urged young black scholars to find their own identity through their own associations, asserting their own traditions and rejecting dependence on white-led organizations and white-controlled resources.[26] The AHSA has been one of the most productive and influential organizations (from an academic perspective) in the field of human rights in general and Southern African concerns in particular.

Many other new, black-led organizations have entered the field of liberation support, all with the cardinal purposes of providing material aid and establishing moral solidarity with Africans under colonial and racial oppression. Black Society, the African Information Service, the Black World Institute, the Congress of African Peoples, the Interreligious Foundation for Community Organization, the Black Caucus, and the African Liberation Committee are but a few of the many new, more militant black American groups. They have provided financial aid to various liberation movements, such as SWAPO (the Namibian nationalist organization), and have begun extensive public reeducation programs, as in the case of the African Information Service, which sent Robert Van Lierop, a black-activist attorney, into Mozambique, where he took pictures and later raised funds to assist FRELIMO in liberated areas.[27]

These groups have not limited their activities to support of the humanitarian aspects of liberation wars, but have also, in some cases, provided resources for the armed struggle. The liberation movements are an outlet for the revolutionary zeal of young American blacks, who have been searching for ways to transmit their revolutionary commitment to Africa.

A New Kind of Cooperation

Black consciousness, if not black power, encompasses all these groups, making the victimization of the black man in Southern

Africa a part of the American blacks' struggle against discrimination at home. This consciousness has united militant and moderate blacks, although it works under different strategies, and it has also created a sense of identity which allows self-confident cooperation with whites in the comprehensive cause of human rights. The black-liberation groups and individuals have found a common cause with the other human-rights organizations. They have helped the development of abolitionist strategies indispensable to the growth of multiracial endeavors, such as those of the ACOA, the Southern Africa Committee, and the American churches. The ideology of liberation, replacing the gradualism themes of the earlier period, has provided an alternative framework for meaningful black-white cooperation.

The Black Caucus in the U.S. Congress (CBC) is one powerful component of this new coalition. Created by a number of NGOs, the caucus works closely with the Washington Office on Africa. Congressman Charles Diggs has provided the informed leadership on southern African affairs the coalition needed. Through Congressional hearings, black rallies, visits to Africa, and even representation at the United Nations, Diggs, his colleagues, and capable former research aide Goler Butcher have presented a formidable case for liberation.[28] Knowledgeable, moderate in manner, with well-researched cases and a clear grasp of the new goals, the Black Caucus has won considerable respect in the Congress and in the foreign-policy bureaucracy. By building support for the liberation alternative of the anti-apartheid struggle, Congressman Diggs, with Senator Richard Clark, has served as a catalyst for action on behalf of the black American Africa constituency. In the United States, this coalition has moved from protest to a position that seriously challenges the communication policy of the gradualists. The coalition politics that emerged from the black-consciousness and black-power struggles of the 1960s has become a force to be reckoned with—by the United States establishment and by South Africa.

Blacks in the United Kingdom

Despite the common base of pan-Negro consciousness in black groups in the United States and in the United Kingdom, there are fundamental historical differences in the nature of the racial conflict in the two countries. In the United Kingdom, resident blacks are essentially immigrants, outsiders in the social system. This group has no immediate revolutionary expectation. The other black element in England, the African liberation leadership, while revolutionary, is necessarily more concerned with African than with English society. There is little sense of unity or common cause between the two groups. The situation contrasts sharply with that in the United States, where blacks are a depressed, alienated minority, with an elite divided between assimilation and liberation, but with a common heritage and common cause within their own society. This, of course, has affected the ideas, methods of organization, and influence on the society at home, as well as the African commitment of blacks in the United States and in England.

The extent of forced assimilation in a conquest system is much greater than that in a society where the minority has largely immigrated voluntarily. Granted that the conditions of racial discrimination are similar in the two countries, but the crucial distinction is the greater *violence* inherent in the American experience—the much deeper loss and repression, the correspondingly much higher level of revolutionary reaction.

The immigrant component has given a strong ethnic identity to the British black community, and it is constantly enhanced and reinforced by the presence of many African students, diplomats, and businessmen in London. Blacks and browns in the United Kingdom, while suffering from discrimination, have been subjected to less pressure for assimilation than American blacks, and have been allowed to keep their ethnic identity of African, West Indian, Hindu, or Sikh.[29] This situation is closely related to the attitude of racist groups in the United Kingdom, which directs their campaigns to repatriate the blacks.[30] The basic white English attitude was vividly summed up by a community-relations worker:

It may be sub-conscious, but many British feel their role in the world has been to go out and civilize the natives and savages, teach them all about the white man's God, and the civilized man's cricket. Those natives were never supposed to come here and live next door.[31]

The insecurity created by the threat of deportation and other forms of white assertion of dominance has generated a new phase of self-defensive black militancy in England. An editorial in *The West Indian World* reflected Indian reaction to an immigration ruling upholding deportation of illegal immigrants:

But suddenly, our feeling of security has been shattered. Before we walked the streets of this country as free citizens, entitled to the protection of the law, like anyone else. It never occurred to any of us that we will be stopped by an official policeman . . . like the blacks of South Africa . . . have to produce the British version of the pass—the passport.[32]

Another basis for the difference between blacks in the two countries is the effect of class on the racial system. British class consciousness, always acute, is at its worst when it comes to providing a place for black immigrant groups. Although the legal barriers to black participation in the opportunities of life have been far less harsh and numerous in Britain than in the United States, class attitudes have rigidly enforced the "colour bar" in England. Nonwhites have been very restricted in opportunity to gain quality education and entrance into the professions and skilled occupations, particularly in the higher-income brackets of society. As Sheila Patterson observed, "Many of the difficulties of coloured immigrants in Birmingham appear to be general to their social class rather than their colour. . . ."[33] This, combined with the growing attitude that "the blacks" should really "go back home," has generated a peculiar class consciousness—what John Rex terms a "racial *Lumpenproletariat.*"

Several outgrowths of this phenomenon are significant. Despair and resignation to poverty and discrimination are two of these. A tenacious perpetuation of social enclosure is another. Among the young who succeed in entering the higher educational system and the middle class, there is a limited identification with race; class becomes the primary base of value formation. In England as in the United States, the educated who enter the professions form a black elite, which is not seriously interested in liberation for others but is dedicated to acquiring the affluence of its white counterpart.[34] The uneducated black majority left behind in the ghettoes face insuperable barriers to entry into the promised riches of society.[35] The response is the growing alienation of the colonial who does not accept the system and has awakened to the realization that the "law and order" around him is not for his benefit.

In the United Kingdom, the outlook in the political arena is no more hopeful. The Labour Party is felt by most blacks and browns to be as racist as the Tories. The immigrants have elected a few local black and brown councillors, but have neither the numbers nor the experience to control (as blacks do in the United States) counties or large urban districts. Immigration restriction since 1962 has cut off hope of change through numbers; the class structure limits hope of change through coalition politics. In short, deprived of a sense of permanence and security by repatriation campaigns, with almost no hope of access to higher education and social standing, and without prospects for a political base, the British black is forced simultaneously into humiliation and resistance.

United Kingdom Blacks and Southern Africa

Given this numbed and impotent condition, it is not surprising that most blacks in the United Kingdom have little concern for African, much less Southern African, issues. African liberation leaders from outside must arouse black consciousness of racial oppression in England as well as in Southern Africa. Among the more prominent of these spokesmen are Oliver Tambo, chairman of the African National Congress of South Africa, and such associates as Reg September, director of the London Office of the ANC. The Pan-Africanist Congress of Azania also has London representatives. These south Africans, along with others like Abdul Minty of the AAM, represent a broad spectrum of black and brown thinking.

The United Kingdom has produced no indigenous counterparts to a Martin Luther King, a Malcolm X, a Stokely Carmichael, or even a Roy Wilkins—leaders who developed a wide following across ethnic lines and into the white world as well, inspiring an awakening not only of conscousness but of conscience, not only of black solidarity but of human-rights commitment. The leadership in the United Kingdom is limited to concerned spokesmen of ethnic groups, whose major preoccupation is the struggle for survival and acceptance of their own communities. There are, of course, younger intellectuals whose voices are beginning to be heard, such as Gus John, Dipak Nandy, Chris Mallard, and A. Sivanandan, but they are the first to admit that they do not represent the black and brown communities. Obviously, the situation here is quite different in a number of aspects from the black political scene in the United States. No real tradition of multiracial cooperation has developed among black groups. They have been either auxiliaries of white-led organizations or remained small ethnic associations; in either case, they have had little influence. If Africa has been low on the priority list of American blacks, among the concerns of British groups, except the liberation-movement representatives, it scarcely exists at all. The reasons for this are apparent in the racial system of the United Kingdom, which creates and perpetuates the "underclass" status of most blacks.

Three Types

1. The *immigrants* are the most numerous of the black groups in England, and are also the least involved in Southern African, apartheid, or other transnational issues. These numerous associations of ethnic groups representing the immigrant communities have proliferated in the United Kingdom over the last two decades. People from the various small islands of the Caribbean tend to group together, as do those of different ethnic or religious background from Asia, India, and Africa. Many groups have federated into wider unions, of which the West Indian Standing Conference, the Indian Workers Association, and the National Federation of Pakistani Associations are outstanding examples. These organizations came into existence primarily to serve as points of unity and strength for the preservation and promotion of the cultural, religious, professional, and class interests of their members. Under the pressures of British white society and government for limitation of immigration and even repatriation, the immigrant associations have begun to search for a basis for political cooperation. Still, their fears and suspicions of each other—sometimes derived from ancient hostilities back in the Caribbean or Africa, such as those between blacks and Indians in Guyana or Uganda—remain great, frequently proving more powerful than their common interests.

The West Indians have shown the greatest natural interest in African problems from a cultural standpoint, although only a minority has an articulate pan-African and liberationist involve-ment.[36] Dr. David Pitt (now Lord Pitt) is one of the better-known West Indians whose career has been built more on cooperation with white-led racial organizations than on association with the communal West Indians. As a British Labour Party politician, Pitt has been a spokesman, at times, for the West Indian view, but he is not accepted by his own people, as was demonstrated by the attitude of the Standing Conference toward him.[37] His cooperation with the National Committee for Commonwealth Immigrants and the Cam-paign Against Racial Discrimination (CARD) made him particularly suspect. Such leaders as Neville Maxwell and Johnny James, rooted in Caribbean thinking, have opposed him, and James was able to use the Caribbean Workers Movement as an effective instrument of radical opinion to press for the rejection of white leadership in CARD—a short-lived, multiracial group that attempted to address the problem of discrimination in immigration policy. The basic West Indian attitude is distrustful of whites and militants in organi-zational expression, uncertain of its directions, and seeking its own identity—an attitude which led to the withdrawal of the Standing Conference from CARD in 1965.[38] On the other hand, it would be wrong to suggest that the Standing Conference represents all the West Indians, for as a federation of organizations, it is itself terribly divided. Nevertheless, the desire for negritude and the pervasive dislike of racism and imperialism in all forms are fundamental characteristics of this group, which has, on occasion, not only found points of solidarity with anti-apartheid NGOs in England, but also, as in the 1970 Stop the Seventy Tour, joined in direct-action campaigns.

This direct involvement of the Standing Conference was particu-larly significant in that it contributed to the cancellation of the tour of the South African cricket team by Wilson's Labour government, which feared serious disruption of domestic race relations.[39] This was an unusual crisis situation, however, with great publicity in the press, and West Indians have a strong interest in sports, particularly cricket. Their commitment on other issues involving apartheid and Southern Africa has been much less dramatic, limited to the more militant groups, such as the Caribbean Workers Movement, which has well-established links with liberation movements in Southern Africa.

East Indians play a less significant role in Southern African involvement. Except for outstanding leaders like Abdul Minty, most are concerned only with Indian affairs or with East Africa, where many have direct ties deriving from a large immigration. As a group, they assimilate into British society more easily than blacks because of a generally higher level of education and achievement, but they retain their own communities. Nevertheless, many of these communities feel bitterly alienated by their loss of property in Africa and the racial discrimination they suffer in England. Like the West Indians, they maintain many different organizations and cultural groupings. One of the most outspoken is the Indian Workers Association, which has its roots in the Indian struggle for independence in the 1930s. The largest is the National Federation of Pakistani Organizations, whose more radical leaders, such as Roy Sawh and V. D. Sharma (a key figure in the creation of CARD), have played an active role in left-wing coalition movements, such as the short-lived Universal Coloured Peoples Association led by Obi Egbuna. This radical wing participates in the anti-apartheid movement through the Indian Workers Association, and South African Indians have contributed some outstanding leadership.

2. The *multiracial* groups in England have always been dominated by the whites. These are organizations formed primarily out of the liberal equalitarianism of many whites in England, who are largely concerned about racial problems at home. Such groups have proved transitory in recent years because of the profound distrust that blacks have of white-liberal leadership. British white liberals, even more than their American counterparts, seem to take for granted a "natural" role of leadership in multiracial situations. The long tradition of black leadership in multiracial organizations (such as the NAACP and the Urban League) in the United States is wholly lacking in the United Kingdom, where the absence of an indigenous black intellectual and middle-class movement has meant, until very recently, that the *black* viewpoint was an essentially *immigrant* viewpoint.

The racial issue of white-liberal paternalism now divides all significant human-rights efforts in England. The experience of such multiracial groups as CARD and the Institute on Race Relations in their attempts to deal with racial or African problems are but two illustrations of the damaging effects of this cleavage. Heineman attributes the collapse of CARD to the hostility between white liberals and West Indians, the rivalries among West Indians and the Asian-Anglo alliance, and the ideological splits among Maoists and other types of Marxists.[40] Marion Glean (O'Connor) does not agree, believing the problem to have been white paternalism, while Dipak Nandy feels that black power was the major destructive element.[41] The views vary according to which side each took in the struggle (in which the central contentions were over British race relations and politics, and had little to do with decolonization or racial oppression in general), but the strains of white paternalism that inevitably tore apart the fabric of multiracial cooperation are apparent.

The problem of liberal-white paternalism was further exemplified in the revolt within the Institute of Race Relations. The IRR was a prominent member of the research establishment, an offshoot of the Royal Institute on International Affairs, with a prestigious board composed of academic, political, and industrial leaders under Philip Mason, a retired Indian Civil Service officer. In 1970, a number of radical scholars, including Robert Mast, Barbara Mac-Kenzie, Jack Kirby, and Robin Jenkins, joined the institute's staff, under a new director from the University of London, Hugh Tinker. This group, in which A. Sivanandan (then the institute librarian) was a key figure, was convinced that race-relations research must be made more relevant to the needs of oppressed minorities and colonized peoples.[42] They also sought wider participation of blacks and browns in the setting and undertaking of research goals. Some, especially Robin Jenkins, were highly critical of the paternalistic, exploitative quality of the IRR's work.[43]

The issues finally came to a head over the publication of IRR's *Race Today,* which the council considered lacking in balance and objectivity. By invoking a democratic referendum to decide the issue in a larger meeting, its staff reversed an earlier decision of the controlling group to end the journal's publication and to discharge the executive director. John Downing, a young sociologist who had recently been appointed to the council, described the incident in terms of the composition and attitude of the race-relations establishment in Great Britain:

The people who did the work, so to speak, all belonged in the centre of British politics: liberal Tories, Fabians, Liberals. They were all reasonable men and women; they understood each other and agreed what had to be done. But it had to be done *to* the oppressed and not *by* them and without denting the granite structures which originate poverty and racism in the first place.[44]

The Institute of Race Relations has become, since the March 1972 coup of the radical group, a critic of white British interests in Southern Africa. The race relations perspective they have adopted, while not monolithic, is in line with the liberation thinking of A. Sivanandan, John Rex, Jack Kirby, and others who see little significant social change in South Africa under the aegis of gradual reform through development and communication, and conclude that the revolution they perceive to be underway is the only solution. A. Sivanandan from Sri Lanka (Ceylón) holds a revolutionary view of the Institute's new task: "to examine the ways and means by which peoples of the Third World countries are being subjected to economic slavery and political subjugation and to address itself to policies and programs that can relieve such subjugation."[45] While sympathetic to black-power concepts, his ideas are much closer to the thinking of the American socialist revolutionary Baraka and the African liberation leader Amilcar Cabral.

Needless to say, when the Institute turned toward this revolutionary-liberation position, the old framework of foundation and academic support disappeared, and the IRR has fallen upon very lean times. Pressures for active involvement within the black community have been very great, leaving little time or money for research and publication. The IRR, like other multiracial nongovernmental organizations, split under the impact of the movement away from liberal paternalism to liberation consciousness. As one of the few points of contact between the black and brown liberation perspective on Southern Africa and the white revolutionary-change view, the Institute, though isolated from the mainstream of liberal English political and academic life, may well have a greater influence on the shape of the new societies of Southern Africa and the Thrid World than the affluent academic establishment. In this, there may be hope for future amalgamation of liberation activism and multiracial cooperation in the United Kingdom, but that day has not yet come.

The basis of mutual confidence and respect necessary for coalition politics does not yet exist in England, according to Chris Mallard, who sees white paternalism as uncompromisingly rampant in virtually all institutions dealing with racial questions, whether of research or action. He perceives the official liberal establishment attempting to co-opt the centers of dissent, research, and action on race relations, working through the Community Relations Commissions and the National Council for Commonwealth Immigrants. Mallard maintains that they hinder black organizational development by endorsing certain groups and branding others as militant and dangerous to the interests of others.

Many local councils, through third parties, have masterminded the collapse of black groups—playing off Jamaicans against Trinidadians, supporting East Pakistanis against West Pakistanis, Sikhs against Hindus, and so on.[46]

He views a policy of "amendment" by white liberal groups as desirable if it brings reform, but fears they will merely be used by the government to obscure the real issues and thwart any meaningful change.

Today, blacks have become the curse of racist-white decency. We are still treated as "lazy, immoral, savage, drug-taking, stinking bastards . . . the black scum spreading over our fair land." Discrimination has increased. Hatred has crystallized into discrimination to rid the country of us. We are ridiculed. We are forced into ghettos, into menial jobs, and into a life pattern which reflects hopelessness, exploitation, man's inhumanity to man. Those of us born in Britain will not put up with the situation any longer. As you have seen, we are beginning to organize into militant groups, associations which will not just concern themselves with defensive activities, but with offensives.[47]

Other militant views have been expressed in periodic newspapers in the 1970s, including *The Backyard News Sheet,* which attacked Courtney Tullouch and Michael X for having "sold out to the police-zionists, fascists," and *Black Voice,* which constantly denounced police violence and called for self-defense, as did *Grass Roots,* edited by A. Kimathi. Black power and solidarity with the liberation struggle of black Africans is a constant theme in these publications. A more sophisticated theoretical paper, *The Black Liberator,* published the Black Workers League Manifesto advocating the establishment of a "multi-nationalist socialist democracy" because "It is not possible to eradicate racism and racialism within the capitalist system."[48]

The class struggle aspect of the black situation in the United Kingdom has also differed appreciably from that in the United States. Marxist-oriented groups, such as the Black Workers League, have often engaged in attacks on one another, and on such organizations as the National Front and the Monday Club. To them, the Communist Party of Great Britain is as racist as the Labour Party. Their ideological themes are heavily influenced by the works of Fanon, Nkrumah, and Mondlane, and their perspective is largely a Peking-Marxist world view, reflected in such groups as the Africa-Europe Research Project, which was established under the patronage of white Christian radicals in the Christian Student Movement (CSM). One paper, *Liberation Struggle,* edited by an Ethiopian, Mejid Hussain, and Dick Hensman, director of the Tricontinental Liberation Institute, presents the African question from a pro-Peking perspective.

Nkrumah and his ideas on class struggle provided ideological insight into the problem of racism in Great Britain, as well as on the differences between the PAC and the ANC in Azania. Under the eclectic direction of a young Zimbabwian, Chen Chimutengwende, the Center of the Africa-Europe Research group offered a basis for research, discussion, and information sharing to a cross section of youth groups in England interested in development, imperialism, racism, and liberation, as well as a nonracial meeting point for the two worlds of black and white. Their ideological debates added little to the endless, doctrinaire nit-picking of Marxist-Leninist groups over how the classless society is to be achieved, but they provided an opportunity for an open discussion and interchange with whites not to be found in most British black nationalist circles at the time.

3. *African liberation representatives* in England, while preserving their own identity as a group, have worked closely with various shades of white opinion to assure that the liberation view is heard and to solicit support. They helped establish white liberal-radical support groups, such as the Anti-Apartheid Movement, which col-

laborated closely with the ANC, Lord Gifford's Committee for a Free Mozambique, Angola, and Guinea, that formed an axis with FRELIMO-MPLA-PAIGG, and the Friends of Namibia, while working closely with SWAPO. These and other liberation groups provided the essential black contribution to what would otherwise have been purely white groups, since immigrants and indigenous blacks are conspicuous by their absence. This collaboration across racial lines unfortunately also created antiwhite sentiment among those liberation groups who were not recognized by British support organizations. The PAC of South Africa and UNITA in Angola, for example, frequently alleged that the British support groups deliberately pursued a divide-and-rule policy or took their orders from Moscow or the British Foreign Office. In short, in liberation circles, the atmosphere was similar to socialist political circles of the last century, where intrigue and suspicion of others constantly poisoned relations. Nevertheless, these groups and African representatives have maintained a constant and most important voice for black consciousness and liberation in the United Kingdom.

Conclusion

The trend away from assimilation and co-optation toward transnational black consciousness and multiracial cooperation for liberation and human rights has been a long and painful struggle for black movements in the United States and in the United Kingdom. In both countries, liberation activists were in conflict with paternalistic white and black human-rights groups, but among the younger organizations on both sides of the Atlantic, a new basis of coalition and cooperation, based on black consciousness and class struggle, has been established. While this has diminished the priority of the racial factor and antagonized some black-power leaders, it laid the groundwork for a much broader anti-apartheid consistuency to emerge, as well as the foundation of a more comprehensive and profound commitment to a universal human-rights endeavor.

African liberation leaders active in all phases of the development of this new spirit have been less doctrinaire than earlier class-struggle exponents, less racially exclusive than many black-power advocates, and less limited in vision than the older liberals and civil-rights spokesmen. They have provided the direction for new coalitions which can be the basis of an effective, transnational liberation and human-rights movement. Black leadership, working in harness with African, nonwhite, and white nongovernmental organizations in a human struggle for the abolition of apartheid and all forms of racial oppression in Southern Africa, now makes the realization of these goals seem more within reach than at any time in recent history.

Notes

1. Fanon, a Caribbean black, speaking of his discovery of his "greater self" through reading Senghor, says:

From the opposite end of the white world a magical Negro culture was hailing me. . . . I had rationalized the world and the world had rejected me on the basis of colour prejudice. Since no agreement was possible on the level of reason, I threw myself back toward unreason.

Franz Fanon, *Black Skin, White Masks* (London: Paladin, 1970), p. 87.

2. Harold Cruse, *The Crisis of the Negro Intellectual* (New York: William Morrow & Co., 1967), p. 371.

3. Commonwealth and colonial subjects have a status in the United Kingdom that allows them to exercise certain political rights after a six-month residency.

4. Kwame Nkrumah, in his autobiography, *Ghana* (New York: Thomas Nelson and Sons, 1957), pp. 53-60, describes the activities with Padmore in the formation of congresses and meetings.

5. St. Clair Drake, in his monograph *Our Urban Poor* (New York: A. Philip Randolph Education Fund, 1967), p. 3, states that progress is partially the result of social-science research allied with Keynesian economics and liberal and labor activism. Drake notes the many failures he believes the system produces, p. 9.

6. Charles Hamilton and Stokely Carmichael, *Black Power* (London: Vantage Books, 1967), p. 8.

7. Chris Mallard, *Black Britain* (London: George Allen and Unwin Ltd., 1973), p. 72.

8. Congressman Ronald V. Dellums of California is one of the most effective spokesmen for the idea of a coalition of all "nigger" groups in American society: blacks, browns, women, peaceniks, professors, students, Socialists. Speech at the YWCA National Convocation on Racial Justice 15 June 1972, New York City.

9. The idea of parity is especially favored by Jesse Jackson. *The New York Times,* 29 August 1973.

10. "Amiri Baraka," *The Black Scholar,* October 1974.

11. *The New York Times,* 28 April 1975.

12. See "Black Workers League Manifesto," *The Black Liberator,* Vol. I, Nos. 2 and 3. "It is not possible to eradicate racism and racialism within the capitalist system. The multi-nationalist, socialist democracy will arise only from class struggle."

13. "The Sixth Pan-African Congress," *The Black Scholar,* Fall 1975.

14. Among the black Americans observing the San Francisco Conference were Ralph Bunche, Walter White, and Roy Wilkins. Such educators as Dr. Mordecai Johnson and Mary McLeod Bethune were also present.

15. *The Atlantic Charter and Africa* (New York: Phelps-Stokes Fund, 1942).

16. Hollis R. Lynch, "Black American Radicals and the Liberation of Africa: The Council of African Affairs, 1937-1955," unpublished manuscript: Adelaide Hill and Martin Wilson (eds.), *Apropos of Africa: Sentiments of Negro American Leaders on Africa from the 1800s to the 1950s* (New York: Humanities Press, 1969), pp. 209-212.

17. Bayard Rustin, "Guns, Bread and Butter," *War/Peace Report* March 1969, pp. 12-13.

18. John Davis and James K. Baker (eds.), *Southern Africa in Transition* (New York: Praeger, 1966).

19. *The New York Times* reported on a number of organizations implicated in CIA funding. Some, like Norman Thomas' Institute of International Labor Relations, did so without knowing they were being used by conduits like the Kaplan Fund, and as Thomas claimed, "they never interfered in any way." Nevertheless, they were used, and the populist public spirit of reform groups was very critical of those who failed to recognize manipulation by the intelligence system. *The New York Times,* 22 February 1967.

20. James Farmer, *Freedom When?* (New York: Random House, 1965), p. 160.

21. *The New York Times,* 14 November 1972.

22. Bayard Rustin, who was his lieutenant in the early 1960s, claims that King was influenced greatly by Luthuli.

23. *The New York Times,* 13 April 1967.

24. Resolutions, NAACP Fifty-Seventh Annual Convention, 5-9 July 1966.

25. NAACP press release, 9 May 1972.

26. Dr. Clarke, an historian and long-time pan-Africanist, is the "elder statesman" of the AHSA. He stated this view publicly in March 1972 at

a conference of human-rights groups in Washington, D.C., and has stressed it in discussion with the writer.

27. IFCO *Report,* 1973, p. 25, and *Daily News* (Tanzania), 15 August 1973.

28. See numerous Congressional hearings under his chairmanship, such as U.S. Business Involvement in Southern Africa, Hearings of the Subcommittee on Africa of the Committee on Foreign Affairs, U.S. House of Representatives, Ninety-Second Congress, May-December 1971.

29. The population of nonwhites had doubled from 1966 to 1973. Approximately 213,300 of the 2 million nonwhites in the United Kingdom were born there, according to the 1966 census. B. J. B. Rose and Associates, *Colour and Citizenship* (London: IRR and Oxford University Press, 1970), p. 99.

30. The Monday Club initiated a petition in 1972 requesting voluntary repatriation. *Race Today,* March 1973, p. 72.

31. *The New York Times,* 31 August 1973.

32. *The West Indian World,* 2 August 1973.

33. Sheila Patterson, "A Hardening Colour Bar," *New Society* March 1967, p. 380.

34. Dr. Robert Hill refuted the Richard Scammon and Ben Wattenburg claim that 51 percent of American blacks had entered the middle class. *The New York Times,* 26 August 1973.

35. Hill's analysis was sustained by the results of a more recent study showing a growing gap between the majority poor-black income and the average white income. However, a class of higher incomes among blacks, in excess of $15,000 yearly, has emerged. *The New York Times,* 31 May 1976.

36. *The West Indian World* represents the African-related heritage of West Indian immigrants in the United Kingdom.

37. Benjamin W. Heineman, *The Politics of the Powerless* (London: Oxford University Press, 1972), p. 87.

38. Ibid., p. 83.

39. Peter Hain, in his book, *Don't Play with Apartheid* (London: George Allen and Unwin, 1971), reports that Harold Wilson's fears about the effect of the tour on race relations, after the involvement of the West Indian Campaign Against Apartheid Cricket, led to his final decision to come out against the tour of the South African team. Also, of course, the work of the South African Non-Racial Olympic Committee (SANROC) and the decision of the Supreme Council for Sport in Africa to boycott the Commonwealth games were important, but the point here is the effect of the action of a small black group.

40. Heineman, op. cit., pp. 213-233.

41. Based on a 17 June 1973 interview.

42. Letter from Robert Mast, associate director of International Studies, Institute of Race Relations, London, to George W. Shepherd, Jr., 30 March 1972.

43. Robin Jenkins became the central figure in the controversy when the council of the IRR ordered his resignation because he made public his negative views of the research conducted by the IRR. Then, *Race Today* became the central issue when the council, dominated by such established scholars and race-relations figures as Lord Boyle, Mark Bonham Carter (chairman of the Community Relations Commission), Sir Frederic Seebohm (deputy chairman of Barclay's Bank), and others tried to suppress it.

44. John Downing, "Britain's Race Industry," *Race Today* October 1972, pp. 328-29.

45. A. Sivanandan, *Race and Resistance* (London: Race Today Publications, 1974), p. 29.

46. Chris Mallard, *op. cit.,* p. 318.

47. Ibid., p. 175.

48. *The Black Liberator,* Vol. I, Nos. 2-3, p. 81.

chapter 5

THE ARMS EMBARGO AND NGO ACTION

Since World War I the Atlantic core nations have constituted a regional security system whose peripheral and semiperipheral areas have first participated in its defense and then slowly broken off from the core, like portions of an iceberg, from Asia to the Middle East to Africa. The core group of powers, which includes the Scandinavian countries (although Sweden maintains an independent security position), has remained essentially the same, with the addition of West Germany, for half a century. These are the nations who colonized the New World and divided up Africa.

After the Boer War, South Africa became part of this Atlantic security system, as demonstrated by her participation in two world wars in cooperation with the Commonwealth regional treaties and Atlantic defense agreements. However, South Africa's contemporary participation in the security system is covert, because she has left the Commonwealth, and there is widespread opposition to her racial policy in the English-speaking world as well as in the United Nations.

In 1963, the United Nations placed an embargo on the supply of all weapons to South Africa, but the Atlantic powers continue to sell her arms, strategic technology, and commodities which can easily be converted to military use.

Abolitionist NGOs and African and Asian nations take strong exception to this. Observance and enforcement of the arms embargo have become one of their prime objectives. NGO influence has been more direct on the arms question than on any other anti-apartheid issue at the United Nations, as this issue commands a wider consensus among them and broader support from the general public than any other. But the continuing tendency of the Western powers to incorporate South Africa as a semiperipheral dependency of the core states in the regional Atlantic security system, despite the proclaimed embargo, remains a chronic and inflammable point of contention.

When the Suez Canal was closed in 1967, the sea route around the Cape became an important security area for the Atlantic nations, and a critical one during the oil shortages and fuel crisis of 1974. The South Africans have shrewdly taken advantage of this situation and sought to use it as a means of gaining official participation in the NATO security system.[1] The argument that the current economic necessity of protecting Western primary interests must lead to utilization of South African bases is vigorously opposed by the Africans and their NGO allies. Nevertheless, the steps taken by both the British and the American governments in strengthening the Simonstown base, despite official withdrawal, and in building a new base on Diego Garcia in the Indian Ocean all point to a continuing amicable relationship with South Africa. Although the United States and Britain deny this, the evidence contradicts their protestations.[2]

The conflict between those groups who advocate the strengthening of the Atlantic defenses in conjunction with South Africa and the NGOs who wish to disengage is a very clear-cut debate, despite the deceptive language of public officials.

The Postwar Atlantic System

South Africa's participation in World War II was an act of identification deeply appreciated at the time by the Allies, particularly because it was a difficult decision for the divided South Africans, among whom there was considerable sympathy for the Fascist cause. Opposition to entering the war, led by General J. B. M. Hertzog, resulted in a close vote of 80 to 67 for participation. Hertzog resigned in favor of General Jan Smuts, who had been deputy Prime Minister. The Nationalists, including B. J. Vorster, bitterly opposed the decision, and the split greatly deepened the alienation between Afrikaners and English-speaking South Africans.[4] Sentimental ties of kinship are greatly strengthened by such travails, and the act of identification with the British struggle in World War II had lasting importance for the generation of Britons who "stood alone" against the Nazis.

In the post-World War II world, South Africa's role in the Atlantic community security arrangement was the status of a semi-peripheral area whose function was to support and supply the needs of the core nations in return for an indirect commitment of defense, should a threat to South Africa also threaten the core.[5] Even this vague commitment, of course, was subject to differing interpretations, to be discussed later. South Africa was not admitted to NATO membership, but, as one of the British Commonwealth nations, played a significant role in the Western defense system.

When South Africa withdrew from the Commonwealth of Nations in 1961, the relationship was not significantly changed, as it maintained most consulting relationships, training programs, and arms-supply patterns with the Western core countries. Most continued even after the United Nations arms embargo against South Africa in 1963. South Africa continued to send contingents for training to the Western powers, particularly to France and the United Kingdom. Joint naval exercises with NATO and South African ships have been held in the southern Atlantic. Standard NATO weapons, including rifles and armored vehicles, have been regularly supplied to South Africa by various partners in the Atlantic core.

NATO

While no formal agreement exists between NATO and South Africa, the Simonstown base agreement, dating back to 1955, indicates extensive British commitment to South Africa in return for the use of the base and facilities. Interpretations have differed among British political leaders as to the extent of legal commitment to supply arms to South Africa under the agreement which lapsed in June 1975. It is nevertheless clear that it was a form of joint defense treaty, indirectly linking South Africa, through Great Britain, to the rest of the Atlantic system. Agencies of these governments, from intelligence to air forces, operate as if this were the case. As J. E. Spence observes:

The 1955 Agreement represented a life line of sorts, in-so-far as it could be interpreted as conferring on South Africa a degree of quasi-formal association with the Western alliance, and in more practical terms, it ensured in the short run a supply of valuable equipment from Britain.[6]

The United States has been more circumspect, opposing any direct role for South Africa in Western defense but supporting its peripheral contingency role in the interests of the United Kingdom.

A number of prosettler groups advocate bringing South Africa into NATO—a goal she has long sought. This point of view is frequently stated by military strategists doing research for right-wing institutions. These are usually retired military officers whose views find considerable support in official circles. In a discussion seminar of the Royal United Service Institution, Rear Admiral Morgan-Giles, M.P., quoted from the *International Defense Review* the following suggestion:

Firstly, all arms embargoes should be withdrawn and every effort made to help South Africa to build up her arms strength. Secondly, a firm pact is needed between South Africa and NATO, agreeing that an attack on her is an attack on NATO. Thirdly, NATO should hold frequent exercises with the Republic off her shores. Fourthly, NATO should keep a standing naval force in the area, as it does in the Atlantic and is now building up in the Mediterranean.[7]

While this view was not necessarily precisely that of Admiral Morgan-Giles, it is a position widely shared in British military and right-wing circles, and could only have been introduced into this discussion because he thought it important.

The more moderate sections of the pro-South African lobby are inclined toward selling arms to South Africa and giving sympathetic moral support to her in the anticommunist struggle, though not wishing to make the identification with the white elite more direct than this. This point of view is frequently expressed in the European—especially British—press, and finds favor among business groups, such as the British South African Trade Association and the Council of British Industries.[8]

The profit motive is easily mixed up with settler-kinship sentiment in the pro-South African groups. Many of them have relations living in South Africa (and would, in any case, sympathize with the white concerns there), and "business as usual" is a major reason why the United States and European governments have continued to supply paramilitary equipment to South Africa despite the arms embargo.

The United Nations Arms Embargo

A "voluntary" embargo against the sale of military weapons to South Africa was finally adopted unanimously by the Security Council in December 1963. It was intended to sever the military-support relationship between the Atlantic system and South Africa, but it has not stopped the flow of arms from the West, nor has it changed the relationship in any fundamental way at present. The embargo, therefore, has had only very limited utility, with the potential of wider implications under crisis conditions. At best, it constitutes a new international standard by which the conduct of nations may be judged, and at worst, it gives the illusion of significant moral action covering a scarcely changed situation. Bruce Oudes observed:

Various spokesmen for the Nixon Administration maintain that these embargoes are still firmly in place. Yet, I have very well-informed sources that tell me otherwise. They say there was a national security decision memorandum issued in 1970 revising earlier guidelines, so that the bureaucracy now tends to approve proposed sales that would have been rejected in previous administrations.

An arms sales ban remains, these sources say, but it is not the broad military embargo of the Kennedy-Johnson years. Which version should the American public believe?[9]

Oudes was referring, in his statement to a Congressional subcommittee, to the increasing evidence that the standards clearly established under the Johnson and Kennedy administrations had been eaten away by those who either placed the development of trade foremost or were critical of such limitations on commercial relations. While his view of what had been established as a clear principle was a bit sanguine, his information about the dual standards proved more than validated when National Security Study Memorandum (NSSM) 39 of the Nixon Administration was published (to be discussed later). Under these conditions, it should be recognized that while the United States and the United Kingdom accepted the idea of an embargo against arms supplies to South Africa, their acceptance was conditional from the very beginning.

The initiative of the Kennedy Administration in implementing the arms embargo, even before the United Kingdom acted, should be seen in the context of the times. The early sixties was a time of maximum influence of new African states and liberation movements. Many nations were just becoming independent, and their presence at the United Nations in New York received wide attention. New African heads of state frequently visited Kennedy, and they invariably raised the question of South Africa.

The Kennedy Adminstration was the first of any Atlantic major power to envision the concept of an embargo against arms for South Africa as a means of instigating social change. The program was first introduced in 1962 on a unilateral basis as a result of increased interest in the emerging African states, and because agitating black Americans gained wider representation under the Kennedy Administration. In August 1963, the United States supported an embargo resolution in the Security Council, but with a substantial reservation.[10] This reservation implied that South Africa could be considered an ally in future conflicts involving the United States' interests, thereby pointing up the underlying core-periphery understanding.

The United States adherence to the arms embargo was specifically placed outside the provisions of Chapter VII of the United Nations Charter by Ambassador Stevenson, who argued that while coercion—approved in that section—would be wrong, the embargo was an appropriate policy under "the Peaceful Settlement" provisions of Chapter VI. This was in line with the general long-standing United States position that apartheid was a violation of human rights, rather than a threat to the peace, as was argued by the African states. The United States voted for the embargo only after it was generally agreed that the action was taken under Chapter VI, and this became the basis on which the resolution of 4 December 1963 was unanimously adopted, with Great Britain and France supporting it on those terms. In this way, the Atlantic security framework was retained by the core states, who were merely censuring the policy of an ally, rather than threatening the use of force against a transgressor of the peace. The distinction is very important in understanding the reservations and problems raised in interpreting compliance with the resolution.

Although the United Kingdom voted for the 1963 resolution, official acceptance of the concept of the arms embargo did not come until late 1964, after the election of a Labour government led by Harold Wilson. The difference between Conservatives and Labour on the scope of the embargo was substantial from the beginning. Many Conservatives directly support the settlers in South Africa, but the position of the leadership has been to resist any attempts to cut off South Africa completely from the security provisions of the Atlantic powers, while at the same time not appearing to condone her apartheid practices. This tightrope position was confirmed by the Heath government, which attempted in 1970 to reinterpret the arms embargo by accepting contracts for naval supplies under the Simonstown agreement. While Labour, under the first Wilson government, supported the arms embargo and opposed the extension of new agreements or obligations with South Africa, it continued to utilize the Simonstown base, promote the Diego Garcia base in the Indian Ocean, and fulfill the contracts for supplies undertaken by the Conservative governments.

The adherence of other Atlantic core states to the Resolution of 1963 has been undercut for years by the policies of France in particular, and to a lesser extent those of Italy and West Germany. These countries are not always responsible for the trade in arms carried on by their nationals, but their enforcement measures have been weak and hypocritical.

France abstained on the critical 3 August 1963 vote and made no pretense of reporting to the Secretary-General concerning her compliance with the arms-embargo measures, as did all the other powers. French sale of military aircraft and the production of submarines for South Africa has been a classic case of profiteering at the expense of other nations who accepted their international obligations. West Germany reported to the Secretary-General total compliance with the arms-embargo resolutions. However, the *rapporteur* of the

Special Committee on Apartheid, in his report of 20 May 1970, noted that the Transall C-160 aircraft obtained by South Africa was manufactured in a German-French combine. It was also noted in the press that a team of South African pilots visited the Federal Republic of Germany in 1969 for training.[11] France, in 1975, modified its position to bring it in line with the other core powers.[12]

In contrast, the Scandinavian nations have played a leading role in drafting and supporting resolutions aimed at strengthening the sanctions and the embargo against South Africa, and have begun a critical assessment of NATO's links with Southern Africa. Norway, for example, particularly raised the issue of Portugal's use of NATO equipment in Africa, thereby challenging the relationship with South Africa.[13]

Enforcement

The major point of critical attack by abolitionist NGOs has been the failure of the Western powers to implement the arms embargo they accepted. The issues vary according to the region of Southern Africa under consideration. For the Portuguese territories, it was a question of actual arms supply of NATO weapons, which was substantially documented, although the Portuguese vigorously denied it. A Dutch group, Angola Comité, under the leadership of Dr. Sietse Bosgra, undertook the most extensive documentation. It issued a biweekly fact sheet, *Facts and Reports,* containing the research material that formed a substantial part of the case made by the British and American NGOs that NATO was supplying Portugal with weapons for her wars in Africa. The United States and the United Kingdom denied the allegations, but the evidence is now indisputable, and the revolutionary government of the Armed Forces Movement openly admitted NATO's role after the coup against Caetano in 1974. This information was available to the Portuguese military and may have played a significant part in the disillusionment of the younger officer corps which led to the 1974 revolution. The role of the Angola Comité deserves careful consideration by those researching this historic event. Since the focus here is South Africa, and because Portugal has severed its colonial ties with Africa, the issue will not be discussed further. It does, however, constitute an important case in point of the activities of NGOs in raising the issue of surreptitious use of NATO to strengthen control of the core over the periphery against insurgency operations.

The South African case is similar. As the Angola War has shown, the South Africans are dependent on the West for sophisticated weapons, a variety of paramilitary supplies, and the nuclear umbrella. This support, plus considerable armament manufacturing of their own, gives them the most sophisticated and powerful armed forces on the continent of Africa. Their forces are strengthened and expanded constantly, as demonstrated by the rise in the military budget from $360 million in 1970 to $948 million in 1975.[14] They are engaged in constant surveillance of their borders and have for years had sporadic skirmishes with guerrilla forces. Some of this activity took place in Rhodesia, where estimates have been made of five thousand South Africans operating with the Rhodesian armed forces, although they began withdrawal in 1975.[15] The intervention of South African forces in Angola in November 1975 dramatized South Africa's basic security problem, leading to her determination to maintain buffer states and minimize Soviet influence. Such conflicts are a continuous drain and bring the Soviet Union, as the ally of African states, into direct conflict with South Africa. South Africa is, of course, no match for the Soviet Union, and therefore she seeks Western protection. South Africa faces future threats from a long land border (the Indian Ocean to the Atlantic), a considerable internal insurgency campaign in the urban centers, and a possible naval assault on her principal ports and beaches, which are also potential landing areas for supplies to insurgents. South Africa's critical need, then, is for sophisticated surveillance equipment to help police her frontiers and for the best-equipped naval and air forces she can develop, to act as deterrents as well as means of resistance should some Great Power decide to aid the guerrilla campaigns directly. The most effective deterrent she can muster is a close alliance with the Atlantic core powers.

The United States and the Arms Embargo

The present debate over compliance with a mandatory arms embargo takes place in the light of this military situation in South

Africa. When the United States accepted the United Nations arms embargo in 1963, it was only under the terms and means of implementation outlined by Rauer H. Meyer, director of the Export/Import Control Office of East-West Trade of the Department of Commerce, in testimony before the Diggs Subcommittee Hearings of the Committee on Foreign Affairs, House of Representatives, 1973:

The U.S. arms embargo policy is administered by the export control authorities of both the Departments of State and Commerce. Materials and equipment which are strictly military in nature are controlled by the State Department, while related or multipurpose items fall within the responsibility of the Department of Commerce. Pursuant to this policy, the Office of Export Control denies for export to that country applications for: military automotive vehicles, military transport aircraft and related items, shotgun shells and parts thereof, and certain machine tools for the production and maintenance of arms and munitions. In addition, Commerce maintains controls over certain multipurpose items (for example, civil aircraft and airborne communications equipment) and does not authorize their export to South Africa if there is likely to be a military use.[16]

The United States government position has been for many years that this adequately covers its obligations under the arms embargo, and that other transactions are a part of normal trade relations with South Africa, which have not been suspended.

However, the first point of criticism by American NGO spokesmen has been that there were certain indirect military-support operations, such as the Space Tracking stations (now being phased out), which are useful for military intelligence concerning ground and sea movements. The Advocaat communication system in Silvermine near Simonstown is equipped by the United States and used by NATO.[17] If only the direct forms of military aid, such as the supply and sale of heavy weapons, the training of armed services personnel, and the seconding of American forces are considered, then the amounts of American assistance to South Africa since the arms embargo have been minor. The debate turns about the use of certain kinds of services related to military purposes such as Advocaat and the kinds of equipment supplied under categories with an apparent primary civilian purpose but also a military-conversion potential. The issue is often over whether or not an alleged civilian purpose is not actually a cover for the military use of such products as airplanes and computers. Judge William H. Booth, president of ACOA, noting the difficulty of obtaining accurate information, stated:

It should not have been the task of the citizens of the United States of America to act out the melodramatic role of intelligence experts in order to insure that the United States adheres to its stated position of denying military support to the white regimes of Southern Africa, but that is unfortunately the position into which we have been thrust.[18]

The NASA satellite-tracking stations near Johannesburg and the optical-camera tracking station in Olifantsfontein were for years the subject of controversy and investigation in Congress under the direction of Representative Charles Diggs of the House Foreign Affairs Committee and a leading spokesman for the Black Caucus. Diggs and others pointed out that these tracking stations had a clear intelligence function and could be used for surveillance of the South African borders and surrounding waters as well as for providing a link in the worldwide communications systems used by the Pentagon to watch the communist world. The existence of these facilities came under criticism from a large number of NGOs in the 1960s, and finally the United Nations Association (USA) National Policy Panel produced a report in December of 1971 requesting the withdrawal of the stations. This panel, composed of a number of distinguished academic and business figures, including William Roth, William T. Coleman, John R. Bunting, Robert Goheen, George Lindsay, and Waldemar Nielson, under the general chairmanship of Cyrus Vance, stated that:

Economic, technological, or other dependencies on the South African government complicate our commitment to racial equality because they tend to develop an interest in the status quo. In this sense, it is unwise for the U. S. to maintain or develop satellite tracking stations in South Africa. . . . The panel recommends that the tracking facilities in South Africa be phased out and alternative facilities be developed as required.[19]

A decision to phase out the stations in 1975 was finally taken in 1974, allegedly for purely technical reasons, though the issue raised by Diggs and others about the integration of personnel attached to these stations was an embarrassing question for the Ford Administration and for South Africa. While the Ford Administration never admitted that its communication programming was a direct aid to South African military operations, its withdrawal indicated that NGO criticism was a factor in at least reviewing commitments and coming up with technical reasons for doing something else.

A related issue has been the technical assistance provided by the United States to South Africa in the development of nuclear power. The capacity of South Africa to develop nuclear weapons is now regarded as very high, especially as France has also given assistance in this area. Much of the nuclear technology and equipment has been given in return for South African exports of enriched uranium. The claim of all administrations that this is for strictly peaceful purposes has been ridiculed by South Africa's critics at the United Nations and particularly by specialists on Southern Africa. They believe that South Africa currently has the scientific capability to develop the bomb and lacks only an ICBM delivery system.[20] However, her Canberra bombers are adequate for a 4,000-mile range. South Africa has not yet tested her nuclear capability, for political as well as financial reasons. Since a test would offend the West as much as the Africans, the South Africans are content, for the moment, with their capacity to produce nuclear weapons in a short period, should the need arise.[21] Through the Atlantic security system, of which they are a silent partner, they enjoy the nuclear umbrella cover against Russian or Chinese aggression while quietly pursuing their own ends.

NGO Criticism

The supply of weapons in the dual-use category has provoked the most protracted criticism of embargo violations. The difficulty arises because the United States government has not attempted to place a ban on many categories of goods that can be used for military and counterinsurgency purposes, as it has in the case of communist states. On the contrary, the United States has sought to maintain normal relations with South Africa by interpreting very broadly the letter of the ban against obvious military weapons.

The American Committee on Africa has for many years investigated and protested before Congress and various United Nations committees major violations of the meaning and spirit of the 1963 arms embargo. Jennifer Davis called attention to the failure of the United States to apply the same standards to South Africa as employed against the People's Republic of China, where the ban includes such items as "locomotives, trucks, high grade computers, advanced telecommunications equipment, petroleum products, and commercial aircraft."[22] Apparently the Nixon Administration considered these strategic materials when commercial relations with Peking were restored, for they were not included in the original list. The ACOA considers any commercial aircraft, telecommunications equipment, and certain types of herbicides to be of such strong military potential as to fall under the arms ban. This thesis has been extensively documented in the paper by Davis outlining the use of Cessnas, Piper Cubs and other small aircraft by the South African Air Commandos.

It must be remembered that flying is an all-white sport in South Africa. The Air Commandos, established in 1964, can best be described as a flying militia. It is made up of volunteers who are not regular military forces, but who are paid by the government when they fly as commandos. . . . Their training entails radio cooperation with army and mobile police striking forces, reconnaissance, practice bombing with grenades, and general cooperation with the police in maintaining the security of both South Africa and South West Africa. Many of these Commandos fly light planes, such as Piper Cubs and Cessnas.[23]

In an area with a very long border and a great deal of bush to survey for insurgency operations, the usefulness of this kind of equipment is obvious, although an administration eager to expand trade and increase communications with South Africa has a tendency to view small planes as nonmilitary items and has determined the matter in favor of sales.

The sale of herbicides is criticized becaue of their extensive use in Vietnam and the Portuguese territories as counterinsurgency weapons. In testimony before the Sub-Committee on Africa of the House Foreign Affairs Committee, Ms. Davis pointed out that not only were exports of dangerous herbicides to South Africa increasing, but also that the Portuguese had employed a South African company, Flink Lugspruit en Boerdery Edmns of Bethal, to supply them for operations against FRELIMO in Mozambique. American sales figures indicated a substantial increase in the amount of herbicides exported to South Africa in the 1970s.

Telecommunications equipment and computer sales to the South Africans amounted to $16,693,865 between 1969 and 1972, and this included electronic search-and-detection apparatus and radar, which is obviously useful for military as well as civilian purposes. Various groups also criticized the use of IBM computers for administrative purposes. The Protestant Episcopal Church, because of its own investments in IBM, particularly deplored South Africa's use of large, commercially owned computers for defense purposes in the Simonstown military complex.[24] This concern exemplifies the opposition of churches to the obvious military uses of equipment developed and sold by American firms operating in South Africa. Such attitudes have contributed to the review of investment portfolios by a number of institutional investors, including universities, banks, and foundations, whose constituency is influenced by gradualist and abolitionist ideas. It should be noted in this connection that the military uses of numerous products sold to South Africa—trucks by General Motors, communications equipment from IBM and GE, several varieties of small planes and helicopters, heavy transportation equipment, such as railway engines, Polaroid cameras for intelligence surveillance, chemicals and herbicides and the like—are increasingly challenged by American churches, universities, and humanitarian groups as contributing to the military and counter-revolutionary capacity of South African apartheid.

The response of American officials to this line of argument is that the ban of trade in these items does not fit their interpretation of the United States' obligations under the arms-ban agreement of 1963, which is limited to "military" supplies and training. (Their attitude was clearly demonstrated in the testimony of Meyer, cited earlier.) The impasse arises out of two essential differences between the anti-apartheid NGOs and the United States government. The United States has been opposed to the application of economic sanctions to South Africa, and a broader interpretation of what constitutes military support would clearly push it in that direction.

The second factor is the American refusal to look at the military-support problem in other than traditional military terms. Nonconventional means are employed to suppress internal insurrection or to conduct antiguerrilla warfare. The United States has been unwilling to face the fact that this is the central issue in South Africa—not the equipping of a navy or the arming of ground combat troops.

The publication of the famous document of the National Security Council, NSSM 39, revealed very clearly an intention of the Nixon Administration to deceive. The NSC determined to develop military contacts with South Africa and one means was to supply dual-category goods "inconspicuously" while publicly adhering to the strict letter of the arms embargo. This duplicity was well known to NGO critics, but not widely publicized until Jack Anderson reported on NSSM 39 in October 1974. The United States would "enforce the arms embargo against South Africa, but with liberal treatment of equipment which could serve either military or civilian purposes," and further, would "conduct selected exchange programs with South Africa in all categories, including military."[25]

The United Nations' surveillance committees—in this case, the United Nations Committee on Apartheid—agreed with the broader interpretation of the abolitionists, but had no way of compelling acceptance of its definition of military support. In 1975 the United Nations majority attempted to pass a mandatory arms ban against South Africa, but this was vetoed by the three Western core powers.[26] However, without agreement on what constitutes military support, the issue of whether the ban is compulsory or not is meaningless. The refusal of Western core powers to accept a mandatory ban illustrates their basic opposition.

The only significant political pressure generated so far in the United States in support of increased enforcement of the arms ban has stemmed from American black groups, particularly in regard to the use of South African bases by the U. S. Navy, and to a more limited extent, concerning the absence of black personnel from the space-tracking stations. The use of the Simonstown base and other port facilities in South Africa came under increasing fire from black groups such as the NAACP and the American Negro Leadership Conference in the late 1950s and early 1960s because of the discriminatory practices South Africans imposed upon American black personnel. In 1967, the Johnson Administration, as a direct result of black American pressure, finally ended visits by American ships and sailors to South African ports for other than emergency purposes. Later administrations have not revived the practice of using the South African bases, but the issue has returned in a new form bècause of the increased interest of both the Russian and American navies in the Indian Ocean and in the protection of the western sea lanes around Africa.

As long as strategists in the United States government plan serious wartime use of South African facilities, it is very clear that the United Nations arms ban will be construed narrowly and great quantities of paramilitary support will flow to South Africa under the guise of peaceful commerce.

The British Arms Ban

British acceptance of the arms embargo was always far more conditional than the American, both in supply of military equipment and uninterrupted trade in paramilitary commodities. The issue has also been more obvious in Britain than in the United States, involving a much wider spectrum of public awareness and opinion, with periodic outbreaks of debate in Parliament and discussion in the press.

The initial British acceptance of the arms embargo in 1963 was qualified by the stipulation that previous agreements for defensive weapons would be honored, particularly those for Buccaneer aircraft. Most important, there was no renunciation of the Simonstown Agreements of 1955 for over a decade after the arms embargo. The Simonstown Agreement not only provided for a British naval base in South Africa, but contained mutual-defense agreements that have since been variously interpreted concerning the United Kingdom's obligation to supply arms to South Africa. The Conservative party has interpreted this as a continuing obligation, while the Labour Party has held that no commitment existed beyond the sixteen Buccaneers. However, both parties, until 1975, regarded the Simonstown installation as a "useful" base and safeguard for British shipping and other interests in the southern oceans.[27] Therefore, the United Kingdom had until 1975 an official "quasi-alliance" policy with South Africa, which directly conflicts with the assumptions of the United Nations arms embargo and has led to a long history of struggle between the British NGOs, who want to abandon all links with South Africa, and the rightists, who wish to extend the NATO alliance system to include South Africa and the southern oceans.[28] The margin of difference, then, has not been great between the two major political parties in Great Britain, though the gap between those groups in British society who regard South Africa as an extension of the Atlantic system and those who advocate abandoning all military ties with her is very great indeed.

The central issue, arising from South African attempts to gain assurance that Great Britain is still committed to her defense, has been the supply of weapons to South Africa. It is generally agreed that South Africa's needs in military supplies can be found elsewhere in the Western world, despite the United Nations embargo. She has, for instance, purchased Alouette helicopters from France, Sabre jets from Canada, and troop carriers from West Germany, but this is not the same as a "mutual defense" agreement, however tacit, with Great Britain. The Conservative government made it very clear from the beginning of the arms embargo that it would continue to honor the Simonstown Agreement. As the then-Foreign Secretary Sir Alec Douglas-Home stated, "It is unreasonable to think that we can have a total embargo of arms to South Africa and still expect that country to continue with the Simonstown Agreement."[29]

The Labour government, faced with enormous pressure not to supply the Buccaneers to the South Africans, held to its policy of honoring prior commitments, but refused to accept further orders. However, Dennis Healey, former Labour Defence Minister, went on record in favor of keeping the naval base as a "valuable" asset, but not reequipping it.[30] When the Conservatives regained power in 1970, they almost immediately initiated arms-supply discussion with South Africa, revealing their intention to strengthen the Simonstown and other agreements.

NGO Pressure

Criticism and pressure from the NGOs range from assessments of the general strategic position to specific issues of supply of arms or support for South African strategy concerning the Cape route and the like. The most searching criticism has been presented by writers like J. E. Spence, who conclude that the real issue is not the supply of weapons, but the continuance of a strategy which carries a tacit agreement to include South Africa in its ideological and military framework. The *Times* summed up South Africa's interests:

The one great priority is not weapons, which South Africa can get from France and probably one or two other countries, but to keep the agreement in being and, if possible, to have it changed in a way ultimately to her advantage.[31]

Foremost among the NGOs who would like to abandon this agreement with South Africa is a strong contingent within the British Council of Churches, drawn primarily from the United Reformed and Methodist churches but supported by a strong minority of Church of England clergy led by a group of bishops, including Ambrose Reeves, Colin Winter, and Trevor Huddleston, who have had bitter experiences with apartheid in South Africa. Since his expulsion from South Africa, Bishop Reeves has served as honorary president of the Anti-Apartheid Movement, where his organizational skill and leadership have been dynamic factors in the growth of that group.[32] The president of the Methodist Conference, the Reverend Rupert Davies, strongly denounced any intention to resume arms sales to South Africa:

It would range us on the side of racist government in the minds of all people in the Third World, and it could also lead to a breakdown of the Commonwealth.[33]

The Methodist and United Reformed Churches and the abolitionist wing of the Church of England played a major role in conditioning the government and the public to accept the arms embargo against South Africa. Led by the bishop of Chichester, a delegation visited the Prime Minister in 1964 and urged compliance with the arms ban and the abandonment of plans to continue to supply Buccaneers to the South Africans, since they could not be considered "defensive" weapons. One of the seminal documents produced by a working group of the British Council of Churches, entitled "The

Future of South Africa," while specifically supporting the arms embargo, did not call for the abandonment of the Simonstown Agreement. As this group agreed with the Labour Party argument that the agreements were "useful though not irreplaceable," it took the practical view that if South Africa should renounce the agreements because Great Britain refused to supply weapons, the loss would not be significant.[34]

The pacifist-socialist wing of the British churches has been a major source of support for the embargo of arms against South Africa. Its influence is felt throughout the universities, press, and student movements. But Michael Scott expressed concern to this author that sanctions might lead to open warfare with South Africa, and his thinking reflects the position of the Working Group of the British Council of Churches which opposed the application of sanctions in its report. Military sanctions, the report argued, could lead to more violence than they resolve. A minority, however, disagrees and favors the use of whatever force may be necessary to abolish the apartheid system.[35]

The 1970 Debate

When the Conservatives came to power in 1970, they immediately opened discussions on arms supply with the South African Foreign Minister, who was the first foreign visitor of the new Prime Minister, Edward Heath, at 10 Downing Street. It was obviously a matter of critical importance in the thinking of Sir Alec Douglas-Home, the Foreign Minister, and defense expert Geoffrey Rippon, as well as of several powerful members of the new Cabinet. When discussions were opened with the South Africans, this until then dormant issue became a major public topic of debate, with the Labour Party in opposition joining with the anti-apartheid NGOs in full hue and cry against this new support for South Africa.

Prime Minister Heath explained that the reasons for the step were a response to the obligations of the Simonstown Agreement and a growing concern for the protection of the sea route around the Cape, which an increasing Russian naval presence in the Indian Ocean now threatened. The Conservative support was to be construed as "for defensive reasons only" and should not be regarded as endorsement of the apartheid politics of South Africa.

There were deeper reasons, however, which were more forcefully expressed by several top ministers, including the Right Honorable Geoffrey Rippon, who stated in *Survival* (the journal of the Strategic Studies Institute) the right-wing view that the new policy was indeed an essential extension of NATO into the southern oceans. He saw the Soviet naval buildup as a threat in several sectors and now particularly in the seas around South Africa. Noting the Atlantic Alliance endorsement of his view in its Washington, D. C., meeting of October 1969, he urged:

Should there be another major conventional war, the sea route around South Africa will be of vital importance. . . . The South Atlantic should now be included to give support and backing to our Portuguese NATO allies and to the efforts of South Africa in action as a bastion against the spread of communism in Africa and her commanding geographical position on two oceans.[36]

Other supporters of active alliance with South Africa stressed the commercial argument for protecting British trade with her and the importance of filling arms orders. Lord Jellicoe, a leader in the House of Lords, emphasized to the United Kingdom's South African Trade Association that there was a close relationship between supplying arms to South Africa and the development of trade,[37] despite some doubts on the part of its executive director (triggered, perhaps by concern for British commercial losses resulting from black African retaliation, especially from the new oil nations of West Africa). The Council for British Industries (CBI) endorsed arms support for South Africa.[38]

Opposition to this strategy was headed by many Labour Party spokesmen, who found a growing coalition of forces outside official Party circles lending them support. Foremost among these was Dennis Healey, who thoroughly discounted the notion of a real Russian threat in the Indian Ocean or around the Cape. He argued that the issue was political influence, and that to arm South Africa would most assuredly spread Russian influence in Africa and the rest of the Third World.[39] He stated that the Labour Government never regarded the Simonstown base as necessary to British interest in a prospective world war, and held to the argument that while it was "not a white elephant," it was certainly declining in utility. In his mind, the Conservative Government under Heath would not withdraw its offer, especially since the African states had made an issue of the matter and it was "not about to back down to a black man," even the respected President of Zambia who headed the African opposition. The British opposition leader noted that there was extensive dissatisfaction among Conservative M.P.s—some thirty to forty were unhappy about the restoration of arms supply and told Heath that a few WASP helicopters was all they could possibly tolerate. The position of Geoffrey Rippon and Patrick Wahl favoring the extension of NATO into the southern oceans, with all the accompanying security links for South Africa, was unalterably opposed by Labour.

The public climate in England did not favor the supply of arms to South Africa, as shown in the public-opinion polls of the *Evening Standard:* 17 percent favored selling South Africa all the arms she requested; 22 percent would sell arms only for defensive purposes; and 48 percent were opposed to any sale of arms.[40] The general attitude of opposition was intensified by the coalition of groups protesting any violations of the United Nations embargo. Foremost among these were the Church and labor leaders, whose statements received extensive coverage in the press, particularly in the *Times* and *Guardian,* where editorial opposition to the action of the Heath government was strongly expressed:

It is in the interest of mankind as well as Britain, that a race war should be avoided in southern Africa. It is not yet inevitable. The question is whether the supply of arms to South Africa would make it more or less likely. All the arguments suggest it would make it more likely. It would greatly strengthen the communist position in Africa and the Indian Ocean, and provide the Africans with the allies that might encourage them to escalate violence.[41]

The arms issue gathered together a much more influential elite than the anti-apartheid movement is normally able to mobilize. Bishops who will condone investment in and trade with South Africa are infuriated at the suggestion that taxes be used to supply weapons or that an agreement of mutual defense should be recognized. One of the most powerful committees consisted of the bishop of Durham,

Dr. Ian Ramsey, who organized a group consisting of the bishop of York, Mr. Jeremy Thorpe, leader of the Liberal Party, The bishop of Stepney, Trevor Huddleston, Lord Soper of the Methodists, Canon Collins, Dame Barbara Hepworth, Mr. and Mrs. Richard Burton, Sir Julian Huxley, Lord Caradon, Sir Alfred Ager, Henry Moore, Graham Sutherland, Benjamin Britten, and Dennis Healey. Alex Lyon of the Labour Party was the secretary of the committee, a powerful coalition of church and Liberal and Labour figures whose voices opposing restoration of arms aid to South Africa could not easily be ignored by the government, though it did not bend to their wishes. Other voices, such as that of the United Nations Association of Great Britain, were raised as well. The UNA campaigned vigorously against the restoration of arms supply in violation of the embargo.[42] Peter Calvocoressi, then president of the UNA and a liberal military specialist, wrote to the *Times* of his concern about the effect on African leaders.

African leaders are faced with the alternatives of continuing their present policies of keeping the Cold War out of Africa or of involving Communist aid in order to fortify themselves in the race war which already exists on their continent.[43]

The reaction of the left and the abolitionists threatened the government with widespread resistance to the decision. At a large rally in Trafalgar Square, several labor-union leaders promised strikes that would prevent the arms from being delivered to South Africa. The National Union of Students announced it was sending aid to the liberation forces, and the Anti-Apartheid Movement, together with abolitionist churchmen, raised the specter of direct action against the government, though little specific detail was given. Drama was added when groups of students, who marched from Trafalgar Square to the Halling Vicker Corporation headquarters, refused to disperse and were arrested. The Trafalgar Square type of demonstration, however, was too periodic and undirected to have much effect—unlike the persistent campaigns of other groups, such as the sports boycott of cricket and rugby matches with South Africa. The threats of trade unions to refuse to work on arms contracts for South Africa and to boycott any transportation of these arms were made on several occasions, but have not been carried through. Nevertheless, such threats may have had some effect in deterring the government from engaging in any large-scale contracts for South Africa. The building of naval vessels, for example, would be far more difficult than selling a few helicopters, because such an undertaking is highly visible and vulnerable to demonstrations.

The African States

One of the most effective forces working against the restoration of arms to South Africa has been the influence of the African states. Through their delegations in London and membership in the Commonwealth, they informed the Heath government of their opposition. Since they were locked in a deadly struggle against apartheid, such a step by Great Britain threatened their own security and forced them to reconsider trade and commonwealth ties with the United Kingdom. Kenneth Kaunda (Zambia), backed by Julius Nyerere (Tanzania) and Milton Obote (Uganda), with assistance from the Nigerians, made one of the most forceful of these representations when, during a London visit in 1970, he broke diplomatic decorum and walked angrily out of a dinner with the Prime Minister. Heath let it be known that he was not going to tolerate African interference in what he considered "British domestic affairs," but the Africans refused to drop the matter and continued to threaten to bolt the Commonwealth or even expel Great Britain unless her Prime Minister reversed his decision and refrained from selling arms to South Africa. The Africans won a delay on a final decision until the January Commonwealth meeting in Singapore, but they failed again to force the British to back down, even with the sympathetic support of the Canadians and Indians.[44] A study group formed to review the "racial policy" of the Commonwealth proved abortive, and the United Kingdom went ahead with its plan to supply limited arms to South Africa despite the United Nations embargo.

The U.N. Committee on Apartheid roundly condemned the English action:

The Special Committee on Apartheid views the recent decision of the Government of the United Kingdom to resume the supply of aircraft and other military equipment to the Government of South Africa as a breach of the provisions of the Security Council Resolutions 181, 182 (1963) and 282 (1970). . . .

To justify its action, the United Kingdom government cites the opinion of its law officers that it is legally obligated to provide the helicopters and spare parts.

Under the provisions of the Charter, members of the United Nations have an obligation to accept and carry out the decisions of the Security Council.[45]

Other divisions of the United Nations supported the protest in a statement by the Secretary-General on 24 February 1971 and in the Twenty-Seventh Session of the Commission on Human Rights in Geneva, and in the Special Committee on Decolonization in New York, March 1971.

Though African opposition to the supply of weapons to South Africa did not prevent the Heath government from ultimately supplying the helicopters, it was an added element in the growing opposition to the policy, which may well have limited the government's freedom to undertake further contracts and engagements with the South Africans. Powerful groups in British society, such as the British Council of Industries, were anxious to provide South Africa with its general defense needs and regretted that French and other European industry than British, obtained these contracts. The Africans and abolitionists, with the help of the churches and the press, created a climate of opinion that made it difficult for the Heath government to go further along this line. Some observers have argued that the failure to prevent any supply of arms exemplifies the ineffectiveness of all these groups, especially the Africans, whose basic security was at stake. This is too harsh a judgment, particularly since the *Times* and other observers concluded that it was precisely the loss of African trust and support that impelled those thirty or forty Conservative Members of Parliament to inform Mr. Heath that they would go thus far and no farther.

The 1970 debate was of critical importance to the future, especially under a Labour Government, and the whole question of recognizing and implementing the agreement with South Africa. The Labour election manifesto of 1972, as well as later statements by the party leadership, reflects the issues of this debate.

Labour endorses the U.N. call for a total international embargo on all arms sales to or from South Africa. We will continue the arms embargo of the last Labour government and ensure that there are no loopholes.

The next Labour Government will withdraw from all relationships resulting from the Simonstown "Agreement" and all military exchange, visits, and technical arrangements will be terminated.

Labour will also end all security cooperation between Britain and South Africa and special police agents will not be allowed entry into this country.[46]

Interpretation and implementation of this policy, of course, rested upon subsequent governments, which are not bound by statements of this kind. On the surface of it, the ending of the Simonstown Agreement by the third Wilson government appears to have been a step toward a tougher British line. This is the interpretation given the change by gradualist opinion. However, the step was taken within the context of expanding commitments in the Indian Ocean and NATO interest in the Cape route so as to cast doubt on the actual extent of the change.

The tendency of the Wilson government to endorse withdrawal in principle while laying down an elaborate smokescreen to cover continuing the practice of the Conservative regime was no surprise to many NGO abolitionists, Labour liberals, and African representatives. The heart of the issue for them, as for the Committee on Apartheid of the United Nations, was and continues to be the maintenance of a working agreement. In this age of secret diplomacy and security agreements, there is grave suspicion of standing arrangements with South Africa to keep her strong in the face of mounting Third World pressures and as a silent ally in the Atlantic security system.

In the fall of 1974, the abolitionists within the Labour Government pushed hard for the ending of all military links with South Africa. The Labour Party voted a motion of censure against the Labour government with five ministers of the government supporting. Prime Minister Wilson was indignant and threatened to sack the ministers.[47] However, the protest had an effect in the ending of the Simonstown Agreement by the Labour government, which did so in mid-1975 simply by not renewing it.

British NGOs

Abdul Minty, speaking to the U.N. Special Committee on Apartheid, outlined the majors points of concern of the British abolitionists, who believe these have not been resolved by either Labour or Conservative government policies. The honorable secretary of the AAM, in referring to the lapsing of the Simonstown Agreement stated:

Britain now says that it is going to end the Simonstown Agreements. We know full well, however, that the British Government is planning other relationships with South Africa, because the Foreign Secretary and the Defence Minister have informed the House of Commons that when the Simonstown Agreement is ended, it will make no difference to British naval vessels going to South African ports, including the base at Simonstown.[48]

Minty went on to reiterate the movement's long-standing requests to the Security Council:

1. All supplies of weapons and equipment to South Africa should be terminated.

2. Military patents and the transmission of technological know-how should be forbidden.

3. The sale of radar and other electronic equipment, which is at present exported by many other countries claiming to support the arms embargo, should be similarly forbidden.

4. Skilled technicians from abroad should not work for the South African arms industry.

5. All visits by military personnel both to and from South Africa should be stopped.

6. All diplomatic missions in South Africa should withdraw their military attachés in South Africa.

7. Investments from Western countries which help to bolster the domestic arms industry should be ended.

8. All collaboration in the nuclear field should come to a halt.[49]

Also, the AAM pressed the issue of a mandatory arms ban. The proposal was later vetoed by the three Atlantic core powers on the Security Council.[50]

As the NGOs have suggested, the Security Council needs to act to plug the loopholes, but the major Western powers consistently refuse to take this step. The reason appears to lie in their continuing perception of a white South Africa as providing a basis for Western security and economic interests and their desire to win concessions from South Africa. The strategic issue was sub rosa until the 1970 arms debate in Britain, followed by the 1973-74 fuel crisis in the Western world, which focused attention on the security aspects of energy and production lines of supply in the Indian Ocean and around the Cape.

An unpublished report of the U.N. Committee on Decolonization stated that the supreme allied commander in the Atlantic Region issued a secret communiqué to prepare for contingencies outside the Atlantic area in reference to the Cape route and the southern oceans.[51] In both American and British strategic circles, there has been a push toward a naval buildup in the Indian Ocean and southern Atlantic to protect oil lines and shipping around the Cape. After much equivocation, the Nixon Administration came down on the side of building a base with the British on Diego Garcia, originally to be only a communications and refueling facility, but since upgraded into a major military base.[52] The stated purpose of the base is to strengthen the Anglo-American supervision of the shipping routes from the Persian Gulf to the Red Sea and through the Suez Canal and the Cape route to the Atlantic. No reference is made to South Africa, but with the departure of the Portuguese and French from Mozambique and Madagascar, there is no major Western facility in the area other than Simonstown.[53]

Admiral John McCain, former U.S. Navy commander-in-chief in the Pacific, stated regarding the Navy's desire to build the Diego Garcia base:

What has happened in Mozambique and Angola makes an American Diego Garcia more important than ever. But it also means that we absolutely need access to the South African naval facilities of Simonstown and Durban.[54]

Because of the danger of a naval arms race and conflict in the southern oceans, a number of NGO spokesmen have attempted for several years to make the case that a "zone of peace" should be established in the Indian Ocean, with a firm agreement among the Great Powers to avoid costly and dangerous competition there. This strategic view is directly supported by both reformists and abolitionists.

Guy Arnold, a former secretary of the Africa Bureau and one of the Labour Party advisers on Africa, pressed for a political rather than military approach to the problem:

The military argument about safeguarding the Cape is downright dishonest: if Britain or any other Western power seriously believes that a major military presence is necessary in the Indian Ocean, then they should put one there themselves, not use the need as an excuse to arm or try to arm South Africa. And as for the Communist argument—for those who think in Cold War terms—the surest way to invite communism into South Africa is for the West to go on supporting a racist-fascist regime.[55]

Pro-South Africa spokesmen in the British military and academic establishment, such as R. M. Burrel of the Department of History in the School of Oriental and African Studies, have long upheld the view that the West must have the Cape as a base. In a seminar entitled "The Security of the Southern Oceans—Southern Africa the Key," held by the Royal Service Institution and attended by a number of leading naval officers and specialists, Burrel stated:

I would like to stress the importance of the Cape route for other things . . . the idea of a neutralized Indian Ocean is a myth and should be completely dismissed. It cannot exist because the British and Russian navies are in the Ocean already and will not leave. In terms of British bases, I see Simonstown as being of overwhelming importance. President Nyerere has suggested the British government should give it up and build a new base, say in Mauritius, but this is impossible, because a base is no longer just a place where ships go for refueling. It has to have security and an industrial backing. This is not going to be available anywhere else except in South Africa.[56]

In the same seminar, Rear Admiral Morgan-Giles, M.P., supporting this view, suggested that Great Britain should supply South Africa with frigates and regretted the loss of the contract to Portugal.

American strategy planners of the Ford Administration adopted this British-South African view of the importance of the Cape route. This constitutes the core of the problem for serious enforcement of

the arms embargo. Melvin Laird, who has been one of the closest Ford advisers on strategy, said in a visit to South Africa, "I
understand the importance of the Cape route from the international
security point of view and the United States is very interested in
Indian Ocean security."[57] The same military thinking based on
realpolitik in the United States led first to the famous Option 2 of
NSS Memo 39 and then to the decision to go ahead with Diego
Garcia and a stepped-up American role in the Indian Ocean.[58]
Presently, then, both the British and American governments regard
South Africa as a useful resource base in time of peace and an in-
dispensable ally in time of general war involving the southern oceans.
As long as that official view remains, the prospect of a universal
arms embargo does not exist.

The Future

The arms embargo is more a symbol of basic policy and attitude
than an instrument of sanctions. This fact has been evident in all
the important decisions of the United Nations, where voting tabu-
lations are relatively meaningless. This does not mean that international action should therefore wait for Great Power unanimity;
but it does warn against reliance on legalistic resolutions and suggests that greater attention should be given to ways in which the
United Nations and NGOs might interact along transnational lines
on a common objective, even when the Great Powers resent and
oppose their purposes and collaboration. Both United Nations
officials and representatives of nongovernmental organizations have
a tendency to discount the potential force and significance of their
interaction because it is difficult to see direct and immediate results
in the policies of the Great Powers. However, there is some indication that NGO positions have led to more cautious and restrained
strategic action by the Western powers. Prior to the Smith acceptance of "majority rule in Rhodesia," there was serious underestimation of the long-term effect embargoes and sanctions can have in
legitimizing liberation movements, raising morale of African ma-
jorities, and mobilizing alternative forces within the Great Powers
and elsewhere in the world.

From the gradualist perspective, the adoption of the arms embargo has placed a moral ban on outright military collaboration,

and the lapsing of the Simonstown Agreement further limits direct military association by the United Kingdom. However, the abolitionists' skepticism about the lack of real change in policy appears to be borne out by the new emphasis on the Cape route in strategic NATO plans of the United States and United Kingdom.

The Angola crisis put the spotlight on the danger of direct Western association with South Africa. NGOs in the United States and the United Kingdom have utilized this serious South African aggressive action to argue for a mandatory arms embargo, basing their arguments on keeping the peace and supporting liberation movements in Southern Africa. As Goler Butcher stated before the Clark committee hearings in mid-1975:

We must not fall prey to the South African game to use the Soviet threat to inveigle us into a defense relationship which, in turn, would be a guarantee of the minority's maintenance of power. . . .

The arms embargo should ban sales to South Africa of all military equipment and it should bar the sales of all items for the use of the South African military, whether lethal or not. . . .

The sale of weapons-grade uranium to South Africa and nuclear collaboration with South Africa should be ended.[59]

Congressman Diggs has submitted legislation to bar such co-operation, and such a step has the support of abolitionists in England and advocates of nuclear non-proliferation. The nightmare of nuclear weapons available to South Africa in a last-ditch stand in defense of apartheid haunts even the mildest of gradualists. To assume the South Africans would not use this fearful weapon on those who threaten their system is placing more reliance on rationality and faith than they deserve. They have acted irrationally before—from their early support of the Nazi cause to their present defense of apartheid.

As the crisis develops, NGOs will step up direct-action campaigns against the shipping of arms, the use of South African facilities, firms supplying paramilitary support, corporate executives who continue military-business links, and leaders who justify a security alliance with South Africa.

They will use the demand of a compulsory arms ban under Chapter 7 of the U.N. Charter as a rallying ground,[60] while relying on direct action to weaken the Atlantic alliance with South Africa. Since Great Power arms support for South Africa is particularly vulnerable to internal political pressures, the impact of NGO action should not be underestimated.

Notes

1. For years, the South Africans have sought an association with NATO. Her refusal to allow African units to bear arms was the initial reason for her exclusion from the Western security system, a decision made by the Western powers, including the United States, at the 1951 Nairobi Conference on pan-African defense. See W. B. Tunstall, *The Commonwealth and Regional Defence,* Commonwealth Paper VI (London: Athene Press, 1959), p. 47.

2. The publication in 1974 of the secret National Security Council memorandum NSSM 39 indicated some of the dimensions of this complicity. See Mohamed A. El-Khana and Barry Cohen (eds.), *The Kissinger Study of Southern Africa, National Security Study Memorandum* 39 (Westport, Conn.: Lawrence Hill and Co., 1976), pp. 28-40.

3. James Barber, *South Africa's Foreign Policy, 1945-1970* (London: Oxford University Press, 1973), p. 8.

4. Ibid., p. 9.

5. *The Simonstown Agreement,* Commissioned paper 9520 (London: HMSO, 1955).

6. J. E. Spence, *The Strategic Significance of Southern Africa* (London: Royal United Service Institution, 1970), p. 15.

7. "The Cape Route," Report of a seminar, 25 February 1970, Royal United Service Institution, p. 13.

8. *The Guardian,* 20 October 1970.

9. Hearings, Subcommittee on Africa, Committee on Foreign Affairs, 20-22 March 1973 (Washington: Government Printing Office, 1973), p. 5.

10. The reservation specified that "the United States as a nation with many responsibilities in many parts of the world naturally reserves the right to interpret this policy in the light of requirements for assuring the maintenance of international peace and security." U. S. Mission to the United Nations, press release 4233, 2 August 1963.

11. Note on Developments concerning the Implementation of the Arms Embargo Against South Africa, U.N. A/AC 115/L285, 16 March 1971.

12. President Valery Giscard d'Estaing announced in Zaire that France would ban the sale of all arms except naval equipment, *Anti-Apartheid News,* September 1975.

13. Norway began challenging Portugal's policies at official NATO

meetings in 1973, and the Scandinavian countries have given direct support to the liberation movements, as noted previously.

14. *Military Balance,* 1971-73, International Institute for Strategic Studies, London, 1973 and 1975. The 1976-77 increase is (Rand) 379-34 millions.

15. Based on reliable estimates given to me in Lusaka, July 1973.

16. Hearings, Subcommittee on Africa, p. 27.

17. *The Sunday Times,* Johannesburg, 21 October 1973, reported Advocaat has direct links with the Royal Navy in Whitehall and the U.S. Navy base at San Juan in Puerto Rico.

18. Hearings, Subcommittee on Africa, p. 78.

19. *Southern Africa: Proposals for Americans,* A Report of a National Policy Panel (UNA-USA, 1971), pp. 53-54.

20. Hearings, Subcommittee on Africa. See also, Jennifer Davis, unpublished paper for the African Studies Association meeting, Denver, 1971, and Ron Walters, "Apartheid and the Atom," *Africa Today,* Summer 1976.

21. Africa Bureau *Fact Sheet,* October 1974.

22. Hearings, Subcommittee of Africa Hearings, pp. 78-85.

23. Ibid.

24. The Protestant Episcopal Church initiated a proxy resolution on this issue against IBM management in 1974.

25. Jack Anderson, *Rocky Mountain News,* October 1974. For the complete text, see *Southern Africa,* July-August 1975, p. 37.

26. *New York Times,* June 7, 1975.

27. In an interview, Dennis Healey, Minister of Defence in the 1964-69 Wilson government, termed the base not essential but "useful."

28. Spence, op. cit., p. 15.

29. House of Commons Debate, Vol. 696, Col. 1419, 17 June 1964.

30. Ibid., Vol. 703, Col. 12-13, 30 November 1964.

31. *The Times* (London), 7 July 1970, and Spence, op. cit.

32. *Annual Report,* Anti-Apartheid Movement, 1971-72.

33. *The Guardian*, 19 October 1970.

34. British Council of Churches, "The Future of South Africa," working group paper, 1965, p. 133.

35. Ibid., p. 77.

36. The Right Honorable Geoffrey Rippon, "The Importance of South Africa," *Survival* (September 1970) (monthly published by Institute of Strategic Studies).

37. *The Guardian,* 20 October 1970.

38. Colin Legum, "Anti-Arms Lobby Grows in City," *The Observer,* 15 November 1970.

39. Dennis Healey, interview, October 1970.

40. *X-ray,* October 1970, p. 1, quoting *Evening Standard* poll.

41. *The Times* (London), 15 November 1970.

42. *The Guardian,* 23 October 1970.

43. *The Times* (London), 20 October 1970.

44. Kaunda was ineffectual at Singapore because of inadequate information. See D. V. Gruhn, "British Arms Sales to South Africa: The Limits of African Diplomacy," *Studies in Race and Nations,* Vol. 3 (1971-72), p. 24.

45. Communiqué of the U.N. Special Committee on Apartheid, 24 February 1971.

46. *Labour Weekly Supplement,* 25 May 1973, p. 6.

47. The ministers were Tony Benn, Judith Hart, Jean Lester, Barbara Castle, and Frank Judd. *The Guardian,* December 9, 1974.

48. Unit on Apartheid, Notes and Documents, No. 17/20 (May 1970) pp. 4-5, No. 30/75 August 1975, p. 1 and 7.

49. Ibid.

50. Abdul Minty, "South Africa's Defense Strategy," *Notes and Documents,* Center Against Apartheid, U.N., January 1976.

51. Fact Sheet, Africa Bureau, October 1974.

52. *The New York Times,* 24 July 1974, and *NATO Review* (Belgium), June 1974.

53. The United States and the United Kingdom, in December 1966, concluded an agreement to make the British Indian Ocean Territory (BIOT) available to both countries for fifty years. See *The Defense Monitor,* Vol. III, No. 3 (April 1974).

54. Quoted in David Johnson, "Troubled Waters for the U.S. Navy," *Africa Report,* January-February 1975, p. 10.

55. "Southern Africa," paper for the Labour Party Conference, June 1974.

56. "The Security of the Southern Oceans—Southern Africa the Key," Seminar of the Royal United Service Institution, February 1972.

57. *The Star,* Weekly Edition, Johannesburg, April 5, 1975.

58. *The Defense Monitor.*

59. Goler Butcher testimony, Hearings, Subcommittee on African Affairs, Committee on Foreign Relations, U.S. Senate, Ninety-Fourth Congress, June-July 1975, p. 268.

60. The Anti-Apartheid Movement in the United Kingdom issued a special appeal for a mandatory United Nations arms embargo in June 1976. They particularly criticized American, German, and British links with the Advocaat Communications System based near Simonstown for surveillance of the southern oceans. In a memorandum to the British government, the AAM listed the goods which they felt should be controlled in an effective embargo. Those items which enable South Africa to develop its own arms industry, they maintained, were exempted in the 1970 Control Order. See *Anti-Apartheid News,* June 1976.

chapter 6 ════════════

TRANSNATIONAL ASSISTANCE TO LIBERATION MOVEMENTS

The commitment to liberation among Western NGOs was well established by the early 1970s. While the major Atlantic powers bitterly opposed this direction and there was considerable dissent among the gradualist wing, the black and the abolitionist non-governmental actors had established a commanding position in the struggle. Their activity had become truly transnational in that they had built direct relations with the African liberation groups in the field. With support from African and OAU committees, they began to transmit aid and funds for the continuing struggle, as it was called, after the FRELIMO slogan *La Luta Continua.*

This development was facilitated by the increased supportive activity of the OAU and the United Nations and the progress of liberation movements themselves. The latter were making rapid headway in the Portuguese territories. SWAPO had firmly established its position in Namibia, and ZANU and ZAPU had made headway in Rhodesia. While differences among leaders and groups plagued them, there was substantial progress, after the hiatus of the late sixties, as the military capability of the insurgents grew rapidly with African and socialist state support. Even smaller Western powers began to provide limited forms of humanitarian assistance, encouraged by the transnational activity of the NGOs, and the growing belief that the liberation movements would soon gain their objectives, particularly in the Portuguese territories.

Major problems accompanied this growth. Not only questions of amounts and types of aid arose but also the matter of what criteria to apply to differentiate among rival groups and claims. Which channels of support to use provided another set of issues. With success itself arose the subject of forms of continued assistance to the new governments. Throughout these questions lurked the problems of Great Power and South African intrigue seeking to use one group against another in the pursuit of rival interests. NGOs themselves, within their national bases, reflected some of these difficult choices and conflicts.

Yet liberation for all of Southern Africa, including apartheid South Africa, by the mid-70s had become again a live option. One major element in this remarkable revival, of what many feared was a lost cause, was the rise of liberation auxiliaries in the Atlantic core.

Humanitarian Assistance

A broad range of groups are involved in humanitarian assistance and for different reasons, and therefore it is difficult to find a definition that fits all their interests. There is general agreement that humanitarian assistance is related to the nonmilitary aspects of the insurgency struggle, although there is no general rejection—and in some cases, active support—of the use of force. Since many church organizations are involved in the humanitarian-assistance program, the manner in which Christians, who generally have not supported revolution and have frequently rejected any form of violence, have come to justify their prominent role in the liberation-assistance program is significant.

In the 1960s the ecumenical movement shifted very rapidly from a liberal rationalization of Western colonial reforms to an acceptance of the idea of full self-determination, regardless of culture or status of development. In the World Council of Churches, the necessity for finding visible expression of support for revolution became increasingly accepted, as representatives from Asia and Africa rose to prominence. The first expression of this was made in New Delhi in 1961.[1] The turning point came at the Mindolo Consultation in 1964, where it was stated, regarding Southern Africa:

For many Christians involved in the struggle for a just solution, the question of possible violence as the remaining alternative has become an urgent and ever-pressing one. Reports indicate that many are convinced that war has already begun.[2]

This conversion of many ecumenical church leaders to the liberation movements' cause resulted in the initiation of the World Council aid programs. What followed had an immensely important influence on the general framework for action, including that of nonreligious bodies.

These groups have come to see liberation movements as the representatives of the victims of oppression who have no means for expressing their opposition other than through leaders who have been driven into exile or have raised the standard of revolution at home and are in prison. Support for these leaders became an expression of confidence in them as an historical force for change, as well as a direct means for alleviating the suffering of the daily victims of deportations, imprisonment, floggings, and torture by the South African and Rhodesian regimes. Humanitarian assistance was seen as a way to help in liberated areas to rebuild villages, introduce school systems, establish medical clinics, and begin to administer areas painfully librated. It was also a means by which young men and women could be educated and trained to serve their people as support echelons in the transition to self-rule.

Nonviolent Aid

Therefore, the distinction between peaceful and violent means of change made so frequently in the West by critics of liberation is highly misleading. An extensive nonviolent dimension to resistance against oppression exists,[3] such as refusal to give information to the oppressors.

Many who support humanitarian programs also endorse directly freedom fighters' activities. But the major impact of a liberation movement may be the nonviolent ways in which resistance is organized—strikes, boycotts, propaganda, and the day-to-day organization of alternative forms of government and social activity for people who have rejected foreign totalitarian rule.

Most humanitarian NGOs prefer to see liberation obtained through a minimal use of force, but they are agreed that peaceful persuasion is not going to bring about this end and agree with the British Council of Churches report: "The time has come to show our solidarity with those seeking radical change and struggling for freedom."[4] Thus, humanitarian assistance to liberation movements accepts the necessity of a total struggle of which one part is armed struggle to reconquer their lost lands. This mobilization encompasses people in many walks of life and situations, using various strategies. The humanitarian liberation spirit is compassionate about lives, on all sides, and works for as bloodless and speedy settlement as possible. But, in contrast to pacific settlement, it does not draw a sharp distinction between force and nonviolence.

The primary military assistance to southern African liberation movements as well as much humanitarian aid comes from the African states and the socialist bloc. However, it is not the task of this study to examine the nature of military assistance, especially as most of it comes from the non-Western world. A very thin line often exists between military and humanitarian aid. The question of how to identify humanitarian aid is, nevertheless, an important one.

The line of demarcation between relief programs of a neutral humanitarian type like the Red Cross, and humanitarian assistance to liberation movements has also been difficult to establish. This is because relief and religious agencies have long operated in conflict zones and have attempted to be neutral. Their access and support has been dependent upon the reality of this neutrality. Both sides in contemporary conflict have attempted to utilize relief agencies for their own purposes, but in most cases this has been successfully avoided.

The United Nations Secretariat developed, for the Oslo Conference in 1973, a set of general ideas and categories for identifying the types of humanitarian liberation assistance with which we are concerned here:

A. Inside the territories controlled by colonial and minority regimes
    1. Legal assistance to persons persecuted under repressive and discriminatory legislation;
    2. Assistance, including assistance for education and training to families of political prisoners, restrictees, banned persons, ex-prisoners and students expelled from schools for political activities;

    3. Grants for emigration of persecuted persons in exceptional cases;

    4. Scholarship and other education assistance to victims of racial discrimination;

    5. Grants to education institutions which cater to such persons, including correspondence colleges;

    6. Appropriate assistance to groups opposed to colonialism and racial discrimination, especially for specific welfare projects;

    7. Research grants for institutions and individuals.

B. Inside liberated areas

    1. Supplies for educational materials, medical equipment and and supplies, foodstuffs, seeds, agricultural implements, supplies of telecommunciation equipment, radios, trucks, etc;

    2. Technical assistance inside the territory.

C. Outside the territories

    1. Assistance to refugees, resettlement, employment, legal protection;

    2. Scholarships and facilities for education and training at at various levels for the indigenous inhabitants;

    3. Subventions to institutions providing places for students from the territories;

    4. Assistance to institutions associated with the liberation movements for education, health, and other activities;

    5. Provision of hospitals, schools, print shops, and other facilities of the liberation movements;

    6. Printing and supply of textbooks, technical assistance to the liberation movements including supply of doctors and teachers;

    7. Other assistance to the liberation movements, such as grants for travel to conferences, printing and distribution of publications, provision of facilities and grants for offices of liberation movement, and treatment of the wounded.[5]

This is a very wide-ranging conception of humanitarian assistance, but it has the virtue of including both traditional nonpolitical and contemporary political categories. Liberation aid is not outside the political struggle. Its central theme is transnational political support from one group to another across national boundaries to achieve a common objective, the realization of human rights by those who are oppressed.

However, these Oslo criteria do not address a more difficult problem, namely the identification of those who are the legitimate representatives of the oppressed to receive the assistance. At the United Nations level, this issue has usually been resolved in favor of OAU determination through the African Liberation Committee. This places great reliance on the judgment of the African states who make these determinations in terms of the credibility of the leadership, organized fighting units, territory controlled, number of supporters from more than one ethnic group, etc. Objective criteria do not always govern their choices, and personal preference, ideology, and readiness of the liberation group to support the political interests of those in power often determine the results, more than public statements, as observed by Vincent Khapoya in his study "Determinants of African Support for African Liberation Movements: A Comparative Analysis."[6]

For those organizations which do not work directly with the OAU, the problem is more complicated. They interpret their role and the activities of the liberation movements with criteria often different from that of the OAU and not always explicit. The issue of criteria is best considered within the context of the various types of liberation aid and will be taken up later.

National NGOs

There are various ways to categorize assistance, including type, size, areas, and countries of origin, but the most useful for this study is a division into (a) single-country-based NGOs, (b) international NGOs, (c) international organizations, and, (d) government aid channeled through NGOs.

The first category consists of the numerous national voluntary programs which have emerged in Western countries (especially the United States and the United Kingdom). Many of these are closely related to the international NGOs. For example, many liberal churches are affiliated with the World Council of Churches, yet all of them have special denominational and local-area ties that draw them into specialized programs of their own. Usually these are related to mission programs and church aid and relief projects established in years past. Especially important are the programs carried out by the British churches through Christian Aid and the American churches through Church World Service. Christian Aid rejects the Program to Combat Racism of the World Council and operates through its own channels according to its own criteria.[7] In 1973, well over $300,000 moved into liberation channels from Christian Aid. One hundred thousand dollars a year is spent by the United Church of Christ, U.S.A., according to one board secretary, in liberation-related work in Southern Africa.[8] Although the largest amounts of money come from the churches, secular relief groups have also made important grants. For example, OXFAM in England and Canada gave $10,000 to the Mozambique Institute in 1974. While the amounts have generally been smaller than those from the Protestant organizations mentioned above, Catholic groups have also supported selected projects.

The two primary American and British NGOs who have, as observed earlier, led the way in liberation support are the ACOA and British International Defence and Aid Fund. They have operated within different contexts, with different constituencies and to some extent different program objectives. Yet the similarities are striking, from the initial universal pacific consciousness to the later development of liberation assistance. Their activities stimulated related interests on the part of the churches, black groups, students, and political associations.

George Houser of ACOA created the Africa Fund in 1967 with Frank Mantero, an American black, as chairman of a group to help Africans "to work against the injustices of colonial and white minority domination." The fund grew rapidly, providing assistance to schools and training institutes of liberation movements, legal assistance to those who were imprisoned, and developing research and analysis to assist this process. By 1975, the fund had a budget of $263,000 and had aided Friendship Institute and Solidarity Hospital in Guinea-Bissau, provided medical services in Angola and educational programs such as FRELIMO's Secondary School at Bugamoyo in Tanzania.[9] A letter from Janet Mondlane, director of the Mozambique Institute, indicated the nature of this aid. She had raised support in the United States for this program among groups who had known and supported her husband.

It is almost impossible to say that one program in the whole process of building a new society is more interesting than another. At the same time, when one is at the secondary school, one feels the vibrations of the gigantic mental and physical growth. Perhaps it is because the school houses, and educates a group of dynamic and eager young people who are ready to act, to carry out that which they have in their minds.[10]

The task since the independence of Mozambique has changed vastly. However, the critical role of the institute continues and Janet Mondlane, as director of social services, is at the center of dynamics of the new nation. Many organizations which worked in close association with the ACOA in giving initial support to the Committee for a Free Mozambique, such as the church-supported Interreligious Foundation for Community Organization (IFCO), are continuing. Other related activities of support are carried out by such groups as the African Liberation Support Committee based on the West Coast and the American branch of the International Defence and Aid Fund.

The major support among NGOs in England was organized by the Defence and Aid Fund which, under John Collins' leadership, focused initially on the need for legal defense and humanitarian assistance to African nationalists in South Africa. Later Defence and Aid expanded by developing a network of social services for the movements from Zimbabwe, Namibia, and the Portuguese territories. The most notable results have been in the assistance to prisoners and their families. Through various devices, the fund, though banned in South Africa, has managed to channel support through courageous South Africans to resistance leaders and their families.

As observed in Chapter 4, black groups are becoming increasingly important in the United States. The International Foundation for Community Organization has aided movements in Angola and Mozambique with technical and educational assistance.[11] Other important black groups in the United States are the Africa Liberation Support Committee which sent a delegation to Dar es Salaam to present over $40,000 in cash to FRELIMO, ZANU, ZAPU, PAIGC, and UNITA. Gene Locke, chairman, claimed over thirty-two chapters in North America and the Caribbean.[12] On the West Coast the Bay Area Liberation Support Movement has been active in sending material support, especially medicines, to FRELIMO, MPLA, and PAIGC. Groups such as the Committee for a Free Mozambique in the United States and the Toronto Committee for

Liberation in Portugal's African colonies and Anti-Apartheid Beweging and Angola Comité in the Netherlands and Informationsstelle Südliches Afrika in Germany, to mention only a few of the numerous national NGOs, perform a critical information and limited fund-raising function. They provide a platform for the liberation leaders and a means by which their views and campaigns frequently reach grass-roots audiences. Since this is the way in which concern is translated into action, their role is to provide ideas and direction to other larger organizations such as labor, churches, and educational associations. They have been very successful in this over the years. Both the American Committee on Africa and the Anti-Apartheid Movement in England have been catalysts in the generation of ideas and programs for humanitarian assistance. As pressure groups go, they are among the powerless, but their ideas and programs have laid the foundation for related nongovernmental action which counteracts official policies and established commercial, media, and prosettler programs of the Western powers.[13]

International NGOs

The international nongovernmental organizations (INGOS), such as the International Defence and Aid Fund (IDAF), International University Exchange Fund (IUEF), the International Commission of Jurists, and the World Council of Churches, have all developed programs of liberation support, inspired by the initial influence of groups based in single countries. The various labor internationals should also be placed in this category. These groups are the most influential because they are the most extensive, having set up international boards of directors and established sets of international criteria governing the operation of humanitarian assistance.

The treason trials of the midfifties created a need to support the dependents of those on trial as well as provide for the defense—a greater need than the national committees could support. The Defence and Aid Fund, created by Canon John Collins in 1956 with the help of refugees from South African oppression, spread to Europe and became the International Defence and Aid Fund with branches in a dozen countries including Australia and the Netherlands.

The International Commission of Jurists (ICJ) and Amnesty International have worked with IDAF on Southern Africa issues.

The ICJ has supplied distinguished observers of "treason" and "terrorism" trials, whose reports have helped bring international legal standards into operation.[14] Amnesty International developed an early interest in a free Namibia.[15]

Several of these groups, especially IDAF, have worked in close cooperation with the U.N. trust funds on Southern Africa. A few governments, such as Sweden, contribute substantially to their budgets. In 1973, two-thirds of the IDAF budget was governmental, primarily Scandinavian. With its close liaison with the United Nations, especially the South African Trust Fund, the IDAF represents a major example of transnational organizational activity, tapping varied sources and bringing diverse interests together in support of the central problem of increased assistance.[16]

Although the IDAF is banned in South Africa, Rhodesia, and Namibia, its leadership has shown remarkable ingenuity in getting assistance to the families of imprisoned Africans and in hiring counsel for their defense. Amnesty International's special concern with the freedom of political prisoners and the general violation of their rights has aroused increasing protest over South African brutality, in Namibia in particular. Amnesty International, together with the IDAF and the ICJ, has provided legal analysis and defense for the rights of Southern Africans, which have relieved the plight of thousands of African families whose chief provider has been imprisoned.

The World Council of Churches' concern for the victims of apartheid, as stated by the Mindolo Commission, has already been noted. The World Council carried out various programs of assistance to movement-affiliated refugees and liberation-movement programs like the Mozambique Institute, largely through the Africa section of the Division of Relief and World Service (DICARWS), under the administration of Dr. Z. K. Matthews, a South African who had been a leader in the African National Congress, and was later Botswana's ambassador to the United Nations. Other liberation leaders, such as Eduardo Mondlane of FRELIMO, Augustinho Neto of MPLA, and Sam Nujoma and Jacob Kuhangua of SWAPO also had close involvement in many aspects of the World Council's program. But it was not until its Uppsala Assembly (1968) that the WCC determined on a program "to mobilize the Churches in the world-wide struggle against racism." The Programme to Combat Racism began a series of grants in 1970 to liberation movements for the purpose of helping with the costs of administration, education, and medical programs. Baldwin Sjollema, as the first director, began an imaginative series of allocations from annual budgets of upwards of $200,000. But the major influence was on other church organizations, international and national, which were encouraged to take similar action,[17] such as the Lutheran World Federation and the Catholic Relief Organizations.

While some negative reaction developed to the WCC program, especially among British, German, and South African churches, the strong positive moral support from Asian-African churches and the financial assistance of many European, North American, and Scandinavian churches, enabled the program of liberation support to grow. In 1972, the World Council of Churches sold its own stock in companies dealing with South Africa and urged its member churches to do the same.

The WCC selection of particular liberation movements for humanitarian assistance was facilitated by OAU guidelines, but in some cases, it has followed its own sense of who was representative and effective. In 1971, the Programme to Combat Racism revealed that out of sixty-six applications, it chose twenty-four, among whom were the following African liberation movements:

Africa Independence Party of Guinea and Cape Verde Islands (PAIGC), $25,000, primarily for improving education and literacy.

Peoples Movement for the Liberation of Angola (MPLA), medical and educational programs, $25,000.

National Union for the Total Independence of Angola (UNITA), campaigns against illiteracy and agricultural assistance, $7,500.

The Mozambique Institute of FRELIMO, seeds, foodstuffs, and development of a new curriculum, $20,000.

Southwest African Peoples Organization (SWAPO), Namibian refugee assistance and education of youth, $25,000.

Luthuli Memorial Foundation of African National Congress (ANC), research, publication, and scholarship grants, $5,000.

For Zimbabwe, $10,000 each for both ZAPU and ZANU, to be allocated after discussions with the general secretary.

Southern Africa, $2,000 in Zambia for awareness building in Zambia and coordination with liberation movements.

Smaller grants were made to support NGOs in Europe, such as the French and Belgian anti-apartheid groups.[18]

This action was extended each year from 1971 to 1975, and the PAC of South Africa was added in 1973 and 1974.

International church agencies, notably the Lutheran World Federation, have assisted in scholarship programs for students from Southern Africa and have aided refugees. This aid is less directly political but important in the view of liberation leaders. Innumerable problems, especially related to the choice of groups and individuals to aid, have plagued these efforts, yet they have continued.

A related INGO of considerable importance is the International University Exchange Fund (IUEF) founded by European student movements in the early 1960s. This organization has primarily provided an educational training and scholarship program for students who have fled the southern African countries and become attached to liberation movements. It has significant support from Canada and the Netherlands, but its major funding comes from Scandinavia. Its budget is well over $300,000 per year, utilized primarily for scholarship aid and the training of Africans in Southern Africa to remain and work with the movements.[19] The IUEF works closely with the liberation movements in providing research and publication aid and financial aid to the southern African student movements based in Botswana. Prison education has been one of their primary projects, to enable political detainees to prepare themselves more fully for responsibility when their countries are free and they are released. They have assisted the black-worker movements and the black-consciousness groups in South Africa, such as the Black Peoples Convention (BPC) and the Black Allied Workers Union, and protested the suppression of these groups in 1974-75.[20]

Amnesty International (under the direction of Sean MacBride, later commissioner for Namibia at the United Nations) has brought the plight of thousands of political prisoners in South Africa and Rhodesia to the attention of the world and facilitated the release of some. It is supported by private contributions of intellectuals and humanists and is nonsectarian and nonpolitical. Its campaign against the use of torture is a restraint on police terror in some cases, although the practice appears to be worsening. The assistance of International Trade Unions—for example, the support of the International Confederation of Free Trade Unions (ICFTU) for the families of trade-union officials detained in Rhodesia—is related to another form of aid. The ICFTU and its rival the World Federation of Trade Unions (WFTU) aid several unions and liberation movements outside their countries by organization, publishing, and monetary assistance. The fact that ideological considerations particularly govern the decision of trade unions to aid one group or leader over another is often denounced by those who do not get the aid, but the flow of funds has been an additional source. It should be especially noted that with their political influence, trade unions are often the mediaries to other funds, especially from governments.

IGOs

A third major category of assistance agencies, the international government organizations (IGOs), have developed liberation support programs as a result of the influence of the INGOs and the Third World majority at the U.N. and are sources of greater support than the voluntary organizations. The United Nations, under the influence of the Afro-Asian majority, first established special funds and then gradually began to require all of its specialized agencies to give support in either a technical or training way to the liberation movements. The two most important funds, the Southern African Trust Fund and the Fund for Namibia, were established enable governments to give aid to the victims of apartheid and colonialism. The specifications were for aid to individuals rather than for direct aid to liberation movements. However, in practice, most of the contributions have been utilized for purposes broadly categorized today as humanitarian assistance to liberation movements: legal defense, education programs, development projects, and support for the victims of apartheid. Grants to several of the INGOs, notably IDAF, Amnesty International, and the ICJ, have been one major means of implementing their work. Contributions had totaled $3,218,199 as of 15 April 1975. Detailed reports of disbursements are not made, in order to protect the recipients and their channels of aid.[21]

The following chart represents the contributions of all members of the United Nations through 1974 to the United Nations Trust Fund for South Africa. One of the striking facts is the difference between contributions of the Scandinavians and the Great Powers. Both the United States and the United Kingdom have obviously preferred to direct such limited assistance as they were willing to give through their own national programs, as is the case with several others.

Contributions to the Trust Fund[22]
1966-1974

COUNTRY	($US) CONTRIBUTION
Algeria	2,000
Australia	13,787
Austria	37,000
Belgium	87,764
Brazil	14,000
Bulgaria	7,000
Byelorussian SSR	1,500
Canada	39,259
Chile	3,000
China	40,000
Cyprus	2,697
Czechoslovakia	2,000
Denmark	554,263
Egypt	3,000
Ethiopia	3,000
Finland	211,000
France	110,000
German Democratic Republic	5,000
Germany, Federal Republic of	55,000
Ghana	5,020
Guinea	6,555
Hungary	4,000
Iceland	2,000
India	6,325
Indonesia	4,500
Iran	20,000
Iraq	1,400
Ireland	18,250
Israel	1,000
Italy	16,283

Contributions to the Trust Fund[22] (continued)

COUNTRY	($US) CONTRIBUTION
Jamaica	3,430
Japan	60,000
Khmer Republic	2,000
Liberia	5,000
Libyan Arab Republic	5,600
Malawi	140
Malaysia	8,000
Mongolia	1,500
Morocco	28,457
Nepal	500
Netherlands	59,499
New Zealand	13,892
Niger	656
Nigeria	32,240
Norway	205,400
Pakistan	20,000
Philippines	11,000
Poland	2,000
Saudi Arabia	5,007
Sierra Leone	8,475
Singapore	1,500
Somalia	502
Sudan	1,500
Sweden	781,308
Thailand	1,000
Trinidad and Tobago	1,250
Tunisia	12,000
Turkey	3,000
Ukrainian SSR	3,500
U.S.S.R	20,000
United Kingdom	40,000
United States	25,000
Venezuela	1,000
Yugoslavia	8,000
Zaire	5,000
Zambia	1,960
Total:	$2,668,725

The first phase of IGO assistance began in the early sixties, with the allocation of funds to refugee relief and training programs, as a result of the flow of refugees from Southern Africa into Zaire, Tanzania, and Zambia and their need for humanitarian relief. The General Assembly established a special education and training project for South West Africa (Namibia) in 1961, and a similar program for the Portuguese territories in 1962. With the endorsement of the education and training program for Southern Africans by the Security Council in 1964, virtually all countries contributed, but the contributions of the United States and the United Kingdom were minor.

The establishment in 1964 of the Special Committee on Apartheid, and the United Nations Trust Fund for South Africa in 1965, with increased funding from member governments, marked the specialized approach to this problem. A broader training program emerged in 1965 as a result of the recommendations of a group of experts on South Africa (representing NGO opinion). With the endorsement of the Security Council in June 1964, the Education and Training Programme for South Africans received substantial support from a broad group of governments.[23]

The second phase began in the seventies. With the adoption of the liberation strategy, existing agencies of the United Nations system were to contribute in some way to the liberation movements, and in a series of resolutions the Security Council as well as the General Assembly, from 1969 on, called for states to increase their moral and material assistance to the freedom movements in Southern Africa.

Specialized agencies became more active in direct humanitarian assistance. For example, in 1973, the FAO sent a small project preparatory mission on behalf of FRELIMO to Tanzania for the purpose of drawing up a draft project to provide for the establishment of an agricultural component within the framework of the ongoing UNDP-funded UNESCO training project to be located in Bagamoyo and Tunduru.

In conversations with the author in 1973, FRELIMO leaders expressed some skepticism regarding the extent of such IGO aid. However, with the advent of independence in 1975 the prospect has opened for full-scale United Nations assistance to the new nations of former Portuguese Africa, utilizing the patterns established during liberation.

The multilateral IGO funds have continued to grow, especially through contributions of most of the world's nations to the Fund for Namibia, despite the skepticism of the United States and the United Kingdom. The United Nations appears to be committed to continuing this transnational form of liberation support.

The close liaison between liberation groups, NGOs, the United Nations, and the OAU was especially demonstrated at the Oslo Conference on Southern Africa in April 1973. The OAU was the instrumental convener of this conference with the help of the Norwegian government and the United Nations Secretariat. Out of the resolutions and papers of this conference emerged a clear picture of the extensive network of transnational actors in the anti-apartheid movement. The OAU's role as a prime facilitator of this cooperation is clearly seen, and many of the United Nations agencies for the first time openly discussed their role in implementing humanitarian assistance. In this conference, NGO participation was limited to spokesmen invited as experts for particular agencies such as the IDAF and the WCC. The close affinity of the thinking of these NGO spokesmen to that of the liberation representatives evidences the cooperation between them.

That there are differences and problems is obvious. NGOs reflect different political views, and their senior officers are drawn primarily from Western countries. This is changing slowly, but there is still a time lag between the resolutions of the General Assembly and the Security Council and implementation of policy by the specialized agencies. Their officers are clearly conscious of conflict between the views of the primary contributors to their budgets and the majority of the members of the United Nations. Nevertheless, the decade of the sixties brought a major shift in IGO policy toward liberation movements, as a result of the movements themselves and NGO pressure, assisted by Third World states. An increasing flow of direct assistance to liberation groups has begun through grants and technical services. Examples are the program of UNESCO educational assistance to FRELIMO and the training of SWAPO members for administrative roles. Through the Namibia Institute, a Lusaka-based creation of the Council for Namibia, several United Nations agencies are involved in the support of this program. The Council for Namibia has been given membership in the World Health Organization and has participated in meetings organized by other IGOs, among them the ILO and International Civil Aviation Organization (ICAO). It also participated in the Third United Nations Conference on the Law of the Sea in 1974. As this trend continues, the council's importance grows and its resources expand, and Namibian representatives, as opposed to South African, are accepted as the accredited representatives of the territory. Through this recognition of liberation goals, the transnational community facilitates the birth of new states.

Unilateral Aid

The fourth category, unilateral governmental assistance, will only be touched upon here, because it is not transnational aid as in the other categories. However, it is often channeled through INGOs and NGOs. This assistance is provided by certain states, like Sweden, to international NGOs such as the IDAF or the IUEF and to individual movements like the PAIGC directly.[25] These unilateral funds from Western countries now total several million dollars annually. Most of the money comes from the Scandinavians,[26] but the Netherlands, Australia, West Germany, and Canada have recently joined this group. These four governments channel funds to liberation movements through national and international NGOs and relief agencies such as the churches and educational programs. The core powers, as indicated above, have often preferred this technique. The United States, through its foreign-aid program, enables the African-American Institute to carry out extensive training and scholarship programs for southern African refugee students. But because of Portuguese and South African protest, its support diminished, leaving a number of southern Africans with unfinished programs. The tendency of governments to use subsidies to NGOs as foreign-policy vehicles has not always been advantageous to these groups, as it has rendered them suspect in the view of several of the liberation movements. Therefore, the humanitarian aspects of liberation aid are probably better preserved by multilateral programs. The entry of Holland and Canada into this field of multilateral assistance is significant not only because of the positive additional resources they have provided but also for the political implications. The Dutch government has contributed substantially to the United Nations trust funds and, through the Netherlands program for dairy assistance, contributed skimmed milk powder and cheese to the Mozambique Institute. In 1974, it was estimated that the Netherlands granted between $4 and $5 million to various liberation groups.[25] The growth of Canadian aid through NGOs is a breakthrough in North America.

In Canada, the Trudeau government is moving toward substantial indirect assistance to liberation movements, providing an example of the prospect, together with its dangers, for a new direction in North America. The government has announced its intention to channel Canadian International Development Agency funds through "reliable" INGOs as well as through NGOs. Canada intends to employ organizations like the IUEF and international church agencies to widen its existing support of the southern African struggle "to achieve human dignity and the right to self-determination. . . ." which would be for peaceful purposes involving "strict accountability," but will offer no cash directly or arms grants.[28] The right-wing furor against this step has been surmounted. Canadian liberation support groups, including the Toronto Committee for the Liberation of Portugal's African Colonies, have been very skeptical of the ability of the government to shake off its commitments to settler regimes under the constraint of NATO. However, some in the Canadian division of the IDAF are more sanguine now that "non-NATO" areas are the targets.

The Criteria Problem

International humanitarian assistance to liberation movements is afflicted with enormous problems at the NGO, INGO, and IGO levels, which have only been touched upon. The total funding dimensions are nowhere near the levels of need. Much of the assistance is in tied grants, or in kind, which are not as easily used by the movements. Movements would much prefer to have cash and be entrusted by their benefactors with confidence in their judgment and dedication, which this kind of financial aid would require.[30] Liberal white paternalism pervades the operation of many of these assistance agencies and limits the options. The cases of misuse of funds are few in comparison with the innumerable examples of sacrifice and commitment on the part of the liberation-movement leaders. Divisions within the liberation ranks create the most difficult administrative problem facing the agencies in deciding who deserves assistance. A professionalism has emerged among a few self-proclaimed liberation leaders, who plead for funds but do little with them other than sustain themselves and their close colleagues, and the tendencies toward deception and intrigue growing out of this are well known. The role of the OAU in sorting out those movements that deserve assistance has provided one means for outside measurement, although many contributors do not follow these OAU guidelines. It is not always clear precisely what these criteria are, and there has been considerable controversy regarding their application. A famous case was the refusal of the OAU Liberation Committee to recognize UNITA in Eastern Angola for at least two years. Two African writers who have attempted to analyze these criteria are Vincent Khapoya and Yash Tandon. They both see control of territory and effectiveness in opening the psychological warfare campaign as primary determinants.[31]

The World Council of Churches' Programme to Combat Racism attempted not to set qualifications on its assistance and to give cash grants. However, in 1971 the program specified some general criteria for the selections:

(1) The aim is to raise the level of awareness and to strengthen the organizational capability of rapidly oppressed people and to support organizations that align themselves with the victims of valid [sic] injustice. (2) The purposes of the organizations must be in consonant with the general purposes of the WCC and its units, and the grants are to be used for humanitarian activities (i.e., social health and educational purposes, legal aid, etc.) (3) The grants are made without control of the manner in which they are used, but are intended as an expression of commitment by the PCR to the cause of economic, social and political justice which these organizations promote.[32]

Some of the assisting groups play dangerous international politics with aid on behalf of national or ideological aims. The infiltration of voluntary NGOs by governments seeking their own national ends is not limited to the CIA; every national power employs this tactic to some degree. They frequently try to use one group against another, attempting to assure that the victorious movement will serve their national interests. This is the most difficult problem for those liberation leaders who wish to avoid becoming the cat's-paws for any foreign power. Infiltration is particularly a problem for the auxiliary NGOs who wish to avoid serving national or intelligence objectives of their own governments. The use of government funds obviously exacerbates the problem. There have been no simple answers, because even the OAU has had tremendous political differences. However, national special interests can best be avoided by utilizing multilateral, rather than unilateral, organizations.

Church assistance programs have found themselves caught between conservative parishioners who object to any liberation programs and the pressure of rival claims for their support.

In order to sort out its own program, one church group suggested the following:

1. Does the movement have the support of the people in the country, cutting across ethnic lines and not representing one ethnic group or privileged minority?

2. To what extent does the movement have an explicit program of action, and to what extent is there correspondence between the program and the actions actually undertaken?

3. Is the movement actually engaged in the armed struggle? Is it in control of liberation areas?

4. To what extent is the movement engaged in the areas it controls in the kind of societal transformation which is necessary for a protracted struggle?[33]

Despite their dilemmas the African Liberation Committee of the OAU states remains the best first guideline in selective support programs. And if this breaks down, the United Nations specialized agencies and funds in conjunction with the experienced INGOs, can give the best direction.

The most acute form of this dilemma over support developed in the division of movements after independence in Angola. Other rival claims exist in Zimbabwe, Namibia, and South Africa. None have faced this choice more poignantly yet perceptively than the African states themselves.

What is happening is clearly the emergence of a new humanitarian force which, as John Collins has put it, "is not nonpolitical but clearly committed to assisting the freedom movements in the white redoubt." The signs of its growth in western Europe and North

America as well as Australia and New Zealand are very apparent. Conservative political reaction, at least initially, is not likely to be able to repress it. There is, of course, an opposite tendency, of Western powers at least, to increase military and financial support for the white elite governments of southern Africa. But the liberation-support movement also has the effect of increasingly challenging the assumptions on which official policies are based. In time the contradictions may become sufficiently obvious so that political changes within the core powers will reflect far more than they do today the values and programs of the humanitarian-assistance groups.

The American NGOs, even considering the work of the liberal churches, lag behind Europe in this program. Careful consideration of the reasons for this is necessary. Leadership in bringing diverse interests together is needed. American racism, fear of communism, and conservative religious thought are each major deterrents, but have not prevented the growth of wide constituencies for African liberation support. Ways need to be found to reach them and to put them in touch with the numerous international channels of assistance.

Liberation leaders are wary of the dualistic policies of some Western states, who support liberation movements but continue the investment and strategic relations of the traditional core-periphery system. Yet they do not refuse assistance, while realizing that these governments have an interest on both sides in this conflict.

The importance of NGO humanitarian assistance cannot be measured or fully compared to other types of assistance. It has grown in importance with the advance of freedom in Southern Africa and has helped bring victory more rapidly in Guinea-Bissau, Mozambique, and Angola. It is closely linked to the political struggle going on within Anglo-American countries over liberation in South Africa, and will be important in the final settlement.

The United Nations has been an essential legitimizing agent for liberation movements, providing them with a forum, recognition and assistance. As a point of contact for NGOs, it has helped to develop relationships that eventually provide substantial assistance. Western government aid has also been greatly facilitated by the United Nations, which provides contacts, information, and neutral facilities. The United Nations, it is true, has often appeared to prefer resolutions to action and failed to enlist various agencies, or provide the scope of aid desired by those involved in the heat of the battle, yet without its transnational, neutral, and multilateral facilities, the humanitarian movement described here would not have become an important variable in the self-determination of Southern African people.

Notes

1. *The New Delhi Report,* Third Assembly of the World Council of Churches, p. 103.

2. "Christians and Race Relations in Southern Africa," Consultation Report, World Council of Churches, pp. 12-13.

3. See Gene Sharp, *The Politics of Non-Violent Action,* 3 vols. (Boston: Porter Sargent, 1973).

4. *Violence in Southern Africa: A Christian Assessment* (London: SCM Press, 1970).

5. "Assistance to the Victims of Colonialism and Apartheid in Southern Africa," pp. 1-12. Mimeographed. The UN Secretariat for the International Conference of Experts for the Support of Victims of Colonialism and Apartheid in Southern Africa, Oslo, April 1973.

6. Vincent Khapoya, "Determinants of African Support for African Liberation Movements: A Comparative Analysis." Mimeographed. African Studies Association, November 1974.

7. The Africa Fund Report, 1975. Letter from George Houser.

8. Conversation with Laurence Henderson, United Church Board for World Ministries.

9. Report from the Mozambique Institute to the Africa Fund, 1974, p. 6.

10. Ibid.

11. IFCO is closely related to the National Council of Churches financially and in leadership. They fund a variety of community-related revolutionary groups, many of which are purely American based. But their role in fostering black American interest and support for liberation should be especially noted.

12. *The Nationalist* (Tanzania), September 1972.

13. A meeting of over thirty such groups in the Midwest at Madison, Wisconsin, in October 1975, showed the continuing growth of this movement.

14. These have been documented in Gerald Gardiner, "The Treason Trial in South Africa," *Journal of the ICJ,* Vol. 1, No. 1 (Autumn 1957), and "The Special Report; South Africa and the Rule of Law," ICJ, Geneva, 1960.

15. Interview with Sean MacBride, May 1974.

16. Based on an interview with officials of the IDAF and their reports in June 1973. They are understandably reluctant to publish detailed budgets,

but the total of the IDAF budget for 1973 was in excess of $1.5 million.

17. See Elizabeth Adler, *A Small Beginning,* Programme to Combat Racism, WCC, Geneva, 1974.

18. Document 25 S WCC, 1971, Executive Committee Action, Programme to Combat Racism, 5-9 September 1971.

19. "Ten years of Assistance to African Refugees Through International Cooperation" (Geneva: IUEF, 1972).

20. The IUEF information service on prisoners and those arrested has been an invaluable source to the liberation groups. See "Report of the Director to the Assembly and International Board, April 1974," 31 March 1975, Geneva.

21. United Nations Trust Fund for South Africa, *Objective Justice* Vol. 7, United Nations, 3 November 1975.

22. Ibid. More recent figures through 31 March 1976 of $3,956,117 from seventy-three governments. The United States and the United Kingdom amounts are unchanged. "United Nations Funds for Assistance to Oppressed People in South Africa," Center Against Apartheid, United Nations, April 1976.

23. Stolke and Widstrand, *Southern Africa,* Vol. 2. (Uppsala: Scandinavian Institute, 1974), pp. 275-277, provide a report showing a total of 744 recipients and a support of $2,629,477.

24. Ibid., Vol. 1, part III.

25. Stolke and Widstrand, op. cit.

26. These contributions are listed in Memorandum, "Swedish Assistance to the Victims of Apartheid and Colonization in Southern Africa." Mimeographed. Swedish Ministry of Foreign Affairs, September 1976. This totaled 30 million Kroner in 1976-77 and 100 million since the program began in 1968.

27. Interview with Bevend Schnitzens, Secretary of Anti-Apartheid (Netherlands), June 1973, Amsterdam.

28. Statement of Michell Sharp, Standing Secretary of External Affairs, 19 March 1974.

29. Interview with officers of the Canadian Branch of International Defence and Aid in August 1974.

30. Interviews with numerous liberation leaders prove they unanimously endorse this point of view.

31. See Vincent Khapoya, *Politics of Decision: Comparative Study of African Policy Toward the Liberation Movements* (Denver: University of Denver monographs, Vol. 12, No. 3 (1974/75).

32. Document 25A, WCC Executive Committee, 1972.

33. From a manuscript submitted by a group of consultants to the African Division of the Board of World Ministries, United Church of Christ, U.S.A., 1973.

chapter 7

TRANSNATIONAL SANCTIONS: THE NONGOVERNMENTAL ALTERNATIVE

Transnational sanctions have grown steadily over the past decade, and there is wide support for disengagement, despite official Western government opposition. Limited cooperation with the sanctions campaign has taken place among smaller Western governments.

The long-standing supposition of many abolitionists, as well as other foes of apartheid, that sanctions could be effective only with universal compliance—that is, if the American and British official policies change—was determined by the narrow framework of traditional international politics. Sanctions undertaken by transnational groups of churches, corporations, trade unions, and international human-rights groups constitute a form of coercion on societies and states which have greater impact than official policy.[1]

A fundamental problem has been how to make a program of sanctions against South Africa a practical as well as a moral undertaking. Ronald Segal, the prime mover behind the 1964 London Conference of NGOs and African states on sanctions against South Africa, concluded that "the Conference has shown sanctions to be necessary, urgent, legal, and practical, but likely to succeed only with the full cooperation of Britain and the United States."[2] This presumption, that sanctions would only be effective when endorsed by the British and American governments, and that those governments could be pressured or persuaded into such action, was the major rock on which this particular design foundered. The two governments have been the prime opponents of such international measures, and have consistently demonstrated at the United Nations their unyielding hostility to such steps.[3] Nevertheless, there has been a return of interest in the seventies in the prospects of sanctions and disengagement because of the changing economic climate. Several related factors are the growing recognition of the power of the transnational actors, small Western powers, and the increased role of non-Western powers, reflected in the détente between the United States and the Soviet Union. Liberation movements have demonstrated they can succeed, despite Western power opposition, under very difficult circumstances. But most important is the weakening of the Western economic system and the dependent South African economy.

The thesis, therefore, has emerged that an effective sanctions campaign can be developed against South Africa, despite the continued opposition of the governments of the United States and the United Kingdom and a lack of cooperation by other Western powers. This entails a different concept of international relations than the one popular in the sixties, which viewed the international systems as dominated by the Western powers. New actors exist. Moreover, there have been changes in our ideas about the determining ingredients of national power and how new tactics and influences can affect a society such as South Africa, producing change and revolution.[4] It is no longer necessary to view a successful international-sanctions campaign as one based on the legal definitions of Chapter 7 Article 41 of the United Nations Charter, as an action in which all the Great Powers must cooperate. The chances are strongly against this happening, and it is not essential for effective action. New forms of nonviolent action have emerged. International pressure is exerted against the contractual and consensual basis of power. This influences opinion, changes economic and financial practices, and strengthens revolutionary forces within and outside of South Africa. Those groups and governments which supply support to South Africa can be pressured into reducing their activity. The investment climate can be altered by international opinion and the retaliation of certain countries against sanctions-busting corporations. Economic changes, such as the energy dependency of the United States and the United Kingdom on the Afro-Arab world, provide a new context in which these activities operate. The development of new positive action "human space" alternatives to force and violence has produced new strategies and given hope to the anti-apartheid groups in the West.

To be effective, transnational sanctions must weaken the role of South Africa in the Atlantic system, thereby easing the task of the revolutionaries both within and outside the apartheid system and their African and Asian supporters. The dependency relationship is the key to the continuance of the white power structure.[5]

The old theory of sanctions was not only legalistic, but viewed the Western powers, especially the United States and the United Kingdom, in a determining role in relation to South Africa. While the new theory, based on a transnational and revolutionary perspective, does realize this significant continuing relationship, it recognizes that peripheral areas have become expendable to major powers when they become liabilities because they are indefensible or constitute a dangerous drain on the core. The elements of drain and liability provide an important means for transnational pressure by NGOs and smaller countries of Asia and Africa, who consistently cooperate over periods of time in sanctions campaigns. NGOs become, in a sense, transnational bargaining agents, able to affect directly the vital interests that major groups, such as corporations, have in continued investments in apartheid or the trade relations of numerous countries.

The effect of international trade and cultural sanctions of this kind can be considerable on the nongovernmental aspects of Great Power relations, weakening and even rendering nominal official support. Governments can make grants and give assistance, but they cannot always maintain the web of private-actor relationships, based on consent and self-interest, that have such an important influence on dependency ties. Over the long run, these can determine investment and trading climate.

Four important international economic changes have taken place (in addition to the rise to more effective levels of influence of the NGOs) to give impetus to the new theory: the new OPEC role; the success of the liberation movements in Rhodesia and the Portuguese colonies; the decline of Western economies into inflation and unemployment; and the unfavorable climate for external investment in South Africa. OPEC's position is most significant for the long run, because the United States and the United Kingdom are progressively more reliant on energy-producing countries in Africa and the Arab world. The economic decline means that most Western industrial countries must now impose increasing restrictions on the exodus of capital, the flight of multinationals from inflation, pollution control, and wage pressures at home. In short, caught in the down cycle, Western capitalism is aggravated by the grip of an increasing energy dependency on Afro-Arab countries. Economies like South Africa are a growing liability because they require investment and loan subsidy and invite Third World sanctions. Faced with pressure and retaliation from the international-sanctions actors in such situations, the Western powers gradually find the liabilities greater than the assets.

Official Policy

Official policies of even the United States and Great Britain are not impervious to pressures from NGOs, and especially from the more powerful organizations, such as the ecumenical churches. However, these governments have had a consistent record at the United Nations of opposition to economic sanctions against South Africa. Moreover, both the Foreign Office and the State Department have lacked enthusiasm for the doctrine of disengagement, even when the United Nations applied it against Rhodesia.[6]

While deploring the moral and political character of apartheid, they have based their opposition to sanctions against South Africa on the ground that it is a poor strategy, that it would worsen the condition of the weakest—the Africans—and only intensify the dominant whites' opposition to change, making the task of the reformers, both black and white, far more difficult. They have therefore opposed resolutions at the United Nations to apply sanctions and all resolutions that would minimize contacts, such as the resolution to expel the South Africans from the United Nations. The view was succinctly stated by the Assistant Secretary of State for African Affairs:

Isolation can breed rigid resistance to change. Open doors can accelerate it. . . . Punitive economic measures are unpopular in this country. We have had experience in the problems of enforcement and control. These experiences do not encourage us to believe that such measures are workable against countries which are important economic entities. We have supported the eocnomic sanctions against Rhodesia, but this is a special case. . . . We can understand the impatience which leads to the demand for the use of force. Nevertheless, we see little prospect of its effective use in bringing change in Southern Africa and we cannot favor its use.[7]

The presumption in this thinking is that a leavening influence will take place among the dominant whites. British government policy of both the Labour and Conservative parties has been expressed in very similar terms. There are, however, other policymakers, especially in the United Kingdom, of a more conservative stripe, who, like Patrick Wahl, embrace South Africa as an ally against the revolutionary and communist forces in the world, as other authoritarian allies have been embraced in the past. They propose South Africa's admission into NATO and regard all sanctions suggestions as subversive.[8]

Some analysts have seen a progressive improvement, away from the hard line against all disengagement, in the official policies of the United States. There have been changes in other areas of policy, such as the acceptance of the arms embargo discussed earlier; however, there is no evidence of significant change in official policy on the economic-sanctions issue.

If anything, under Nixon and Ford, the evidence shows a strengthening of American economic ties with South Africa, as advocated by NSSM 39,[9] Option 2, and the continuity of the anti-sanctions policy of the American and British governments has been remarkable, especially given the presence of certain abolitionist stalwarts in the third Wilson Cabinet formed in 1974.[10]

It could be argued that the rising influence of NGOs and liberation pressures from Arab and African states has intensified official opposition to the anti-apartheid strategies—for example, the bitter reaction of the United States and the United Kingdom when they employed their vetoes against the move to expel South Africa from the United Nations in October 1974.[11] The unyielding policies of the United States and the United Kingdom indirectly nourish the growth of NGO dissent, which can take advantage of the moral argument of support for the victimized majority and opposition to those who give oppressors aid. The official position has a dissembling moral quality about it, of agreement to an arms embargo and participation in an international sports ban against South Africa. However, spokesmen for anti-sanctions governments have been increasingly forced to rely on their veto power in the United Nations, when they try to defend the policy, in which there has been no basic change in over thirty years, against virtually all the rest of the world.

NGO Sanctions

It is within this changing situation that the sanctions activities of the various NGOs should be considered. In the past evaluation of that activity has been based on the assessment of its immediate impact on South Africa or the policies of the Western powers. This has led to a major underestimation of the real processes of change. What has been dismissed as ineffectual protest and conscience salving on the part of small groups must be placed in the meaningful context of its contribution to a growing transnational impact.

There also exists the danger of overestimation of the effects of transnational action. This can be prevented by a realistic assessment of the staying power of the South Africans, which has yielded ground only to establish new defensive positions, i.e., giving up "petty apartheid" and launching a détente strategy with the new African states.

Both the banks and sports campaigns were significantly successful in terms of ending some forms of financial and sporting contacts with South Africa. They did not, of course, succeed in cutting off all relationships between the financial institutions and South Africa, nor in excluding the South Africans from all sports contacts. However, they met certain effectiveness criteria in that they involved a substantial number of people, educated the public, compelled certain sanctions actions by the transnational institutions involved, and influenced limited public-policy changes.

The Bank Campaign

The campaign in the United States against those institutions which engage in loans to the South African government has been premised on the assumption that this support for apartheid was using other peoples' money the banks had no right to employ. It has had a remarkable effect, because of the sensitivity of banks to public attitudes and the punitive actions of groups and individuals. However, these banks have resorted to secret arrangements, some of which have come to public light, while others doubtless lie hidden in depths of international finance.

When ten American banks announced in 1966 that they had made loans to South Africa, amounting to $40 million, the Committee of Conscience Against Apartheid was established by the American Committee on Africa, which included a number of distinguished clergy and trade-union figures, such as Henry Pitt Van Dusen, then president of Union Theological Seminary, and A. Philip Randolph, the dean of black American civil-rights leaders. Individuals were encouraged to protest to their banks and threaten to withdraw their deposits unless the banks changed their policy. The action of the United Methodist Board of Missions in threatening to withdraw its $10 million investment portfolio from the First National City Bank led to a number of similar actions by liberal Protestant denominations. It is estimated that some $23 million were removed from the banks involved.[12]

In the end, the banks capitulated and did not renew the arrangement with South Africa, on the pretext that South Africa no longer needed the money. In actual fact, they proceeded to establish secret agreements. The effect of this first round was to establish the fact that a segment of the public would take punitive action against banks which lent money to South Africa.

The more complicated picture of international loans was the arena of the second round of activity, growing out of the exposé of the so-called Hanover Document, which came to light in 1973 as the result of some information sent to the Corporate Information Center (CIC) associated with the National Council of Churches. According to these secret documents, obtained from the European-American Banking Corporation (EABC) of New York, there were six major transactions, involving banks in the United States, Europe, England, and Japan. The American banks, according to Don Morton, contributed approximately $70 million of the total. Four of these American banks—Wells Fargo, Central National Bank of

Chicago, Merchants National Bank and Trust Company of Indianapolis, and City National Bank of Detroit—tried to remain anonymous.

The primary purpose of these loans, according to the banks, was to assist the balance of payments and provide funds for the expansion of certain industries, such as wire, steel products, and the like, in South Africa. The CIC said of these loans:

Contributions to South Africa's economic strength are indirect contributions to its military and policy systems, designed to perpetuate domestic racial helotry. These policies are also directed at retaining control over neighboring Namibia and aiding the Rhodesian regime.[13]

Several church groups proceeded to extend the campaign against the banks participating in the EABC scheme. When a group of church and civil-rights leaders confronted the Maryland Bank of Baltimore with their opposition, its president suddenly announced, "We will divest ourselves of the South African government loans presently on our books."[14] Most other banks were not as conciliatory in their reactions, and many new pressures began to build up against them.

In England, a similar set of actions was undertaken by the AAM and student groups at several universities. Their major target has been Barclay's Bank, which has extensive dealings with South Africa. The activities in England, however, have not had the backing of the large church denominations and institutions with substantial funds. The trade unions have indicated support for the investment campaign, but have taken little action. Certainly they have not gone to the point of withdrawing substantial investments from Barclay's or the Standard Bank as evidence of their support. Consequently, the protests have been more activist in the United Kingdom, consisting of picketing and occasional sit-ins by student groups, which have generated some press attention, but have had little effect on the banks.[15]

The difference between American and British banks is the extent of their holdings in South Africa. American banks generally have only a marginal interest in South Africa and may calculate that they would lose more from an adverse public campaign than they would gain by continuing relations, but the British banks have a large stake in South Africa and have not been subjected to the same kind of major financial pressure.[16]

As the advocates of communication with South Africa point out, there is little difference between lending money to a government and investing in industry in that country, except that the former can be more easily cancelled. Most of the NGOs involved in the bank campaign, however, have begun to review the nature of their investments in companies doing business with South Africa. The bank campaign was clearly an initial phase of the subsequent challenge to the corporations.

Sport Boycott

The nature and impact of the sports campaign was quite different in the United States and the United Kingdom. Sport is a matter of wide and strongly felt attachments throughout the world. It symbolizes many of the virtues of society, such as excellence, courage, and skill. With the common attachment to teams and individuals often as strong as patriotic sentiments, nations use sports as a means to demonstrate their accomplishments and even superior ways of life. South Africans are extremely sport conscious; it is a style of life for them. At the same time, they have used international competition to demonstrate, as the Nazis did before them, their phony notions of racial and cultural superiority.[17] A severance of sporting contacts, then, between South Africa and other nations, has sensitized them to their isolation from the rest of the world more than any other issue. Initially, the goal was the improvement of competitive opportunities for nonwhites. The South African Non-Racial Olympic Committee (SAN-ROC), with Dennis Brutus as president, was formed, with the object of demonstrating how the general cultural and political isolation of South Africa from the Western world could affect the Afrikaner racist pride and therefore exact a price for the continuance of this false and obnoxious doctrine.[18]

These campaigns of sportsmen and political groups in the United States and the United Kingdom to sever the competitive ties with South Africa and to ban it from the supreme contest of international sport, the Olympic Games, has been ably described by several authors, including Dennis Brutus, Peter Hain, and Richard Lapchick. The details, therefore, are well known, but certain conclusions need to be drawn in relation to this study.

The sports campaign is a truly transnational phenomenon, because it involves direct relationships between privately organized sporting associations, whose policies may or may not have government sponsorship. In the case of the British and American groups, their activities were generally counter to government policy and aimed, in some cases, at changing it. South African groups are much more closely controlled by government policy, but even here, the politics of sporting associations and clubs were frequently in conflict with government policy and sought to change it. This was obviously true in the case of nonwhite associations, but the campaign produced considerable internal controversy over how to handle the external pressures and some significant advances in the way sports are played in South Africa.[19]

British sports in South Africa were by far the most developed, ranging over a variety of major sports from rugby to cricket, and therefore the British campaign was most effective in terms of numbers and influence in South Africa. The American campaign became significant because of the participation of a number of outstanding black athletes and, of course, because of the prominent position the United States occupies in the Olympic Games and other international associations. Both the United States and the United Kingdom, through SAN-ROC, became major influences on the Asians and Africans, who, in the last analysis, swung the balance of power.

Since the sixties, there have been very few appearances by South African teams in the United States. A basketball team toured the United States in 1975, and there have been regular appearances by Gary Player in golf; and Arthur Ashe's visit to South Africa in 1974 received widespread attention. Ashe was severely criticized for playing in South Africa by Ray Gould, who states, "We feel that Mr. Ashe is terribly misguided in his efforts to bring about a rapprochement between white and black South Africa."[20] South Africa reversed the earlier refusal to give Arthur Ashe a visa in order to show their policies toward blacks were changing and to win the sympathy of the outside world. Ashe felt he could bridge this problem by making contacts with black South Africans during this tour.

On the question of South Africa's participation in the Olympics, the United States, under Avery Brundage, equivocated and connived with the Europeans on the Olympics governing committee to keep South Africa in the games. When the South Africans were suspended in 1968, the United States protested, but South Africa was expelled in 1970.[21] This became a real test of the two contending strategies: the State Department's Option Number 2, of "open windows," and the boycott campaign of disengagement. While it was not a complete victory for the boycott abolitionists, it came very close to it. Its impact in terms of more significant change in South Africa after the ban is a decisive argument in favor of isolation.[22]

The new rules of sending multinational teams abroad have pacified few of South Africa's critics, and the discrimination in sporting clubs within South Africa among the racists, although it enjoys some modification, remains as unacceptable as ever. The special significance of the British sports campaign is in the large numbers of sympathizers who have been aroused, especially during the Stop the Seventies Tour campaign, started in 1969, when huge demonstrations were organized by Peter Hain and the Action Against Racism Committee, working closely with the AAM, SAN-ROC, and several ethnic groups. This was a very broad-based coalition, from churches to the Young Communist League and the West Indian Campaign Against Apartheid in Cricket.[23]

A special feature was the nonviolent direct-action campaign, participated in by students and the militants, which led to the tearing up of pitches, interruptions, and picketing. The fear of major violence between the pro and con groups finally forced Harold Wilson, in February 1970, to come out against the tour. After considerable disruption and fear of its effect on the elections, the tour was finally cancelled by the British Cricket Council.[24]

The British policy on South African competition in international contests has never opposed South Africa consistently, however, because the sports associations are governed by elite groups which tend to reflect government policy. The British government clearly favors an open-door policy of contacts and internal pressures, not a policy of disengagement from South Africa. It has consistently opposed the sports-boycott campaign, though after the Stop the Seventies Tour campaign, it became very cautious about promoting exchanges.[25]

The final observation on the sports campaign is that, like banking, it spread to other countries and to transnational organizations. While not all sports federations have excluded South Africa, the most important, the Olympics and the International Amateur Athletic Federation, have done so, and every South African knows that his government's policies are not respected abroad. The opposition to South African contests in Australia and New Zealand has grown to the point where both governments have had a policy of not playing with apartheid teams. Scandinavian countries and the Netherlands have taken a similar stand.[26]

Many South Africans resent this, but it has led them to attempt various reforms, which will be discussed in the last chapter. Blacks and whites now do compete in certain sports, and nonwhites mix with whites as competitors and spectators in international events. These changes were brought about by boycotts and the expulsion of South Africa, rather than by playing and compromising with apartheid.

However, many people who support an international boycott in sport do not carry the principle over into trade and investment. This has been especially apparent in Great Britain, where the sports campaign received massive popular backing, while only a fraction of the same people would extend this to other forms of sanctions. The distinction arises because many Anglo-Saxons place a high value on the concepts of fair play and equal opportunity to compete. This is most obviously denied to nonwhites in athletic competition under apartheid. However, in the production of goods and the investment of money, the black is regarded as a commodity of labor who cannot enjoy equal status with the white. This is, of course, nonsense and a racist white myth about black productivity and capability in nonathletic endeavors. White Englishmen and Americans have shown their readiness to accept the nonwhite as a sports hero, like the gladiators of Rome, but the recognition of the ability of blacks to progress in other fields, even with education, has remained very restricted. There is also the obvious reason of self-interest linked to jobs and income, which are regarded as necessities, while sport is an entertainment, a luxury. These interests reflect class interests and are based on short-run assumptions; yet they govern much political behavior.

Economic Sanctions

The abolitionists have succeeded in creating a new issue out of economic sanctions, despite the consistent opposition of the major Western powers. They have demonstrated that the rapid expansion of the South African economy has been stimulated by Western investment, and they argue that this growth primarily benefits the dominant whites and the overseas investors, instead of increasing the welfare of Africans and reducing the discrimination blacks endure under apartheid. They have therefore urged upon their own governments, Multi-National Corporations (MNCs), and upon the United Nations, the implementation of a universal ban on investment and trade in South Africa, as a means of inducing change and giving assistance to the freedom fighters both within and without the Afrikaner domain.

During the height of the debate over the role of British companies in South Africa (triggered by Adam Raphael's exposé articles in *The Guardian*) the anti-apartheid movement reiterated its position on broad-based economic sanctions as the best way to deal with the exploitation of apartheid. Abdul Minty, speaking for the AAM, stated:

All international links with the Apartheid system, and especially economic links, help to maintain the status quo in South Africa. . . . Overseas investors will side with the white regime because by their investments, they have already intervened on the side of the status quo. The movement has therefore always demanded the total withdrawal of overseas investments in South Africa, because they help sustain the racial tyranny and will inevitably come into confrontation with the aspirations of oppressed African people for freedom and democracy.[27]

The AAM had the following set of demands:
1. Make no new investment in South Africa.
2. Cease the recruitment of British workers for their southern African subsidiaries.
3. Make no loans to South Africa.

4. Continue to expose the exploitation of black workers.

This was to be done through the cooperation of church councils, which would disinvest, trade unions, which would discourage emigration, and local government councils, which would sell their stock in companies doing business with South Africa. These suggestions have been more controversial than other forms of sanctions because their implementation would affect a great many powerful interests. It cuts to the very center of the debate between the reformists and the revolutionaries. Numerous transnational groups who oppose apartheid cling to the hope that the system of economic exploitation will reform itself out of economic necessity. This view was stated in an editorial in *The Guardian:*

Whether in the end economic growth and good employment practices can undermine Apartheid remains an open question. Again, those industrialist employers who are most determined to bring gradual change cannot afford to say so openly. But the thesis put forward among others by Mr. Harry Oppenheimer at least suggests the way in which change is most likely to come . . . sustained economic growth is leading to cracks in the traditional South African way of life, which can be solved only by a fundamental reshaping of that society.

. . .

The ANC approach, if adopted, must lead to great African suffering in lost jobs and further displacement from urban areas, and eventually, in bloody fighting for which Africans are untrained and unarmed. Nor is there any guarantee that this course can succeed, at least in the lifetime of those alive today. The gradualist approach is less bloody and more likely to accomplish change.[28]

African leaders in exile are quick to call this the typical paternalism of British liberalism, and to state that Africans must be the judges of what their people are prepared to bear. Reg September, the ANC representative in London, wrote to *The Guardian* and specifically requested that investments be withdrawn and they be left "free to deal with their oppressors."[29] From inside Africa, however, Chief Gatsha Buthelezi has become the spokesman for that African opinion which wants investments to be continued, and he has been engaged in active campaigning for cooperation with the gradualists within and outside of South Africa, who believe, as Ralph Horowitz has put it, "that a successful campaign to withdraw foreign investment would entrench one of the world's most abhorrent regimes for yet more generations.''[30]

The issue has been joined on the effects of industrialization, which all agree is taking place rapidly, and the way in which races and classes will be affected by this process. This debate has been a long-standing one among South African opponents of apartheid, but now has entered the transnational field through the sanctions issues and the proposals of the abolitionist NGOs to disinvest from corporations operating in South Africa, compel withdrawal, and seek boycott actions against those who fail to comply with the universal standards set up by the United Nations.

Some think this controversy has hurt the anti-apartheid campaign, dividing the gradualists from the abolitionists and giving legitimacy to corporate reformist claims. It has done this to some degree, as we shall see. However, it has also revived among NGOs what had become a stale and lifeless subject as a result of the monolithic government opposition to economic sanctions in Britain and the United States. Suddenly, an opportunity for direct pressure on the corporations themselves was opened by the activist groups, leading to significant reactions. This came at a time when the OPEC nations, especially Arabs and Africans, revived the trade-boycott tactic through collective action, not previously taken seriously in ruling circles in the West. The two movements thrust sanctions against apartheid onto a new, transnational level, which the South Africans, as well as officials in the United States and the United Kingdom, have now taken very seriously.

The Oil and Energy Boycott

The idea of an oil boycott against South Africa was revived in the mid-1970s after the successful demonstration of the OPEC nations in 1973 that a unified strategy could be developed among them and implemented for even a brief period of time. Most of the nations are Arab and African, and they have had a generally consistent record of opposition in principle to apartheid, especially the North Africans. There are, of course, immense difficulties in applying such a sanction action against South Africa. These difficulties have blocked the implementation of the idea in the past, and many of them are still operative. Nevertheless, the Arab and African attack on Western resource control and the activities of several of the abolitionist NGOs have modernized and strengthened the proposals. Apartheid has become a symbol of the attack on the entire Western system of racial and class dominance. South Africa, therefore, is an ideal issue to dramatize the struggle between the Third World and the West for a new world economic order.

The idea of an oil boycott of South Africa has been a favorite proposal of NGOs and African nationalists for many years. South Africa has no domestic oil sources and, despite attempts to develop alternatives and convert coal to oil, is still 20 percent dependent on oil imports for all her energy needs. Once a significant number of oil-producing Arab and African states had become independent, the proposal began to take on a new form. Previously, the objective had been to try to persuade the Western powers to participate in the ban; now it seemed possible to enforce their compliance.

There was considerable interest in the oil-sanction proposal at the 1964 London Conference, which debated the subject at length and finally agreed on a line of action which recommended that oil sanctions be adopted, along with boycotts of other key commodities, industrial machinery, and chemicals. However, it was suggested that such a program would work only if there were "universal cooperation" and an "effective police system."[31]

Brian Lapping discussed the necessity for universal cooperation and an implementation system that would include either a naval blockade or a United Nations supervised method of surveillance and enforcement.[32] It is significant in this connection that the British Council of Churches has never endorsed the general principle of economic sanctions and, in the case of an oil boycott, published a report which stated that the "conditions for a just war" that would be inevitable in an attempt to enforce a blockade of oil "do not at present obtain." They opposed the spilling of blood as long as there was "any conceivable alternative."[33]

This, of course, presupposed that an effective scheme would necessitate a blockade and the use of direct armed force. The same presumption existed at the London sanctions conference—that sanctions would need to be universal and backed by Western powers. The experience of the Arab and African oil embargo denied this assumption, demonstrating that relatively weak countries could have a major effect. It also demonstrated the potential impact of nongovernmental groups in support of such a campaign and in undermining support for governmental aid to apartheid programs.

Though South Africa has become less dependent on oil for energy use—she had a 75 percent dependence on the Middle East sources in 1973—an effective Arab and African boycott could be very potent in the key industries, such as transportation, and cut into any business boom. Her reserves would last no longer than six months, it is estimated.[34] The extent to which European countries and the United States will continue to assist South Africa, working through Iran, her principal supplier, is the major question. The ability of NGO groups to protest and resist such assistance is one factor. The international forces working against the boycott of South Africa include the alliance between Israel and South Africa, as both find themselves similarly threatened by a coalition of Arab and African states.

This clearly weakens the NGO pressure on the United States and the United Kingdom, since the issues become confused in the American liberal mind, which opposes South Africa but supports Israel. The African and Arab states of OPEC have not removed South Africa from the 1973 boycott, and it is conceivable that, with the help of former Portuguese territories and effective pressure on Iran, the sanctions could be tightened. This would not have the total impact of the previously conceived universal scheme, but it could very well be the first phase of an accumulating set of pressures to weaken the South African economy. South Africans have not found significant oil resources of their own and face costly difficulties in a shift to nuclear and coal alternatives. The NGO pressures in the Western countries against supplying the South Africans can be expected to hold, though there is considerable opposition to OPEC oil-boycott tactics in the public mind and even among the more militant opponents of apartheid. The United States has already facilitated the development of South African nuclear reactors and can be expected to provide her with additional means for making a rapid transition to nuclear power. This has backfired, given the increased NGO opposition in the United States to the uses of nuclear power. The exploitation of nuclear resources in Namibia at the

Rossing Mine has come under attack and provided the basis for extending the boycott to the antinuclear lobby.[35]

The Anti-Investment Campaign

The protest over investment in South Africa goes back to the early fifties when the African petitioners at the United Nations, together with the NGOs, first argued that Western corporate money was helping to exploit nonwhites throughout settler Africa in a system based on forced labor and racial discrimination. In these early days, the attack on investment was more of a moral-political protest. It was not foreseen that significant pressure from within corporations could be mounted.

The Campaign Against Investing in Apartheid, as it is called by the abolitionists, has stirred the greatest interest in sanctions actions since the London Conference of 1964. The attack on corporations within the Western world has been exclusively NGO, and the defense of the corporations is primarily nongovernmental in origin as well, although it is seconded by the governments of the United States and the United Kingdom. A set of NGOs, both new and old, have emerged to defend the "reform and communications" strategy, giving Western governments powerful allies in maintaining their communications policy against the advocates of disengagement. There are different interpretations of its significance, but the corporate investment campaign has demonstrated more fully than other types of policy action the ultimate significance of transnational, nonstate actors.

In a real sense, the proposition that transnational groups, rather than Western governments, will determine the ultimate fate of South Africa rests on the nature of this debate and struggle over the role of corporations.

The economic motive is a powerful aspect of the continuing dependency relationship between South Africa and the Atlantic community. Many bureaucratic and military interests, from corporations to individuals, benefit from South African investment. During times of expansion and growth, such interests have been unshakable. However, recession, retrenchment, and economic crises in the Western economies have weakened these forces, and the sling of the abolitionists is a real threat to what appeared previously to be an invincible Goliath.

South Africa's rapid industrial growth of the past two decades has ended. The contributing factors are the energy crunch, labor unrest, inflation, the fall in gold prices, a gradual drop in immigration, and a decreased flow of investment.[36] Any greater cut in the flow of investment and technology could have irreparable effects on the economy. It is this struggle over the level of investment and technological growth, rather than the withdrawal of industry itself, which has made the sanctions campaign significant.[37] Moreover, South Africa's economy has reached a point of the semiperipheral in relation to core powers. With increased loans and investment, the South Africans hope they will be less open to external pressures. The reverse is actually happening.

The corporate withdrawal campaign developed first in the United States, before spreading to England and Europe. Ralph Nader and his public-responsibility movement provided the spiritual genesis for the broad disinvestment attack on the corporations.[38] The demise of the unquestioned belief in the beneficence of the corporations has been long in coming. All the other disillusionments, initiated with Vietnam and Watergate, have affected faith in the corporate-military leadership.

The abolitionist groups which launched the disinvestment campaign were at first morally motivated against investment in racism. Later as the campaign became more closely associated with liberation support, it took a more anticapitalist and anti-imperalist character.

The new disinvestment strategy employed the populist method of direct attack on the corporations themselves. This meant that criticism of specific activities of corporations, such as racial discrimination in employment, was raised in stockholder meetings by groups of stockholders who disagreed with the corporation's policies and sought to change them through resolutions.[39] Other activist-student and black groups advocated disinvestment boycotts and legal actions. During the 1960s, expanding American corporate activity in South Africa provided the basis for critical research on the companies, which concluded that apartheid was strengthened, not weakened, by foreign investment.[40]

Tim Smith, a Canadian working for the CCSA (Council of Christian Social Action) of the United Church of Christ, U.S.A., was one of the first of the new, radical researchers to visit South Africa. Before the South African government banned such activity, he did a series of company studies. Smith quoted a General Motors executive as saying to him, "I don't mix with them blacks at home, and I don't mix with them here." He concluded, concerning General Motors activity. "GM is a mirror of the intensely discriminatory laws and customs of South Africa—low wages, the South African tradition of treating workers as 'labor units' to assist GM in making some of the highest profits found in the world."[41]

GM claims that it is a progressive company in South Africa, but it had not budged one inch to protest the conditions under which 80 percent of South Africa's population must survive. A series of investigations and publications of groups such as ACOA and the Southern Africa Committee stimulated a number of church and university actions.[42] Black groups at several universities sought to pressure their institutions into supporting the proxy resolutions and demands for reform. The most publicized incident concerned the Polaroid Corporation.

The Polaroid Revolutionary Worker's Movement, formed by black workers, challenged the corporation's activities in South Africa, in particular the supply of some materials used in surveillance in the "pass system." Polaroid published expensive advertisements across the country, explaining its position and indicating it would investigate the situation. After the visit of a team of Polaroid representatives to South Africa, the company announced its intention to stay in South Africa, give up its government contract, and help reform the system by opposing apartheid through better wages, black employment, and African education.[43]

The response of the Polaroid workers was to reject this solution. They announced that they would "enforce an international boycott against Polaroid until it completely disengages from South Africa or until South Africa is liberated in the name of the people.[45] George Houser summed up the attitude of most of the abolitionist groups by urging rejection of "the Polaroid approach because what is important is that Polaroid has publicly committed itself to proving the soundness of the argument that it is putting into practice the theory that American firms doing business in South Africa can help to end racism there.''[45] This, Houser argued, has been consistently proved to be a wrong assumption.

The gradualists interpreted the effects of Polaroid's actions differently, seeing in them the prospect of change and reform for blacks in South Africa. A substantial debate emerged within the ecumenical movement of the Christian churches over reform versus disengagement. The World Council of Churches, as previously noted, endorsed clearly, in its Utrecht Statement of the Executive Committee in 1972, the disinvestment strategy. However, considerable dissent from this position arose among the liberal Protestant denominations in the United States and the United Kingdom, despite the support given this approach by social-action agencies.

A statement of disagreement, affirming a "corporate persuasion" approach, was sent to the WCC by four boards of the United Church of Christ, drafted by Howard Schomer, who became a primary reformist spokesman. "Corporate reform should be judged on the basis of performance," the statement read, because "we have found great differences between the sensitivities, principles, practices, and potentialities of the several corporations whose involvement in Southern Africa we have taken pains to study."[46]

The CCSA of the United Church replied that information was already adequate in regard to certain companies, such as IBM, which were not only racist employers, but supplied apartheid with essential materials and military support in the form of computers for surveillance.[47]

A policy of selective corporate action emerged out of these differences. In 1975, fourteen denominations and Catholic orders joined in a stockholders' resolution against IBM management policy, requesting an end to computer sales to South Africa. They also joined in requests for certain companies, such as Standard Oil and Getty, to withdraw from Namibia.[48]

Although certain differences in interpretation of reform remain, the two sides came closer together as a result of the accumulation of information and evidence that certain companies were beyond reform and engaged in intolerable apartheid-support actions. However, the reformists continued to maintain that significant improvements were instituted in the working conditions for Africans as a result of their pressures, while the abolitionists minimized the changes in the powerful support the multinational corporations gave to apartheid. As Canon Burgess Carr, general secretary of the All-African Conference of Churches, put it, "U.S. corporations have done business as usual . . . unmoved by the massive racial oppression."[49]

The corporations themselves launched a vigorous counterattack, employing, as George Houser had predicted, the reformist arguments of Polaroid. The reactions ranged from the initial outright rejection of the intervention of the churches in business affairs, by such industrial leaders as Henry Ford II, to claims of anti-apartheid intent by a vice-president of the National City Bank of New York.[50] A representative of IBM reported in a seminar of the African American Institute that IBM "has no fondness for apartheid, but has chosen to stay in South Africa and do its best to constructively improve conditions." He outlined these improvements, which showed that IBM, compared to other companies, has a progressive record, and noted that 25 percent of IBM's business in South Africa is with the government.[51] Later, IBM objected to the church request to end sales to the South African government, on the ground that this in effect would mean withdrawal.

The impact of the anti-investment campaign in the United States has been variously interpreted, depending on the criteria and goals employed in its assessment. If the votes on proxy resolutions are considered primary, the results have been slim indeed, ranging from 1.9 percent favoring the IBM "end of sales and leases" resolution to over 6 percent favoring Continental Oil withdrawal from Namibia.[52] The proxy resolutions, however, are only one aspect of total impact on the investment climate. Three major American oil companies withdrew from Namibia in 1974 and 1975, and two of them specifically cited church pressure at home as one factor.[53] A much wider impact on employment practices has been noted in several studies of reforms in American corporate employee policies. American NGOs, then, have had a major impact on reform of company practices and a limited impact on new investment, which might have major importance in the future. General Motors' announcement to the churches, in March 1977, that they would not expand production as long as apartheid continued, indicated a major reconsideration of MNC policy was underway. Chrysler had already announced it was ceasing production.

The corporate issue in the United Kingdom emphasized reform rather than withdrawal, primarily because its corporate investment and economic stake in South African industry is more extensive than that of the United States, and also because of the continuing influence of Manchester liberalism on the British left. Outside of the AAM and its auxiliaries, no major association took the withdrawal or disengagement position. The churches had few advocates of this stand, even among the denominations that had been inclined toward the abolitionist position on other matters. Even the trade unions were apathetic and reformist in their approach within the Labour Party. The few advocates of disinvestment limited their attacks to such specific targets as the Rio Tinto Zinc investment in the Rossing Mines in Namibia.[54]

The AAM, as noted, cooperated with the liberation movements and particularly with the ANC in its disengagement position. The other major African and human-rights associations have been heavily in favor of the reformist logic. Several new groups emerged to deal with the issue by bridging the various approaches, of which the Study Project on External Investment in South Africa and Namibia and Christians Concerned About South Africa are representative.

Leading figures in the anti-apartheid movement became divided over the issue, and its net effect may have been to damage the movement, rather than expand it as the sports and arms embargo campaigns had done. Two major anti-apartheid leaders, Michael Scott and Colin Legum, working primarily through the Africa Bureau, were the initiators of the External-investment Project through a group which originally planned to undertake a series of conferences on the investment issue, but wound up doing a series of studies through an international consortium. While the project attempted to utilize different views, its focus was primarily on the economic conditions of change and the role of corporations in the total process of changing apartheid.[55] Christians Concerned About South Africa, led by Trevor P. Jepson, a Quaker and secretary of the Joseph Roundtree Charitable Trust, working from an anti-apartheid moral perspective, set out to educate businessmen in the ways they should adapt their company practices to the requirements of justice in South Africa.[56] The impact of both these groups, contrary to some of their founders' intentions, was to give considerable impetus to the reformist thesis of the MNCs and businessmen in South Africa.

Lively debates developed among the intellectuals in the Africanist community, and in theory the disengagement forces appeared to have the upper hand (as at the seminar held at Bristol University in late March 1973), but given the way in which the media and political parties dealt with the issue, the gradualists carried the day with the public and certainly the American and British governments. This led to the conclusion of several AAM spokesmen that the investments issue had been successfully turned against them and the boycott campaign. One view was dramatized by *The Guardian* exposé of the British companies in South Africa in 1973. Adam Raphael, a South African by origin, in a series of major articles in *The Guardian,* brought to light a mass of facts concerning the poverty and exploitation of Africans and the discrimination in hiring, promotion, and wages policies of British firms in South Africa. The ensuing political uproar in Parliament was soon directed into a select committee, which held extensive and well-publicized hearings. These, however, gave the corporations and their representatives the opportunity to refute charges made against them and to make claims of extensive reform.[57] The major result was to give considerable credence to the Heatherington thesis, quoted previously, that investment is a useful instrument of political reform in South Africa, preferable to the waste and tragedy of loss of jobs for Africans through disinvestment, and loss of life through guerrilla struggle.

The churches, as institutions, did very little to refute the reformists' claims. The British Council of Churches rejected the lead of the World Council of Churches on investments, and instead issued ambiguous statements in which recognition was given to various approaches. The Church of England especially opposed the call of the WCC for disinvestment, and there was a strange silence from most of the anti-apartheid bishops, such as Huddleston, Reeves, and Shepard.

British corporations are not subject to the same proxy resolution requirements that the Securities and Exchange Commission imposes on American firms, and therefore, stockholder pressure has not been generated. However, similar campaigns have been mounted vis-à-vis such firms as Rio Tinto Zinc and Barclay's Bank.[58] There has been no counterpart in the United Kingdom to the Continental Oil or even Polaroid consideration of withdrawal. British firms remain, instead, supremely self-righteous about their role as profitable—and even reform—agents, as shown at the annual meeting of Barclay's Bank.[59]

The trade-union response by the TUC was highly reformist. Its concern centered on the conditions of African labor, and after a delegation visited South Africa in 1974, it issued a report that called for reform and the recognition of African trade unions. However, the delegation dodged the whole question of continuing investments and dealt very inadequately with the problem of white domination of South African trade unions. This contrasts with the position of the TUC at meetings of the ILO, where it has voted in support of a total boycott and economic sanctions against South Africa. Perhaps like the churches at WCC sessions, the further they are removed from their constituents, the easier it is to vote their consciences.

The investment campaign, then, was ignited by the abolitionists either to force the withdrawal of Western corporations or to limit the amount of external investment in South Africa, but the major effect has been to provide the basis for a great deal of rationalizing of the inequities of British and American firms' continuing apartheid in their labor practices and exploiting cheap African labor. The limited improvement in employment opportunities, wages, and working conditions for a Coloured and African elite has been used by the South Africa Foundation, the MNCs, and the moderate reformists in both these countries to demonstrate the value of investment and expanded production. The British and American governments have seized on selected changes to validate their "communication thesis" while ignoring the evidence of the deteriorating situation of most Africans and nonwhites. This evidence shows that in the last decade of industrialization, the African standard of living has steadily declined in comparison to whites. The urban riots beginning in 1976 reflected this. (See Chapter 9.)

Therefore, the success of the investment campaign within the total boycott program of anti-apartheid NGOs depends upon what the objective is considered to be. If the objective is the gradualist limited improvement for some African workers, then it has been a moderate success, at least in the short run; if the objective is the abolitionist goal of revolution against apartheid, the strategy has produced considerable support for the reformist thesis.

While the American and British publics are better informed on the evils of apartheid, the reform policy has produced many leaders who are persuaded that more investment, rather than less, is the way to reform South Africa. Corporations in the United States are shaken by the possibility of adverse publicity at home and its effect on black workers, but in general, they are more self-righteous than ever and convinced that morality and profits, though not politics, mix well together.

The Future of Sanctions

The effectiveness of economic sanctions against South Africa by NGO groups and their allies is related to the increased vulnerability of the South African economy, its declining growth rate, unfavorable balance of trade, and the changing climate for investors created by riots and strikes. During the prosperous industrial boom of the past decade, the expanding market for raw materials and the high price of gold, the development reformist logic had considerable appeal. This has gradually changed, especially with the difficulties in the American and British economies of capital shortage, inflations, and unemployment, which discourages foreign investment and aggravates the weaknesses of a dependent economy such as South Africa's. A weakening of the South African investment climate has been induced both by the fall in the price of gold and by the 1976 race riots. The cost of South African raw materials has risen, while Western investment has fallen drastically, making South Africa dependent upon loans, which the United States and the United Kingdom and private banks have readily extended. Under these conditions, NGO attacks are apt to be far more effective in creating an adverse investment climate than they have been in the past.

The strongest economic pressure for change to date has been the demand of African, Asian, and Arab states for a reorganization of resources and wealth in the world (the New Economic Order).

Economic decline in the West has made it more vulnerable to these types of pressures, since the relative power of the United States and the United Kingdom to control the world economy has been reduced. This means the prospects for bargaining and confrontations have increased. The new anti-apartheid NGO strategy may well be campaigns in support of the Third and Fourth World attempts to adjust the inequities of the world economy through self-reliance campaigns. Apartheid in South Africa is a vulnerable anachronism to protect in such a world, a symbol for the attack on racism and injustice everywhere.

Notes

1. Leonard Kapungu, in his study of sanctions against Rhodesia, concludes that Western powers violated the norms and procedures of the ban on trade by failing to enforce the Security Council resolutions. See *The United Nations and Economic Sanctions Against Rhodesia,* CIRR (Cambridge, Mass.: Heath Lexington, 1973).

2. Ronald Segal, *Sanctions Against South Africa* (Baltimore: Penguin, 1964), p. 14.

3. The United States and the United Kingdom vetoed a resolution of the Security Council which sought to extend sanctions to South Africa, under Chapter 7, *The New York Times,* 7 June 1975.

4. Alastair Buchan, in "The Emerging International System," *International Interactions,* Vol. 1, No. 4 (1974), p. 195, has noted that in international relations "a particular international system has rarely lasted for more than one or two generations."

5. Ben Magubane, "The Continuing Class Struggle in South Africa," Denver *Race and Nations,* monographs, September 1976, p. 45, describes these sources of conflict, i.e., the strikes and labor unrest of 1973-74.

6. The United States exception over chrome imports indicated the lack of official enthusiasm, and the British government's ruling out of the use of force at the outset of UDI reflected this nominal policy on sanctions against Rhodesia.

7. David Newsom, U.S. Department of State Bulletin, 11 October 1971, pp. 6-7.

8. Based on an interview with Patrick Wahl in May 1973 at the House of Commons. See his recent book, *The Indian Ocean and the Threat to the West* (London: Stacy International, 1975).

9. This was a secret document, but was reproduced as *The Kissinger Study of Southern Africa* (Nottingham: Spokesman Books, 1975).

10. Judith Hart and Frank Judd are known supporters of sanctions; yet there has been no change in official British policy.

11. Their primary argument was the violation of the principle of universality in expulsion. Again, in June 1975 Britain, France, and the United States vetoed another resolution attempting to place sanctions under Chapter 7, *The New York Times,* 7 June 1975.

12. *Stop Banking on Apartheid* (New York: ACOA, 1975).

13. "The Frankfurt Documents," CIC Brief, *The Corporate Examiner,* July 1973, Corporate Information Center, p. 30.

14. *The Corporate Examiner,* May 1974, p. 5, and January 1974, p. 4. The Merchants National Bank and Trust Co., Indianapolis, The City National Bank of Detroit, and the Central National Bank of Chicago also announced a policy of no future loans to South Africa.

15. Martin Bailey, *Barclays and South Africa* (London: Haslemers Group and Anti-Apartheid Movement, 1975).

16. Victor Feather, executive director of the TUC, announced they were reviewing their investments with ten companies doing business with South Africa, *The Guardian* (London), 9 September 1972. The TUC sold their holdings in the Trade Union Trust because the trust refused to dispose of shares in companies with interests in South Africa.

17. Richard Lapchick's thorough study compares the Nazi period to South African policy, *The Politics of Race and International Sport* (Westport, Conn., Greenwood Press, 1975) pp. 3-20.

18. Right Reverend C. Edward Crowther, "Apartheid, the Politics of Sport," *Notes and Documents,* U.N. Unit on Apartheid, No. 18/71, April 1971.

19. Mixed sporting contests have taken place, and spectators were not segregated for some of the international matches. See *The Star,* 9 April 1973.

20. *Daily World,* 19 December 1974.

21. Lapchick, op. cit., p. 217, found out that all white national representatives except the socialist states voted for South Africa's participation.

22. A conservative Member of Parliament, Brocklesby Fowler, stated that "sports was not comparable to politics" in an interview in 1973. Many disagree and consider it to be in fact an extension of politics on an international scale.

23. Peter Hain, *Don't Play with Apartheid* (London: George Allen and Unwin, 1971), p. 121-122.

24. Ibid., p. 173.

25. A rugby team toured South Africa in 1975. The reciprocal event in England is not possible unless teams are multiracial from start to finish.

26. "World Against Apartheid," *Notes and Documents,* U.N. Unit on Apartheid, No. 10/71, 1971, p. 6-9.

27. *Anti-Apartheid News,* April. 1973.

28. *The Guardian,* 28 April 1973.

29. *The Guardian,* 24 April 1973.

30. *The Guardian,* 22 March 1973.

31. Segal, op. cit., p. 249.

32. Ibid., pp. 148-152.

33. *The Future of South Africa,* British Council of Churches, (London: BBC, 1964), p. 77.

34. Barbara Rogers, in *White Wealth and Black Poverty: Study in American Investments in Southern Africa* (Westport, Conn.: Greenwood Press, 1976), a study of South Africa under sanctions, believes most reports of South Africa's reserves are grossly exaggerated, as is her capacity to switch quickly to other fuels, nuclear or coal.

35. *Anti-Apartheid News,* May 1975.

36. A conservative economist in the London *Financial Times* reported this sharp falling off of capital inflow into South Africa, beginning in 1970, and equated it with the anti-apartheid movement. *Financial Times,* May 1970. More recently, net capital inflow from the private sector declined sharply in 1976, *Times* (London), 6 July 1976.

37. Figures on recent external investment show a downward trend.

38. See Bevis Longstreth and H. David Rosenbloom, *Corporate Social Responsibility and the Institutional Investor* (New York: Praeger, 1973). See also H. David, "Soweto Before and After," *X-Ray,* July-August 1976, p. 1.

39. In the United States, this culminated in the collective efforts of several institutional investors, coordinated initially by the Church Project on Investments in Southern Africa.

40. See "Apartheid and Imperialism: A Study of U.S. Corporate Involvement in South Africa," *Africa Today,* Vol. 17, No. 5 (September-October, 1970).

41. Tim Smith, "General Motors and South Africa," pamphlet, Council for Christian Social Action, United Church of Christ, New York, 1971.

42. See *Church Investments, Corporations, and Southern Africa* (New York: Friendship Press, 1973).

43. *Financial Mail,* 22 January 1971.

44. Quoted in "Polaroid and South Africa," pamphlet, Africa Research Group, Cambridge, 1971.

45. George Houser, "The Polaroid Approach to South Africa," *Christian Century,* 24 February 1971.

46. Memorandum to the World Council of Churches, "1972 Central Committee Resolutions Concerning Investments in Southern Africa," from The United Church Board for World Ministries, 14 September 1972.

47. Memorandum to the World Council of Churches from George Shepherd, chairman, International Relations Committee Council for Christian Social Action, 28 November 1972.

48. News release, National Council of Churches, 14 January 1975.

49. *Pro Veritate* (periodical), Christian Institute, Johannesburg, June 1974.

50. *Newsweek,* 24 May 1971, p. 78.

51. AAI Africa Policy Information Center, mimeographed unpublished proceedings. Institutional Investors Eastern/Southeastern Study Group, 3/29/72—statement by W. B. Ewald and J. L. Sherry, Jr.

52. *The Corporate Examiner,* Vol. 4, No. 6 (June 1975).

53. Letter to author from vice president, Continental Oil Company, December 1974. Later, Texaco and Standard Oil indicated their intention to end prospecting.

54. The left-wing British Labour leader, Anthony Wedgewood Benn, apologized for having negotiated the Rossing Mine agreement while he was in the Cabinet, but after Labour's return to power in 1974, he did nothing to revise it.

55. A series of studies began emerging in 1974, among which were Roger Murray et al., *The Role of Foreign Firms in Namibia,* and John Spence, *The Political and Military Framework* (London: Africa Publications Trust, 1974).

56. This group held a seminar, "Corporate Responsibility and the Institutional Investor," at the London Business School, November 1973.

57. *Wages and Conditions of African Workers Employed by British Firms in South Africa,* hearings of Select Committee on Trade and Industry, Vols. 1-4 (London: HMSO).

58. Bailey, op. cit.; also, *The Rio-Tinto Zinc Corp., Ltd., Anti-Report* (London: Counter Information Service, 1972).

59. See "Diary," *The New Internationalist,* May 1975.

60. The South African Trust Fund (Safit), based in Switzerland, was a net seller of South African shares up to March 1976, despite the fact that the purpose of the trust was to promote investment in South Africa. *Rand Daily Mail,* 5 May 1976.

chapter 8 ═══════════

THE TRANSNATIONAL EMERGENCE OF NAMIBIA

The revolution in Namibia is in the fullest sense transnational. Its existence as a national identity and the struggle for its independence was developed by transnational actors, working with liberation leaders. The United Nations Council for Namibia and the NGOs form the nucleus of the coalition of groups assisting the independence of this former trust territory against the hostility of South Africa and the covert and at times open opposition of the major Western powers, who fear an anti-Western takeover.

Because of its origins as a German colony, then a mandate under the League of Nations, and later under the United Nations, this territory of Namibia, formerly called South West Africa, has not become part of South Africa. Instead, it has become a battleground between the crumbling empires of the past and the liberation forces of the future. It has a small population, fewer than one million people, and the wealth of the country is in mineral resources, especially uranium and copper. Like Angola on its northern border, Namibia is a source of growing economic rivalry.[1]

The outcome of this struggle will influence what happens ultimately in South Africa, which is a reason why South Africa has been very slow to respond to the considerable international pressures. Although Prime Minister Vorster has stated Namibia will be "independent," what he means by "independent" is at sharp variance with the aims of the South West African Peoples' Organization (SWAPO) and the United Nations. The South Africans are the prisoners of their Bantustan thinking, which conceives of African states as subsidiaries to the industry and wealth of South Africa.

Since 1975 the United States and Great Britain have increasingly criticized South African policy while urging Namibian independence, but have generally sought accommodation with South Africans rather than confrontation.

South Africa is in illegal occupation of Namibia, where it has imposed a policy of fragmented Bantustan development on a people who want the United Nations to rule as a transition to independence of a united Namibia. The United Nations has rejected South Africa's claim to jurisdiction as well as her policies and is searching for an acceptable transition to independence.[2]

The objective of the struggle has become, not the existence of a Namibian state, but who will rule. This will be determined by the nature of the transition. How the power shifts, whether under United Nations auspices or not, may well decide who inherits authority. This in turn will decide the fate of corporations and the distribution of the wealth South Africa and the Western powers are eager to retain.

The history of the NGO role in the struggle illustrates the influence anti-apartheid has had on helping to pressure South Africa and the policies of the NGOs' own governments.

The NGOs have, for two decades, pressed both the United Nations and their own governments to take a course of action based upon liberation principles. Although partially recognized at the United Nations in recent years, the counsel of these groups has been largely ignored by the officials of Western powers. However, the importance of these ideas and programs has gained international recognition with the U.N. Secretariat, smaller European powers, the Afro-Asian world, and among political opposition. While their views and proposals are much influenced by the majority United Nations position and particularly the nationalist and liberation leaders, there is a distinctive importance about them which deserves careful consideration.

These anti-apartheid proposals have been based upon (a) the self-determination principles of the United Nations, (b) the prime responsibility of the United Nations in this issue of Namibia to act together with the peoples of Namibia, (c) the inevitable disintegration of racial empires for which South Africa's Bantustans are no alternative, (d) the necessity of enforcement by United Nations members, and (e) support for liberation movements.

Self-Determination and Bantustans

The South African concept of independence for Namibia is derived from the Bantustan idea, which has been the basis of her acceptance of a so-called self-determination for nonwhite peoples. Merle Lipton outlined succinctly the theory of the nationalist government:

South Africa does not consist of one nation with a common citizenship and rights, but many nations (a multi-national state) each of which wants (or should want) to retain its identity and determine its future. The last hope for harmony does not lie in forcibly mixing up these peoples (who differ in colour and culture) but in allocating to each its own state, a homeland; and the freedom to develop along its own lines. Hence the present Republic of South Africa is to have carved out of it seven or eight Bantu states, for the various black nations (another eleven will be set up in Southwest Africa). . . . White South Africa will institute a classic policy of "decolonizaton" in regard to the various black nations, culminating in self-government with, it is presumed, seats for all in the Organization of African Unity and the United Nations.[3]

The theory of Bantustans is an attempt to get away from the outright racism of apartheid which the South African government recognizes as very damaging to its image abroad, especially at the United Nations, but also reflects the attempt within white South African politics to devise a solution.[4] The Afrikaners are trying to transform the urbanized African into a tribal member who will somehow return home and make a living in scattered, often arid lands where there is nothing. This defies credibility. Whites, who constituted 17.6 percent (1970) of the population, will retain over 83 percent of the arable and productive region of South Africa. A majority of white liberals and several African leaders now appear to favor reluctantly accepting the reality of this framework of Bantustans as an established fact and to bargain and press for concessions from the nationalist government within them. The most famous of these is Alan Paton, who argued in the London *Times* that, as much as he opposed the concept, Bantustans do give a limited opportunity for African opposition to be expressed.[5] Most African leaders oppose independence for Bantustans, despite the granting of independence to the Transkei.[6] The Black Peoples Convention and the South African Students Organization have come out against the Bantustans, in all their aspects, and have criticized those black leaders who regard them as a solution.[7]

Even dissenting white opinion now generally accepts the Bantustan policy as given and attempts to modify and improve it in terms of benefits to the blacks. The SPROCAS Reports reflect this thinking on the part of some of the most progressive people in the churches, universities, and institutions among various races. Out of such groups they hope a stronger political force will arise, capable of achieving gains for the oppressed.[8]

Some see the Bantustans as united in a federation and acting as a political party within South Africa. But most liberal and progressive opinion has accepted Bantustans as inevitable, as the studies of Lawrence Schlemmer reveal.[9] Moreover, the white electorate has no intention of really developing these areas, since they oppose putting more money into them, and that is the only way improvements can be made.[10] Therefore, this is racial separation or apartheid in another form in which the whites simply hope to put a partition between themselves and the reserves they now choose to call homelands or Bantustans.

South Africa's "New Policy"

Under pressure from the United Nations and the people of Namibia, Prime Minister Vorster announced a new policy in September 1974 that was a modification of the previous Bantustan policy for South West Africa. He stated that "the people of South West Africa will decide their own future" and move toward a constitutional development which would be the basis of an eventual united, independent Namibia.[11]

A year later, South Africa issued a Declaration of Intent to establish a constitutional convention, after several African councils and organizations indicated they would cooperate.[12] The objective of this convention was to write a constitution that would integrate the various tribal groups and diverse populations while preserving their separate ethnic and racial interests.[13]

The unrepresentative character of the Turnhalle Convention, which excluded SWAPO, led to a great deal of suspicion about the real intent of South Africa's policy and whether any basic change from a "homelands" separate development had been made.[14] Participation by Chief Clemens Kapuuo of the Herero Council and a leading nationalist gave the discussions some credibiility. However, the Damara Advisory Council refused to participate, and SWAPO denounced the basis of this convention as a fraud, as did the white right wing. The Turnhalle Conference report was later rejected by several groups, including SWAPO and the Council for Namibia.

The United Nations also rejected the Turnhalle constitutional talks because they bypassed the directive to South Africa to hand over the whole process of transition to the United Nations, under the Council for Namibia. The council called for a national election to an all-Namibian assembly, which would decide the future of Namibia. The election would be held under the supervision of the United Nations to assure that all groups, including SWAPO, were fairly represented.[15]

Despite South Africa's announced intention to grant "independence" on 31 December 1978, to a government emerging from this process, just as with the Transkei, the conflict and the problems will remain. The United Nations has refused to accept the credentials of the Turnhalle group, as have the African states of the OAU. NGOs have opposed this group, and support has grown for the liberation movements of SWAPO.

The South West Peoples Organization (SWAPO) of Namibia wishes to make it categorically clear that the announcement by the racist regime of South Africa—through its equally racist Nationalist Party—to hold so called multi-racial talks on Namibia's constitutional picture at this time, is a well-calculated and deliberate political maneuver, aimed at misleading world public opinion.[16]

Gerson Veii of the rival organization, South West African National Union (SWANU), which also opposed the talks, argued: "if the whites are sincere they should release all political prisoners and allow the exiled leaders to participate in the so-called new deal."[17] Thus, the South Africans are far from any settlement with the United Nations or the people of Namibia or the anti-apartheid movement. The basic problem is that South Africa insists upon preserving white and Western interests in control and has refused to deal with SWAPO, especially the external revolutionary wing. SWAPO, in turn, demands exclusive recognition by South Africa. The impasse is political and cannot be resolved by a constitutional formula established outside of the jurisdiction of the United Nations.

There are, of course, immense pressures coming to bear on South Africa after the MPLA victory in Angola. Western governments are eager for a settlement of a dangerous conflict. The opposition in South Africa constantly needles Vorster's failure. Moreover, the military cost and risk of having to defend a border with Angola across the Caprivi Strip to the boundary with Zambia grows every year. And SWAPO, given time, will increasingly radicalize the African population to enlarge its internal support.

The capacity to settle the issue does not lie in South African or Western hands. It will have to be a decision freely arrived at by the Namibian people and legitimized by the United Nations.

Who Speaks for Namibia?

The question of who speaks for the Namibian people is obviously very important. The South Africans have some support as indicated by the testimony received by Ambassador Alfred Martin Escher, the special representative of the Secretary-General of the United Nations, who visited Namibia for seventeen days in October 1972 and received a vast variety of viewpoints. A careful assessment of his report to the Secretary-General[18] shows that the groups who supported South Africa, such as Chief Councillor Phileman Elifas of the Executive Council of Ovambo and Chief Councillor Linus Shashipo of the Kavango and Chief D. Goreseb of the Damara Legislative Council, were not representative of the wishes of most of their people.[19] For example, later elections to the Ovamboland Council showed heavy resistance to the "self-government" plan of South Africa. Mr. Vorster had announced a "new elective element since South Africa is often criticized because the system of government in Ovambo does not provide for elective representatives." The overwhelming boycott of the election in July 1973, despite considerable repression of meetings and arrests of SWAPO sympathizers, showed where the people stood.[20]

The Federated Coloured Peoples Party of South West Africa and the South West African Non-European Unity Movement (SWANEUM), under the leadership of D. Beznidenhaut, indicated to the Escher mission that they feared the unity of Namibia on the basis of one-man-one-vote would reduce the Coloured population to "the vote of a mute minority."

Support for the "homelands" policy was strongest among the white population, which numbers 90,000 out of a total of 745,000. This group controls the central farming region and major centers, such as Walvis Bay, and wants South Africa to continue her administration because it fears "the latent hostility existing among the non-white groups."[21] Not all whites agree with this; for example, the German Evangelical Lutheran Church, a group of 10,000 whites, has supported Black African Church demands for United Nations rule.

SWAPO

SWAPO is the most representative movement among Namibians with a base among the largest tribe, the Ovambo, and representation among the more important smaller tribes, i.e., Damara and Herero. It is the only liberation movement recognized by the OAU and the United Nations. Founded in 1960 as a national movement, it had its origins as the Ovamboland Peoples' Congress, formed in 1957, to organize against the contract-labor system. Originally a peaceful protest movement, it hoped to gain independence from the United Nations, but after persecution and arrests of their leaders, especially in 1966 and 1967, SWAPO turned to the organization of a guerrilla wing. Sam Nujoma, the president of SWAPO, in addressing the Brussels Conference, described this decision:

It was only after all our efforts to reach a peaceful solution that my organization, whose history of non-violence I have already outlined above, decided to embark upon armed resistance as the only remaining means open to us.[22]

SWAPO's major activity since 1970 has been external, based in Zambia and Angola. Although heavily persecuted, it has not been banned to date in Namibia, although the leadership is imprisoned and harassed. Its military operations, beginning in 1966, were confined to the Caprivi Strip but have since spread to Ovamboland from bases in Angola. The first commander of SWAPO armed forces, Tobias Hainyeko, was killed by the South Africans in May 1967 while attempting to cross into Namibia.[23] Since that time, new tactics, with more sophisticated weapons, have been developed, and the Peoples Liberation Army of Namibia (PLAN) claims to have killed 150-200 South African soldiers. Some of the arms captured by SWAPO from the South Africans were exhibited at the 1973 tenth anniversary meeting of the OAU. The exhibition included Bren guns and the NATO all-purpose machine guns with which South African forces have been equipped.[24] PLAN military activity does not claim to control territory but their engagements are for harassment, training, and reconnaissance purposes, as well as letting people on the inside know that resistance to South African military rule is possible and growing. PLAN faces a major South African force of 12,000 to 15,000 troops, who have cleared a 1,000-yard wide "no go" area along the Ovamboland side of the 320 miles of border.[25]

SWAPO is the most militant of the nationalist organizations, with supporters among all the major tribal groups, although concentrated in Ovamboland. Others, such as the South West African National Union (SWANU), have support and some following, especially among the Herero, and they carry out limited external diplomatic activities. However, the OAU recognizes only SWAPO for external support. The extent of military resistance to South African occupation should not be overestimated but it is growing and receiving increasing external aid. As South African forces are spread between Angola and Rhodesia, their capacity to cope with increased infiltration has been weakened. Thus South Africa's attempts to dismiss the importance of the guerrillas is repudiated by their own extensive mobilization along the border.

South Africa's belief that she can wipe out this resistance as she has elsewhere, in Pondoland, for example, is unrealistic because the guerrillas have a sanctuary in Zambia and have moved freely through Angola since its liberation. The nationalist spirit is strong and growing, with increased hope of ultimate success, even without utilizing Cuban or MPLA intervention. SWAPO has the backing of the Peoples Republic of Angola and Zambia, which provides facilities for housing refugees, and the organizational activities of the "freedom fighters." This sanctuary was not destroyed during the South African 1976 invasion of Angola. The channel is important for the increasing support of SWAPO from other African states, Western countries, especially Scandinavia, and the socialist states of eastern Europe and Asia. The church groups have increased their aid as well. This external support is critical to the morale of the nationalist SWAPO movement in Namibia and has helped sustain it, despite heavy South African suppression. South Africa continuously harasses the internal SWAPO leadership. They are called terrorists and are frequently arrested and tortured, and two were condemned to death. External assistance by INGOs, such as the IDAF and the ICJ, in these trials, has been an important assist in keeping alive the spark of resistance. Joel Carlson, in his book *No Neutral Ground,* relates some of his experiences as the trial lawyer for several of the Namibian defendants in the South West Africa treason trials.[27]

NGO Transnational Aid

The transnational dimension of the growth of nationalism and liberation in Namibia has been very important. SWAPO leaders today emphasize their own struggle and believe that Namibian freedom will ultimately be won only by the struggle of the people and not at the United Nations debates, but if it were not for the United Nations legal, diplomatic, and liberation support, there would be a different kind of struggle. In all probability, South Africa would have incorporated the territory de jure as well as de facto, making it much more difficult for Namibians to gain a hearing and international support.

The role of NGOs in the development of international concern for Namibians dates back to the early fifties, when Michael Scott represented the Hereros at the United Nations and presented the petition of their famous chief, Hosea Kutora. Later, petitioners such as Mburumba ua'Kerina (Getzen), who first represented

SWAPO at the United Nations, and J. Kosengwizi (SWANU) were assisted by the American Committee on Africa, the Africa Bureau, churches, and black groups in presenting their views. They gained support for several legal actions, resulting in a series of International Court of Justice advisory opinions. Although the initial decisions were not very favorable to the nationalist cause, in the end the entire United Nations system held against South Africa and revoked South African authority for the mandate.

The decision emerged out of two decades of petitioning and debate. In the sixties the growing number of African states led to increased pressures for South African withdrawal and United Nations rule. Initially, the strategy was gradualist and within the pacific action framework. Proposals ranged all the way from requesting South Africa to implement the ICJ's ruling (resolution 447A, 13 December 1950) to calling for South Africa to accept a trusteeship arrangement, and later at the sixth session, 19 January 1952, asking South Africa to negotiate. As South Africa resisted and the African states became more impatient, the resolutions turned to demands for withdrawal, and finally, in December 1963, the General Assembly, by a vote of eighty-four to six with seventeen abstentions, called for action by the Security Council and sanctions. When these harsher measures failed and the Ad Hoc Committee for South West Africa of fourteen members could not agree, the United Nations in 1967 established the Council for Namibia with eleven members and a commissioner, who moved toward the final legal transfer of the mandate to the United Nations.

When this action failed also, the United Nations changed from a policy of negotiation and accommodation to increased confrontation. This dates from Security Council Resolution 276 of 1970, which determined that South Africa's occupation was illegal, a decision that was reinforced by the ICJ advisory ruling in 1971.

Dialogue

When the United Nation's clear-cut legal claim was established and supported by the United States, although not until later by the United Kingdom and France, the issue became one of enforcement, with the gradualists still advocating negotiation and the African and transnational liberation groups pressing for more forceful measures. Within this context the new Secretary-General, Kurt Waldheim, initiated a dialogue between South Africa and the United Nations, which led to division among African states and NGOs and initiated a series of debates over negotiation. The policy of dialogue led later into the South African détente period, which further widened the gap between those who proposed to achieve Namibian independence by negotiation and pressure and those who believed that forceful support of liberation was the best strategy.

There had been some support initially among African states for dialogue and the Escher mission, especially from Gabon, Zaire, and even Tanzania, but as South Africa's intention became clear, this soon disappeared. SWAPO was initially noncommittal, not wishing to offend powerful friends, and some of the internal groups in Namibia associated with the national convention hoped that the United Nations could persuade South Africa to accept international administration. In May 1973, Sam Nujoma, president of SWAPO, made it unequivocally clear where the liberation movement stood:

I, as the President of SWAPO of Namibia, on behalf of the Namibian people, categorically reject further diplomatic contact, dialogue or negotiations with the enemy which is based on inequality.[28]

The Council for Namibia on 27 March 1973 decided to call for the immediate termination of contact, and it further demanded that South Africa cease extending to Namibia its policies and practices of racial discrimination, including the creation of Bantustans and of the so-called advisory council.[29]

Finally on 12 December 1973, the Security Council unanimously voted to end the contacts of the Secretary-General with South Africa. The Secretary-General noted that the Council for Namibia, Namibians themselves, and the OAU felt there was no further point in continuing the dialogue with Pretoria. While the United States supported the Security Council action, it was clearly not the view of the Western powers that the door should be finally closed. An American official in the State Department indicated that the United States regarded this as a pause in the United Nations campaign of peaceful persuasion: "The U.S. remains supportive of peaceful discussion over differences with South Africa although we recognize she is in unlawful occupation of Namibia.[30]

The issue over dialogue preceded the détente debate and reflects the differences among Western NGOs over Namibia, despite their unanimous endorsement of a free and independent Namibia.

The gradualists have faith and hope in South Africans coming to their senses and opting for an accommodation. Therefore, moderate church and civil-rights leaders responded to dialogue with South Africa and commended the Escher mission, and supported the Secretary-General in his attempts to persuade South Africa to set a date for withdrawal and handover of authority to the Council for Namibia.

The abolitionists joined with SWAPO in its denunciation of such tactics. The American Committee on Africa was particularly critical of the continuation of the Security Council dialogue with South Africa, because it provided time for South Africa to continue to establish her "homeland policy" through the creation of tribal councils. The ACOA asserted that the Escher mission showed that South Africa dictated the framework of all discussions. No amount of dialogue on such a basis could possibly advance United Nations objectives for Namibia.

Despite the careful phraseology of the proposed agreement we believe that it legitimates or appears to legitimate the illegal South African occupation of Namibia. It creates a situation in which the U.N. Representative is totally dependent on South African approval for the exercise of his mission, and will have to obtain South African approval even to travel to Namibia.

This is a step backwards. It nullifies the basic position taken by the U.N. when it terminated South Africa's mandate and ended completely all South African authority in the territory by Resolution 2143 and 3248. It is not consistent with the advisory opinion of the International Court of Justice of June 19, 1971, which found that South Africa was illegally in Namibia and that its authority should not be recognized. The proposal for the appointment of a special representative not only recognized de facto South African control but recommends doing business with it. The U.N. is thus giving up its basic legal position on Namibia and gives South Africa unwarranted confidence in its right of control over the territory."[31]

The ACOA objected particularly to Mr. Eschers apparent acceptance of Vorster's determination to press ahead with the homelands policy, establishing ten homelands under the pretense that they would be self-governing. The ACOA further pointed out that, while seeming to devolve authority, Vorster's plans in no way indicated an acceptance of the unification idea. In addition, the ACOA expressed its concern about the maintenance of all the restrictive legislation, influx control, martial law in Ovamboland, and the imprisonment of political leaders like G. N. Maxuilili, the acting president of SWAPO.[32]

The conclusion that there was a fundamental impasse here between the United Nations and NGO view of a united independent Namibia and Vorster's homelands concept was borne out in later discussions, in April 1973, between the Secretary-General of the United Nations and Hilgard Muller, South African Minister for Foreign Affairs. Although there was a shift in terminology by the South Africans, in which they stated they had "no intention of imposing any constitutional system, particularly one which was not in accord with the Charter request for recognition of the principle of equal rights and self-determination," the Secretary-General in his report agreed with the Africans and NGOs that "the statement does not provide the complete and unequivocal clarification of South Africa's policy in regard to self-determination and independence for Namibia envisaged in Resolution 323 (1972)."[3]

The establishment of an advisory council by South Africa consisting of representatives from the major homelands and the Coloured and white populations appeared to confirm the earlier commitment to a "homelands" policy.

South Africa's intention to create tribal councils leading to Bantustans was given a startling blow in the SWAPO-inspired boycott of the elections held for the Ovambo legislature on 1-2 August 1973. Many of the opposition leaders were imprisoned, the Democratic Co-operative Development Party (DEMKOP), which is also in opposition, joined in the SWAPO boycott, and the result was that only 2.3 percent of the 42,000 potential voters of Ovamboland cast their votes. This brought into serious question Vorster's contention that a new election element was being introduced in Ovamboland. This combined liberation, African, and NGO opposition to dialogue ended this particular accommodation ploy and opened the way for another phase.

Confrontation Proposals

The abolitionist NGOs, in close consultation with the liberation movements and United Nations officials, put forward a number of confrontation proposals for enforcement action to assert the authority and jurisdiction of the United Nations and the rights of the Namibian people to independence.

Sean MacBride, then representing the International Commission of Jurists, laid the basis for many of these steps he later had responsibility to implement. At the Ad Hoc Subcommittee established in pursuance of Security Council Resolution 276 (1970), in New York, he set forth several proposals. MacBride urged especially the strengthening of the council and the commissioner's office and drew attention particularly to the need for research on social conditions and the need to train Namibians in the administrative skills for self-rule. An opinion from the International Court of Justice against South African rule, appealing to those elements in South Africa who have some regard for legality, MacBride argued, would strengthen the United Nation's hand. He charged South Africa with genocide against children and requested that the Genocide Convention be invoked. When questioned about support for liberation movements, he replied, "While it was helpful to provide assistance to the liberation movements, the United Nations should go beyond that. It was the responsibility of the organization to take the initiative and use all the means at its disposal to free Namibia."[34]

Michael Scott, in 1970, speaking for the Africa Bureau, made a number of important recommendations. Among these was that the Council for Namibia should be strengthened by the presence of at least two of the Western powers. The only Western country to have served on this council previously was Turkey. But Scott's argument was that the presence of those powers with the greatest influence with South Africa would of course add weight to its decision. The isolation of the Western powers from the council, Scott felt, was one of its weakest points in dealing with South Africa. Also all governments should recognize the Council for Namibia "as the one body with direct responsibility for the administration of the territory." Further, Scott maintained that "all member states should recognize the Council as constituting the legal government of Namibia and

South Africa should be regarded as the "illegal occupying power."[35]

A strengthened council should then move to establish its jurisdiction over a variety of matters covering business investment, trade, taxation, and communications. Scott's proposal implied the cooperation of countries which carry on extensive commercial relations with Namibia through South Africa.[35]

Elizabeth Landis, a vice-president of the American Committee on Africa, published an elaborate set of proposals which emphasized legal and economic actions to be taken by the Council for Namibia. She urged Western countries that join the council to act as its enforcement branch by requiring their own government departments, companies, and courts to recognize the rulings of the council as Namibia's sole administrative authority. For example, the United States should *not* permit American companies operating in Namibia to write off taxes paid to South Africa from their profits but should require that, in order for these taxes to be written off, they should be placed to the account of the Council for Namibia at the United Nations.[37] Once the Council for Namibia established its authority in these areas, activities such as the granting of commercial concessions by South Africa would be considered less valid. United Nations member guarantees and supports for trade and development would, of course, be withdrawn, and contracts, such as that for the zinc development concession of Rio Tinto Zinc, would have to be redrawn or abandoned entirely. All of these measures are not sanctions in the traditional sense of the word, but are direct actions taken in cooperation with the correct authority in international law governing commercial relations. The fact that over 50 percent of the economy of Namibia is dependent upon the exports of British and American firms means that these steps would have a considerable impact on the economy of both Namibia and South Africa.

Brussels

The breadth of NGO support in the Western world for strengthening the Council for Namibia and supporting an active policy was revealed at a conference on Namibia held in Brussels in June 1972.[38] This conference was attended by a wide variety of NGO groups from eastern and western Europe and the United States, and representatives of liberation movements (primarily SWAPO). Delegations included members of Parliament from several Western countries, research centers, relief organizations like OXFAM, IUEF, and Christian Action, and various political parties from the Communists to the Liberals, national unions of students, international trade unions, and women's organizations, as well as all the major anti-apartheid organizations. Representation from the Third World was present but purposely limited, for the organizers wished to reflect European—especially western European—thinking. The conference issued a report which contained the strategy of sanctions and liberation support outlined by liberation leaders and abolitionist groups. They called upon trade unions "to refuse to handle cargo obtained in contravention of United Nations decisions on Namibia." The report requested, "Groups should campaign to make Governments break off their support for companies involved in Namibia."[39] They especially called attention to institutional investors and their responsibility to put pressure on their companies. The blockade of Walvis Bay was supported, and the Cunene River Basin scheme, which is to bring power from Angola into Namibia, was challenged. For the first time, an international conference called attention to the need to restrict South Africa from participating in the benefits of GATT and EEC. International agencies like the IMF were requested to consider terminating agreements concerning the sale of gold which benefit South Africa. Numerous other legal and political measures, including support for SWAPO and internal-political movements, were endorsed. However, the Brussels Conference was ambiguous on the issue of dialogue and assumed that both accommodation and confrontation could be pursued simultaneously.

Oslo

An antidialogue strategy emerged at the Oslo Conference in 1973, convened by the OAU and the United Nations. It shifted the emphasis away from contacts to what the United Nations majority could do itself, using United Nations agencies to assert its authority against South Africa. The refusal of most Western powers to implement these suggestions was circumvented by the formulation of a coalition between Afro-Asian states and increasingly powerful groups of NGOs committed to pacific-action pressures.[40]

The experts who presented papers at the Oslo Conference were especially representative of the transnational revolutionary views of NGOs. Liberation leaders also played prominent roles in the discussions, and for the first time at an official international conference, were given delegate status comparable to that enjoyed by the representatives of member states. This was opposed by Britain, France, and the United States and contributed to their absence from the conference. There were, however, representatives in attendance from a number of Western governments including Austria, Australia, Denmark, Finland, Iceland, Mexico, Norway, Sweden, and Turkey. The eastern European countries were of course present and active participants.

The terms of the conference limited the invitation list to the five states of Scandinavia, states which served on the Security Council, the United Nations Council for Namibia, the Special Committee on the Situation with Regard to the Implementation of the Declaration on the Granting of Independence to Colonial Countries and Peoples, the Special Committee on Apartheid, and the Coordinating Committee of the Liberation of Africa of the OAU. Under this formula, sixty-five states were invited. Congressman Charles Diggs was included among the group of experts although he was not an official representative of the United States. In addition to liberation-group representatives and invited experts, each of the major United Nations agencies dealing with matters affecting colonialism and apartheid was invited.

Western government participation was the first tangible evidence of a widespread break on the part of small Western powers from the pattern established by the dominant Western powers concerning Southern Africa. Their commitment to all the proposals of Oslo was, of course, limited by national considerations. However, the unexpressed dynamic was a growing recognition of long-term interests in trade and investment in black Africa and the Arab world, which would be damaged by close identification with apartheid. Also a stronger awareness of their dependence on a maturing international system helped clarify this issue for these countries. None of these European states wished to be involved in any way with the continuation of colonial war, whether in Southern Africa, the Middle East, or Southeast Asia, and their presence at Oslo showed they were looking for a way to carry out the United Nations majority view.

There was a great deal of repetition of previous ideas and discussions, but a number of new suggestions were also put forward concerning strategy. Several were adopted.

Elizabeth Landis stressed in her paper the necessity for transforming the Council for Namibia into a "full-fledged government or quasi-government-in-exile." This, the General Assembly could do by redrafting its resolution establishing the council with an eye to experiences elsewhere such as in New Guinea and Eritrea. The quasi-government would have powers of representation of Namibia on all international agencies and conferences. It would redraft legislation covering commercial and diplomatic relations between the mandate and other countries.[41] To do this, of course, Landis pointed out that an adequate budget would have to be adopted and a full-time permanent commissioner with a full staff appointed. A new style would have to be adopted, she said: "A Commissioner whose function is to help the Council assume its proper role in ending South Africa's occupation of Namibia must differ in temperament, attitudes and talents from a Commissioner conducting a mere holding operation. . . ."[42] The position would demand innovation, courage, and immense ability.

This suggestion was well received by the conference with the provision that representation of the Namibians should be provided on the council.

The transnational government idea has, however, a number of problems which Africans and liberation leaders have pointed out. Since the issue is who will control Namibia, the lines should not be too rigidly or permanently drawn between those struggling inside and those fighting outside for independence.[43] Since the South Africans are attempting to form a puppet regime and to have them carry the fight against SWAPO, the dangers of antagonisms solidifying among Namibians is very great. There should be no question but that the United Nations backs SWAPO and the liberation approach. However, the United Nations should attempt to be a reconciling force among rival African groups. These differences are, of course, intensified by the South African policy of recognizing and promoting their separateness. Unfortunately, these differences persist, as in the case of the Congo in the 1960s and Angola more recently, after freedom from colonialism has been won. Therefore, it is important to bring a wide representative government into existence and to give assurances on this objective prior to the takeover. This can best be done through an election supervised by the United Nations. SWAPO has insisted South African troops be withdrawn, and they can be replaced by a peacekeeping force of the United Nations for the purposes of a transition. Persuading or forcing South Africa to accept United Nations control of the transition is indispensable to a peaceful solution.

NGO Auxiliary Campaigns

NGOs have proposed various support activities to reinforce United Nations claims. Several of these have been implemented despite opposition by the Western governments concerned.

Barbara Rogers, in her paper for the Oslo Conference, suggested a number of actions including developing a Karakul wool boycott, as the Brussels Conference recommended.[44] Friends of Namibia in England had attempted to obtain support in Denmark and London for campaigns against the auction of the pelts, though these were not very effective. She argued that with official action by the Council for Namibia on a transitional government, this action could be made more effective because it would have official sanction. Another suggestion for economic action mentioned by Rogers was action against South African exploitation of the Namibian fishing waters. For example, the Council for Namibia could make an agreement with a fishing state such as Norway for fishing rights in Namibian territorial waters. "If South Africa were to attack such a vessel, outside South African territorial waters but within the territorial waters of Namibia, such an attack would constitute an act of aggression."[45] Namibia might become a party to a South East Atlantic Fisheries Agreement. She suggests that "The FAO should provide technical assistance in drawing up the agreements and should provide all documentation on fishing in South Africa and Namibia."[46]

Any such interference with the rights of shipping authorized by the council would be adequate grounds for Security Council enforcement action.

A campaign has been launched in western Europe, England, and America against companies which have investments in Namibia, none of which recognize the authority of the council. The Council for Namibia has disallowed past concessions and decreed that no exploitation can take place without its authorization.[47]

In the United States, Congressman Diggs took up the suggestion that tax credits to American corporations operating in Namibia should be disallowed on the jurisdictional ruling of the ICJ. With the help of the State Department and the International Division of the Treasury, Diggs took the matter to the Treasury Department. "The acceptance of the Court's opinion, they argued, required the government to refrain from any affirmative acts which would imply recognition of South Africa's right to govern Namibia."[48] The Tax Policy Division, after eighteen months of deliberation, finally ruled against this request from Congressman Diggs, largely on the grounds that Congress had not provided for such distinctions in the law.[49] Several American organizations, including influential church groups, have since set out to amend the tax law to enable this type of pressure to be brought to bear on American corporations operating in Namibia. Later action by the United Nations to establish clear authority over the resources of Namibia enhanced the prospects of adopting such legislation, since this created a duly constituted authority, capable of utilizing such payments in ways employed by other governments. In Great Britain the British Labour Party, while out of power, announced its determination to terminate the Rio Tinto Zinc contract for the development of uranium deposits. They also pledged not to enter into any new contracts which would imply recognition of South Africa, and to review all treaties dealing with South Africa "including double-taxation" to seek to exclude Namibia "from all provisions."[50] This policy, however, has not been implemented.

Nongovernmental action in England against Rio Tinto Zinc was taken by the church commissioners of the Church of England, who sold stock in the company in part because of their dissatisfaction with the southern African policies of this company, which was widely publicized through the *Anti-Report* of the Counter Information Services.[51] The *Anti-Report* stated in part:

A new company formed to operate the mine would be controlled by the Industrial Development Corporation of SA with RTZ as managers and secretaries. . . .

Thus the final control over the output and use of the uranium from the mine is in the hands of the South African Government which otherwise has no access to large reserves of uranium. This has an ominous significance in the light of the declaration of 12.4.1971 in the Rand Daily Mail by Dr. A. J. Roux, Chairman of the SA Atomic Energy Board, who said, "it would be impracticable and almost impossible to make nuclear weapons from plutonium. The reason for this was that much of the material and equipment needed to make use of plutonium for military purposes would have to be imported from abroad. Such an installation would be subject to international inspection. Although the SA policy was to use her enriched uranium for peaceful purposes, the new process recently developed in the country put her in a position to make her own atomic weapons."[52]

Assisting South Africans to develop nuclear weapons, the report perceived, was against the principles of many Englishmen, and the protest was bound to spread.

In the United States even stronger demands for corporate reform and withdrawal from Namibia have been developed by NGOs within the churches and civic groups whose concern has been touched off by South Africa's unlawful occupation. American investments are a significant proportion of the total, since mining accounts for sixty percent of all exports, and the American Newmont. AMAX corporations and the South African Consolidated Diamond Mines of South West Africa Ltd. together account for ninety percent of all mining. Other significant American firms in the mining industry are U. S. Steel and Bethlehem Steel, and Nord Resources of New Mexico. A United States policy determination to discourage further investment in Namibia was outlined by American Ambassador to the United Nations Charles W. Yost in August 1969.[53] This, however, has not been implemented and the reality of this policy was stated by Assistant Secretary of State Richard Newsom in a letter to George Houser: "Such efforts obviously rely on our powers of persuasion. In the last analysis, the decision whether to invest in

South West Africa remains with the individual; under United States law it is not illegal per se to invest or do business in the territory.''[54]

Among American churches, considerable soul-searching has developed regarding their investment portfolios, especially with respect to firms such as Newmont and AMAX. This concern is the product of a wide social-responsibility movement, which focuses on situations where the social criteria of the church are in conflict with the practices of companies abroad in which the churches hold stock. Firms operating in Southern Africa have come under particular scrutiny as a result of the United Nations decision regarding Namibia and the growth of social-responsibility concern described earlier.

In the early 1970s, several churches looked carefully into corporate practices and decided to try to do something about their low wages and racial discrimination. Some of the groups concerned, especially the Episcopal Churchmen for Southern Africa and the Council for Christian Social Action (UCC), decided that firms such as Newmont Mining Corporation, AMAX, and U. S. Steel should be asked to withdraw from Namibia. Other church groups felt this was too drastic and ineffectual at this stage. But in 1972 and 1973 they did agree on proxy campaigns to request reforms in the employment and general social and racial policies of Newmont and AMAX.[55]

The withdrawal-from-Namibia position was forcefully argued by the Council for Christian Social Action (UCC) within its own denomination, and its views have had considerable influence in the wider church, closely paralleling those of the Programme to Combat Racism of the World Council of Churches.[56] In a memorandum prepared for the General Synod of the United Church of Christ in July 1973, the CCSA stated: ''We support efforts of the Boards to discourage new investments in Angola and Namibia, but we fail to understand why that same logic should not be extended to press companies already in Southern Africa to withdraw.''[57]

The churches' joint project on investments circulated proxy requests for Newmont to pay taxes directly to the United Nations. The taxes in the case of the Tsumeb mine have amounted in the period 1946-1971 to $166,510,287—which is twice the total wages paid, including those paid to whites.

At the stockholders meeting of Newmont Mining Corporation in

May 1973, Howard Schomer, representing the 65,600 shares of common stock owned by the United Church of Christ, moved the following resolution:

Be it RESOLVED that in its operations abroad, the Corporation will practice principles of fair employment, including equal pay for comparable work, equal employee benefit plan, equal treatment in hiring, training and promotion, and equal eligibility to supervisory and management positions, without regard to race, sex or religion. In any country where local laws or customs involve racial discrimination in employment, the Corporation will initiate affirmative action programs to achieve meaningful equality of job opportunity."[58]

Newmont management had fought and prevented the circulation of this proxy resolution which also called upon the company to pay taxes to the United Nations Council for Namibia rather than South Africa. Even these moderate reform resolutions were heavily defeated in the voting, but not before Schomer was able to place some pertinent facts before the stockholders and the public. He pointed out how the company had been taken over from its German proprietors in 1946, and since that time had earned over $1 billion in market sales:

Of this amount ($1,030,713,360) to be exact, only 8.5% was given to the laborers (some 6,000 or more in recent years) in cash or kind. The actual figure is $87,423,116. The tax bill—most of it to the foreign occupying power, the Republic of South Africa—was higher than $166,510,287 or 16.2% of gross revenue. Materials, power and all other operating costs came to another 20.3% or $209,085,514. . . . This left gross profits of $530,042,133 or 51.3% of gross revenues, almost totally exported to the parent companies. . . . Dividends passed on to Newmont shareholders have been normal, but the big profits from Tsumeb have permitted Newmont itself greatly to increase its holdings.[59]

Schomer had visited Namibia and was able to point out how the contract and compound system of labor for Africans was bitterly resented and that the African leaders—such as Lutheran Bishop Leonard Auala—are demanding basic changes in policy. In addition Namibians are worried about the rapid depletion of their resources; within twelve to fifteen years the copper will be gone, and they want United Nations control over this. Schomer proposed for the UCC that a Tsumeb Mine Educational and Community Development Foundation for the Ovambo and Kavango Tribes be established which would hold as a private trust some of these enormous profits. Others have suggested that the United Nations should play this role and that the companies should contribute to the Fund for Namibia. However, the companies have not agreed to contribute to any fund for the Namibian people and have flatly rejected all of these proposals in favor of continued high profits with minimal reforms, in the hope that within ten years, they will have milked the country of its valuable minerals, and when the Namibians finally do gain control, they will be gone.

An ACOA study, *Namibia, U. S. Corporate Involvement,* stated:

1. U.S. companies give direct support to the South African government in Namibia by the taxes they pay;

2. U. S. companies in Namibia strengthen the economy of South Africa by injecting large amounts of capital and developing significant sources of foreign exchange and earnings;

3. U. S. companies in Namibia operate in areas strategically vital to the continuation of white domination by force. Oil from Namibia currently being sought by Chevron and Etosna, is potentially of great importance in securing South Africa's military position and increasing its general economic self-sufficiency, thus reducing its vulnerability to international sanctions and boycotts;

4. U. S. economic involvement in Namibia serves to legitimize the illegal South African Government, and inevitably brings about a closer integration of the South African economy with those of the West. One result of this interdependence is the increased willingness of Western governments to come to economic and military aid of the white regimes against the legitimate demands of the people;

5. Finally, because U. S. interests in Namibia are heavily concentrated in the extractive industries, the problem is particularly urgent, since resources are being rapidly depleted and the profits are nonrenewable. Herero Chief Clemens Kapuuo has appealed to the international community to prevent companies removing the assets which the people of Namibia will need when they win their independence.[60]

This campaign against corporate exploitation in Namibia has had an effect which is both immediate and long term. While the major companies have ignored the Council for Namibia's rulings on the exploitation of resources, they have introduced substantial changes in the labor contract system in Namibia.

A duly constituted transitional government of Namibia under United Nations auspices could create a new force in the struggle. However, at this stage, many of the liberation-support groups have little confidence that the United Nations can go beyond its current verbal gestures. For this reason, they prefer to rely on their own nongovernmental pressures and direct support for liberation-movement activity inside and outside the country.

Liberation Support

A course of action was suggested by the SWAPO representatives at the Oslo Conference, which requested United Nations and organizational assistance for their struggle. Their recommendations were affirmed in such a way as to make SWAPO clearly the recognized representative movement in the territory.

(1) The international community should support the liberation struggle of the people of Namibia. The South West Africa People's Organization, being the liberation movement of Namibia which is recognized by the Organization of African Unity, should be accorded appropriate recognition as the authentic representative of the people of Namibia.

(2) Accordingly, there should be an active commitment by all Governments, international organizations and national bodies to channel all aid for Namibia—financial, material or otherwise—through the South West African People's Organization.

(3) The United Nations should take steps for the implementation of its decisions to enable the United Nations Council for Namibia to act as the legal authority of the Territory and exercise those powers now illegally exercised by South Africa pending the independence of Namibia. In that connection the South West Africa People's Organization should be closely associated with the Council.[61]

A great deal of consideration at the Oslo Conference was given to ways in which the United Nations and NGOs might develop more extensive support for liberation movements. SWAPO, as the leadership of the Namibian people in their external struggle, is the organization most widely recognized and the only one carrying out armed resistance. Even if all else fails, the support of the liberation movements will continue. The Council for Namibia has given considerable attention to the needs of SWAPO, which is the only group the OAU recognizes externally. The work of the National Convention and several other organizations internally is recognized as effective, as the Ovambo strike and boycott of elections has attested, but it has come into increasing conflict with SWAPO because of the convention's participation in the South African-sponsored constitutional talks.

United Nations Aid

A new way of assisting Namibia was found in the creation of the U.N. Fund for Namibia in 1970, which was established to give special attention to problems of Namibian independence, to provide assistance to Namibians who have suffered from persecution, and to finance a comprehensive educational and training program for Namibians with particular regard to their future administrative responsibilities in the territory.[62] Contributions were slow in coming at first, but by 1973, the General Assembly placed $100,000 in the fund, and in addition twelve countries had contributed, with the Netherlands making the largest grant.

As much as the liberation movement appreciates the support raised by the United Nations, there is a good deal of criticism of the way in which the money was spent and the difficulties in getting funds for what is needed. Leaders of SWAPO and several of the NGOs indicated to the author they were unhappy with the fact that the funds for Namibia had not been used for purposes they deemed important, such as the establishment of a farm-educational-medical complex for SWAPO in Zambia. Some excellent plans have been laid out, but implementation has been very slow on the part of the governments concerned, as well as the council and other United Nations agencies.[63] The FAO has discussed the possibility of assisting in the agricultural training at the school, and UNESCO is interested in helping with the training of teachers, as is ILO for the development of a trade school. These agencies—it was hoped—

would also provide scholarships for the school. The Fund for Namibia agreed to transfer $20,000 to the Botswana government for the establishment of a medical clinic for Namibia at Makunda with the help of WHO and UNICEF has agreed to provide equipment and drugs.[64] This coordination was stepped up as the result of the implementation of an NGO appeal for a strong and experienced commissioner for Namibia.

The Turnhalle Proposals Opposed

The appointment of one of the leading NGO advocates to the position of comissioner for Namibia marked a major step toward strong transnational action. He immediately initiated several far-reaching measures, based on the assumption that Namibia would be liberated by the efforts of SWAPO and would be an independent unified nation with all groups and forces participating. One of the most important actions taken by the Council for Namibia under MacBride's direction was the decree on Namibian natural resources which was modeled on some of the earlier NGO recommendations. This decree was based on the principle that the resources of Namibia belonged to her people and prohibited the search for extraction, processing, and exportation without the consent and permission of the United Nations Council for Namibia. This meant, of course, that all the mineral mining companies such as Newmont and RTZ were in violation of this United Nations authority.[65]

The new United Nations approach of MacBride also improved the training and research function by the establishment in Lusaka of the Namibia Institute under an international board with a Namibian director, Gottfried Geingob. The institute provided the means to coordinate research on all aspects of Namibian development related to self-rule and to prepare Namibians for their new expected roles.[66] Once the Namibians take over their country, the entire economic and educational system from contract labor to Bantustan education will have to be restructured. This approach received the support of even the major Western powers, who contributed funds for the institute. The Fund for Namibia has received increasing support from Western countries despite the fact that it is a major instrument of the liberation policy.

South Africa's response to all these pressures for liberation was to announce its goal of "ultimate independence" for Namibia and to initiate the Turnhalle Conference, "constitutional talks" moving toward self-rule, working with chiefs, parties, and councils prepared to work with them. Their chief spokesman has been Mr. A. N. du Plessis, leader of the National Party in Namibia, who submitted his proposals in the form of a letter to the Secretary-General of the United Nations stating in part "the time was now opportune for the Whites of South West Africa, acting in a more positive and practical manner, to undertake with representatives of the other population groups of the Territory, more particularly on South West Africa's future, a pattern of constitutional development."[67]

The Council for Namibia has rejected this framework because it does not regard the South African and German populations in Namibia as citizens of that country and therefore not proper leaders for such a transitional process. The council, of course, recognizes SWAPO as the preeminent national group, while South Africa rejects it.

The response of SWAPO has been to denounce the constitutional talks and all those who participate in them. They have stated that SWAPO will not negotiate with South Africa unless SWAPO of Namibia is acknowledged as "the sole authentic representative of the Namibian People." They view the so-called multiracial council as "Bantustan in another guise."[68]

Thus the liberation leaders have abandoned any illusions about a grant of independence. They believe they have to fight for their country outside, and resist within. They warn the world against Vorster's détente, which they see as a modern version of divide and rule. Reform is seen as presented through African chiefs such as Chief Kapuuo and whites like Mr. du Plessis while the real representatives of the people are arrested and executed.

The liberation leaders work with the United Nations and especially the Council for Namibia and regard the United Nations' legitimizing role, funding, and training aid as extremely important to them. But the struggle they believe must be won in Namibia by the sacrifices of their people, as was the case in the Portuguese territories and elsewhere.

There is a great deal of misunderstanding about this SWAPO attitude among gradualists at the United Nations and in the Western world. They believe the South Africans should be met halfway and step by step, rather than by confrontation. Détente appears viable to them, and the idea of a peaceful transition is very appealing. However, most of the NGOs were disillusioned in the failure of dialogue in 1973. They now feel that a liberation struggle will have to be fought, and it may well involve South Africa on several fronts, as well as at home, before any firm ground for compromise can be found.

The decision by South Africa to grant independence under a transition government by 1978 to the so-called multiracial group emerging out of the Turnhalle Conference has not altered this stand-off but has intensified it.

Notes

1. For the basis of mineral wealth, see Roger Murray, et al., *The Role of Foreign Firms in Namibia* (Uppsala: African Publication Trust, 1975).

2. G.A. Resolution 2145 (27 October 1966) revoked the mandate for South West Africa by 114 votes to 2. On 20 March 1969, the Security Council gave its imprimatur to the revocation in Resolution 264, adopted 13 to 0, with France and the United Kingdom abstaining. The legal basis of these actions was strengthened by the International Court of Justice in the second phase of the South West African cases. See John Dugard, *The South West Africa/Namibia Dispute* (Berkeley: University of California Press, 1973), pp. 379-397.

3. Merle Lipton, "Independent Bantustans," *International Affairs,* Vol. 48, No. 1 (January 1972), p. 1. Also, see Rhoodie and Venter, *Apartheid, A Socio-Historical Exposition* (Capetown: HAUM, 1959).

4. Prime Minister Vorster has made it very clear that independence is to be the goal. *Hansard,* 7 and 15 October 1970.

5. Letter to the *Times* (London), 22 July 1971.

6. Interview with Gatsha Buthelezi, February 1973, New York City.

7. "Aims and Organization," mimeographed, Johannesburg, SASO, 1972. Also interview with BPC leader, London, March 1973.

8. *South Africa's Political Alternatives,* Report of SPROCAS Political Commission, Christian Institute, South African Council of Churches (Johannesburg: Raven Press, 1973), p. 39.

9. Schlemmer found that roughly 66 percent of white voters in South Africa considered the idea of independent Bantustans a good one. Among Progressive Party supporters the proportion was 46 percent in favor and

18 percent opposed, respectively. "White attitudes to the Bantustans," *Third World,* Fabian Society, London, June 1973, p. 42.

10. Only 30 percent of both English and Afrikans were willing to pay more taxes for the support of the Bantustans.

11. Letter to the Secretary-General of the United Nations, 26 September 1974, United Nations document A/9775-5/11519.

12. *Windhoek Advertiser,* 23 September 1974.

13. *X-Ray,* November-December, 1975.

14. *Pretoria News,* 10 September 1975.

15. International Conference on Namibia and Human Rights, held at Dakar, 5-8 January 1976.

16. *Namibia Bulletin,* 29 January 1975, p. 4.

17. *Windhoek Advertiser,* 25 September 1974.

18. Statement of the government of South Africa to the Secretary-General of the United Nations, 30 April 1973, United Nations document S/10921, 30 April 1973.

19. Ibid.

20. *Southern Africa,* August-September 1973, p. 26.

21. UN S/10832, p. 16. Mr. de Wet, commissioner general for the Native Peoples of South West Africa, stated (p. 17):

Whereas the United Nations was demanding immediate independence, the South African Government considered that, despite the substantial progress made within the past decade, the Territory and its inhabitants wre not yet ready for it. . . . It was financially and economically linked to the Republic of South Africa, which had the technical knowledge and the financial means to pursue its development for the benefit of all its inhabitants.

22. Namibian Documentation No. 2, International Preparatory Conference, Brussels, 14-15 February 1972, published by SWAPO.

23. *Namibia Revolution,* The Permanent Secretariat of the Afro-Asian Peoples Solidarity Conference (Cairo: UAR, 1971), p. 9.

24. Andreas Shipanga, *Namibia and SWAPO* (Vancouver, B.C.: Liberation Support Movement Press, 1973).

25. *Who Is SWAPO?* Africa Bureau Fact Sheet, No. 48, London, July/August 1976.

26. Aaron Mushimba, SWAPO's national organizer in Namibia, and Hendrik Skikongo were sentenced to death 12 May 1976. See *Anti-Apartheid News,* June 1976.

27. Several organizations, especially the International Commission of Jurists and Amnesty International, have sent observers to trials in South Africa. Judge William Booth, president of the American Committee on Africa, was one such observer. See his *REPORT,* mimeographed. ACOA

March 1972. Also, see Joel Carlson, *No Neutral Ground* (New York: Crowell, 1973).

28. *Namibia News,* May-June 1973, p. 6.

29. United Nations press release, 14 December 1973, WS/637.

30. Interview with Kaiser, Southern Africa Division, U.S. State Department, 21 January 1974.

31. "Statement of the American Committee on Africa on the proposal for a special representative in Namibia," mimeographed. ACOA bulletin, New York, 24 July 1972, p. 1.

32. Ibid.

33. Report by the Secretary-General on the implementation of the Security Council Resolution 323 (1972) concerning the question of Namibia. United Nations documents/10921, 30 April, 1973, p. 7.

34. Ad hoc subcommittee established in pursuance of Security Council Resolution 276 (1970) S/AC, 17/SR, 14, 7 August 1970.

35. Michael Scott, "New Initiatives for the 1970's," *Proposals for Action in South West Africa* (Namibia), edited by Richard Hall (London: Africa Bureau, 1970), p. 31-32.

36. Ibid., pp. 37-39.

37. Elizabeth Landis, "Namibia: The Beginning of Disengagement," *Studies in Race and Nations,* Vol. 2, No. 4 (1970-71).

38. The report of the conference is found in *Report of the United Nations Council for Namibia,* Vol. 11, G.A. Twenty-Seventh Session, Supplemental No. 24 (A/8724), pp. 18-32.

39. Ibid., p. 24.

40. "Organization of the Conference," Report of the Secretary-General, International Conference of Experts for the Support of Victims of Colonialism and Apartheid in Southern Africa. United Nations document A/9061, 7 May 1973, p. 3.

41. Elizabeth Landis, "Namibia Legal Aspects," mimeographed. Oslo, UN-OAU Conference documents, April 1973, p. 4.

42. Ibid.

43. Interview with Chief Clemens Kapuuo, November 1973, Denver, Colorado.

44. Barbara Rogers, "Namibia: Economic and Other Aspects," mimeographed. U.N.-O.A.U. Conference documents, April 1973, p. 5.

45. Ibid., p. 4-5.

46. Ibid.

47. "For the Protection of the Natural Resources of Namibia," Decree No. 1. *Namibia Gazette,* No. 1 UN Council for Namibia, 209th meeting, 27 September 1974.

48. *Southern Africa,* August-September 1973.

49. Ibid.

50. "World Peace," *Labour Weekly Supplement,* 25 May 1973.

51. Based on an interview with Elliot Kendal, secretary for African Affairs of the British Council of Churches, 22 February 1973.

52. The Rio Tinto Zinc Corp., Ltd., *Anti Report* (London: Counter Information Service, 1970), p. 8. Roger Murray was responsible for most of the research on this document.

53. The Rio Tinto Zinc Corp., Ltd., *Anti Report* (London: Counter 1970.

54. Richard Newsom to George Houser, 24 September 1970.

55. See proxy resolutions, "Church Project on United States Investments in Southern Africa," New York Corporate Information Service, 1973. Appendix II and III, p. 6.

56. Don Morton, *Partners in Apartheid, A Christian Assessment.* (New York: CCSA, United Church of Christ, 1973.)

57. Memorandum, "Response by the CCSA to the Social Impact Statement of the Four Boards, United Church of Christ to the World Council of Churches," 28 November 1972.

58. Press release, United Church of Christ, 7 May 1973, pp. 1-2.

59. Ibid.

60. *Namibia, U.S. Corporate Involvement* (New York: ACOA, 1972), p. 30.

61. *Southern Africa,* Vols. 1-2, UN-OAU Conference, Oslo, 9-14 April 1973, edited by Olav Stolke and Carl Widstrand (Uppsala: Scandinavian Institute of African Studies, 1973), pp. 240-241.

62. See Table 4, "Voluntary Contributions and Pledges by Governments January 1-March 23, 1973, for U.N. Trust Fund, U.N. Educational and Training Programme for Southern Africa and U.N. Fund for Namibia." *Southern Africa* 11, op. cit., p. 284.

63. Based on interviews in the field with NGOs in London and with SWAPO and United Nations officials in Lusaka, July 1973. The situation may have improved rapidly since my visit. One SWAPO official mentioned they could not even get funds to dig a well on a farm they had been granted by the Zambian government. At the time, they had been promised a second site for their education complex but "nothing was moving."

64. Brief by the regional office of the Council for Namibia, "Fund for Namibia Projects and Related Questions," mimeographed. U.N., Lusaka, 1973.

65. Council for Namibia, 209th Meeting, 27 September 1974.

66. *Namibia News,* July-August 1975.

67. Letter to Secretary-General, 26 September 1974 (A/9775-5/11519).

68. *Namibia Bulletin,* 29 January 1975.

chapter 9

ANTI-APARTHEID IMPACT ON SOUTH AFRICA

A prevailing white South African belief is that abolition anti-apartheid is counterproductive because it creates antagonism toward reform and a "laager" defensive mentality among the ruling Africaners.[1] A related view is that external sanctions do not influence significantly the political dynamics of South Africa.

These views are based upon a gradualist theory of social change and assume the elite responds to reason and moderate pressure. However, the opposite appears to be the case. Change in policy has been adopted by South Africa time and again only after an accumulation of transnational pressures. External NGO pressures are linked to internal groups in South Africa—churches, institutes, etc.—as has been demonstrated, thus broadening the impact.

The effect of external pressures on the breakdown of order must be carefully considered. As discussed in Chapter 1, the presumption that only peaceful change is legitimate is superficial Western social science. It is now necessary to determine what kind of external pressure has had the greatest effect in breaking down apartheid.

Which strategies have strengthened the hand of the opponents of the settler system, both internally and externally? It is here that we must search for the fault line. From the outset, this study has analyzed effectiveness in opposing apartheid among groups, outside South Africa, working across national boundaries, in a truly transnational revolutionary manner. The assessment now must be made of anti-apartheid strategies in terms of the South African response.

The whites now have power, but it is highly probable that, in the long term, it will be primarily the blacks who decide whether and on what terms the races can live together. Therefore black responses must not be left out.

The transnational power of liberation has reached into South Africa despite the attempts of the South African government to suppress and exclude it. The external-internal movement has breached the defensive "laager" at several points. Thus, the nature of South African response extends on a continuum or spectrum from revolution to reform and reaction.

The Spectrum of Responses

In considering the full spectrum of responses to the external challenge to South Africa, it is well to keep in mind that the abolitionists have long had major spokesmen among South Africans of all groups. The anti-apartheid movement, in the true sense, was begun by black and white South Africans within South Africa, and when repression made it impossible for some to work within their own country, they became the backbone of its organization overseas. Also, many courageous individuals of all races have continued to maintain their opposition inside the country, despite the heavy penalties.

The revolutionary point of view is openly to be found among spokesmen of organizations in exile, but it is extremely difficult to gain accurate estimates of the strength of this point of view inside South Africa because of the consequences. Spokesmen for revolution cannot be expected to express their opinions in South Africa, and the scholar has no right to place their lives in jeopardy by either enquiring or by publishing direct findings. Despite claims to the contrary, scholars and journalists also risk reprisals on themselves.

When I visited South Africa in 1971,[2] I was closely watched, and consequently I did not make any attempt to contact the underground. I used the occasion primarily to gather data among the legitimate groups, with the clear understanding that additional information would be put together from exile sources. I am skeptical of the findings of South African scholars who have worked on revolutionary groups primarily within South Africa, simply because they have no way of bridging the information gap between blacks and whites. In other respects, their information is well developed and extremely valuable. One has to be aware of biases, as Western social-science research in Third World revolutionary conditions is notoriously ethnocentric. It is surprisingly slow in correcting its use of data based on government statistics and information from the limited source of "acceptable spokesmen."

On one occasion, when I interviewed a group of African leaders connected with the Institute of Race Relations, they would only talk freely when all the whites had left the room. However, even under those circumstances, many Africans cannot be assumed to be speaking freely, since they could not be sure of what a stranger from abroad would do with the information. Moreover, informers are said to be always present in a group gathering of this nature. South Africa's extremely efficient secret police have established one of the most elaborate informer systems to be found anywhere in the world. Nevertheless, on several occasions, I encountered a surprising amount of forthrightness, and individual spokesmen risked their freedom in the statement of their views.[3]

The reactions of other groups such as the Coloured and Indian minorities are similarly guarded and complicated by paternalism. In any analysis the significance of each group's response must be determined by the author's theoretical suppositions about the importance of these groups to the ultimate outcome in South Africa. In the long run the black majority view will be decisive, but in the short run, the Bantustans, divisive policies, and police repression diminish its importance.

One of the assumptions stated at the outset of this study is that fundamental solutions to racial conflict emerge out of racial class changes rather than out of individual attitudinal changes. A change in attitude may facilitate change, but it cannot substitute for changes in the power position of groups.

"Class" control over the political and economic system is the point at issue, and change in this control is what must be considered significant. In South Africa, where the basic policy is separate development (meaning the exclusion of nonwhites from the white society and its decision-making process), it is easier to detect the operation of class control than in other systems that profess equality and assimilation. However, even in South Africa, it is important to be as precise about the class differences as possible in order to keep our attention focused on what is fundamental as opposed to ephemeral indications of change. Some of the leading studies of South Africa by major social scientists have failed to do this and as a result have led to optimistic conclusions, not sustained by developments.[4]

External Influences

Nongovernmental groups exercise their influence through indirect methods, in contrast to governments, which have direct means of influencing diplomatic processes at their command.

The transnational movement permeates cultural activities, the economy, political opposition, military policy, and revolutionary expectations. The government response is to try to control and limit this infiltration of its domain. This response is, in itself, one involving change. However, a fully effective transnational campaign influences a broad spectrum of group responses, many of which cannot be controlled by government. It strengthens the opposition and prepares the revolutionaries for their major task of constructing a total alternative to the existing governing elite.

Within the South African ruling groups there have been several broad responses to the external pressures, such as the rise of the Progressive Reform Party, the emergence of a *verlichte* ("enlightened") camp within the Afrikaner Party, the adoption of a homelands policy by the government to offset the racialism charges against apartheid, and finally an outward policy toward Africa, seeking friends and acceptance on the African continent. Other official policies, such as a powerful police and army to contain the threat of revolution and attack from abroad are also influenced by the anti-apartheid movement.

The Sport and Culture Boycotts

The sport and culture boycott has had a broad impact on South African society, affecting segregation practices in sport and in what is called cultural "petty apartheid." However, the significance of these reforms is debatable.

South African whites are extremely culture and sports conscious, and denying their teams and artists the opportunity for international tours and culture contests shocks them. Not all international participation has been eliminated by the boycott, of course, but declining participation is costing them dearly.

Many white South Africans, especially English speaking, have long opposed discrimination in sports. Under pressure from sports associations and promoters, the South African ruling groups have agreed to modify the rules of sports contests along several lines. By employing the fiction that black representatives of Transkie or Kwa Zulustan are "foreigners," they allow their teams to play against white teams in what are termed "international" contests. However, the Coloured teams, ethnically primarily Afrikaner speaking, cannot compete for Afrikaner club positions or play for these clubs. The South African Non-Racial Olympic Committee (SANROC), led by several prominent South African Coloureds, has vigorously exposed this fraud, both inside and outside South Africa.

South Africa has agreed to allow nonwhites to represent South Africa abroad in the Olympic and international competitions. However, there is still a major barrier to Africans within South Africa making up these teams, since the opportunities for competition are still largely segregated. As long as the school system and the sporting-club associations practice apartheid, it is impossible for competition to become open among the races.[5]

Those who see some advances in the system point to the new opportunities for spectators to be unsegregated and for racial groups to play against each other. Liberal and progressive white groups in South Africa cite these changes as major concessions.[6] A number of black South African athletes have been happy to take advantage of these changes and have agreed to compete for Bantustans rather than for South Africa. But African leaders remain critical of the limitations on their athletes.

The African leadership in exile and in prison continues to advocate a strict boycott of sports and cultural relations with South Africa on the grounds that the basic discriminatory system has not been changed. The government motive in making these token reforms, they maintain, is to induce other countries to reestablish communications. These African leaders also oppose attempts by individual sports stars, such as Arthur Ashe, to help the black athletes within the existing system, on the grounds that little real help is possible and the legitimizing of pseudoreforms does more damage in the long run to the future of black athletes than the little encouragement personal contacts can give.[7]

One can only conclude that change in South Africa's sport policy is primarily a charade. It is founded on the separatist doctrine that seeks to cast nonwhites out of South African society. It is true, as the liberal whites in South Africa argue, that wider opportunities have been opened for competition with whites, but the fundamental inequality remains. Black athletes cannot receive the kind of recognition, rewards, and importance they would gain in multiracial societies, because they cannot join the clubs, play in the major contests, and receive salaries available to whites in the professional category.

The effect of the international sports campaign to boycott South Africa cannot be said to have succeeded, for the essential class and caste discrimination remain. But the boycott keeps up internal pressure on the South Africans to eliminate the major restrictions. Insofar as there has been any progress at all, it has been as a result of the boycott. Those athletes who refuse to compete in South Africa are expressing solidarity with the silent majority. The boycott validates the action of the Olympics Committee and the International Amateur Athletic Federation in banning South Africa.[8] Discrimination is demonstrated to be a costly policy for South Africa to follow and for those who persist in playing with apartheid.

Cultural Exchange

The refusal of popular singers, musicians, actors, and scholars to visit, tour, and work in South Africa has had considerable impact on the decision to abandon strict racial segregation fof visiting cultural representatives. Since the 1970s, black Americans can travel in South Africa, stay in white hotels, and eat in some of their restaurants. Even certain intellectual events of an international nature take place in nonsegregated facilities.

Liberal and progressive South Africans have praised these changes as a step forward. They point out that international pressure can be thanked for forcing the government to recognize that it must drop the frustrating barriers of "petty apartheid."

On the surface of it, there would appear to be a stronger case for cultural exchange than for sports, because this could lead to the increased knowledge and therefore power position of the nonwhite community. The issue has been debated in several different ways by the British African Studies Association, which has rejected a boycott proposal, and the (American) African Studies Association, especially as it effects long-term academic and scientific appointments.

The exile organizations are very clear that exchange strengthens the apartheid system. They continue to advocate boycott. Led by C. P. Snow, authors in England have signed a pledge not to perform or allow their works to be performed in South Africa. They argue that, although a boycott does work a hardship on many young nonwhite intellectuals unable to travel abroad, yet there are several considerations that make a boycott worthwhile. Works and publications are censored so that only those ideas considered harmless are circulated. Long-term appointments of scholars to South African institutions help a segregated system to survive. Although many white anti-apartheid academic and cultural groups feel strengthened by these visits, most of their membership is able to travel abroad and hence are not dependent on visits for such "strengthening." Moreover, the South African government has clearly used the visits of prominent white critics, blacks, and Africans to demonstrate that détente is working; therefore, the foreign visitor may be unwittingly contributing to the credibility of the South African government's policy. This was what happened when the president-elect of the African Studies Association (ASA) visited South Africa in the spring of 1975. This tour led to a thorough review of ASA's policy on contacts and official visits. It was finally concluded that such visits must be weighed with an eye to their possible use by South Africa in justification of its contacts and détente policy.[9]

The South African government is engaged in a struggle of psychological warfare to maintain its legitimacy in the West and to assert a new legitimacy, on the basis of internal reforms, with the new states of Africa and Asia. If cultural and political leaders, especially those known for their opposition, visit South Africa or invite South Africans to the Western world, the abolitionists fear a process of legitimizing and acceptance can take over.[10] Thus, a policy of boycott finds support in the black-consciousness movement in South Africa, as well as among supporters of the liberation movements.

Cultural exchange, however, is pushed by liberal whites and the Bantustan chiefs, who use their contacts abroad to exert leverage on the government for change at home. They are prone to exaggerate the significance of these exchanges. The basic framework of discriminatory education and cultural opportunities has been unaffected by exchange. The real revolutionary advocates are not permitted in or out of South Africa.

The one point of agreement between the internal reformers and the external abolitionists is that study and travel abroad by South Africans of all races should be facilitated in order to mature their anti-apartheid consciousness. Even the Verkrampte ("Conservative") Afrikaners are mellowed by such an experience, and most blacks and nonwhites, if they return, are better equipped mentally, spiritually, and professionally to resist. However, those who make it abroad should not be considered the true representatives of South African opinion, and the host institutions abroad should be wary of those who come as propagandists for the South African government.

It should be particularly noted that African liberation representatives in the transnational movement have never opposed all contacts.[11] Those contacts that facilitate revolutionary ideas and programs are warmly encouraged. The revolutionary value of certain programs such as the education of black South African students abroad is a top priority. However the exile organizations have criticized any visits to South Africa that do not have a useful revolutionary purpose, such as collecting information, giving aid to the victims of oppression, and strengthening resistance.[12]

The black-consciousness groups in South Africa have also asked for limited contacts, with the full realization of the way in which the South African government uses them in psychological warfare.[13] They have been eager to visit the United States and the United Kingdom, and the opportunity for some of the regime's critics to travel abroad has strengthened contact between internal and external anti-apartheid groups.[14]

The Arms Embargo

Considerable liberal and progressive white opinion in South Africa, especially among the churches, supports the arms embargo against South Africa. They are unhappy about the rapid expansion of the military budget and resist the demands of the military for possible "unjust wars." Favorable opinion about the arms ban arose among Africans as well. But the right-wing and government reaction is to build "self-sufficiency," a nuclear capability, and to establish new strategies of interdependence with NATO and the American and British interests in the Indian Ocean.

The Afrikaner government and English-speaking establishment is furious with the United Nations and the anti-apartheid movement, which they consider to be the cat's-paw of Communism in weakening the Western strategy in southern Africa and the Cape. South African military spokesmen discount the influence of the ban, but privately diplomats go to great lengths to find ways of bypassing it. The basic South African policy is to strengthen ties with the Western powers. The arms supply from the West is regarded as more of an assurance of continuing Western support than a military necessity. When the British Conservative government came into office in 1970, the South Africans lost no time in attempting to reestablish military shipments.

South African whites are very confident that they can obtain all their defense needs from Western countries such as France and West Germany, even if the arms embargo should be tightened by the United States and the United Kingdom to include paramilitary equipment.[15] Moreover, they believe they will, by the 1980s, be producing virtually all of their own equipment. The development of tactical nuclear weapons will be well advanced by that stage.

Self-sufficiency, however, is impossible and therefore much of this is psychological warfare, as they recognize their basic reliance on the Atlantic powers for defense against a communist power. During the Angola war, the South African press expressed a good deal of alarm over their country's vulnerability. The intervention of Cuban troops with Russian weapons in Angola in 1975-76 brought a direct clash with the South African troops and the first serious losses for the South African army on their own continent since World War II. The order to mobilize and create a "no-man's land" along the northern border of Namibia indicated the seriousness of the situation to the South African military. In addition, the growing "naval threat" of the Soviet Union in the Indian Ocean, as perceived by South Africa, has led to a strong campaign on their part to involve the Western naval powers, especially the United States, in defense of the South African strategic position.[16] The arms embargo could impede the kind of aid they believe they need to confront communist powers. They especially see their own navy incapable of defending their long coast,[17] and therefore the arms embargo seems aimed at maintaining that weakness.[18]

In 1975-76 they almost doubled their expenditures of the 1974-75 military budget to over $1 billion and have increased the mobilization of the white population into reserve units. Their great weakness is manpower, and they intend to meet this by expanding the use of the Coloured corps. In 1974, they began the training of an African combat corps which will do supply and guard duty and is trained in the use of firearms, which they carry while on guard duty. The use of Africans and Coloureds in the armed forces as combat units and the training of officers is a reform which might be said to be related to the overall attempt to show critics that changes are being made. However, the realities of South Africa's long border with African states and the prospects of warfare with guerrilla armies is a better explanation.

The chief reaction to external anti-apartheid military pressures from the West is to substitute informal for formal relations. Earlier formal relationships have been progressively abandoned by the United States and the United Kingdom—i.e., visits of naval units to South Africa by the Americans and the British Labour government's decision to give up the Simonstown base agreement. There are extensive reports of the attempt by South Africa to encourage greater integration of the South African defense system with NATO.[19] Visits by South Africans to Washington and by American Congressmen to South Africa in 1975 were attempts to gain greater American response to the needs of defense of South Africa within the wider context of the Indian Ocean.[20] The vast importance of psychological warfare to South Africa in the struggle against the threats of guerrillas and the Russians is well understood by the South African military, and the arms embargo is a ticking time bomb to their security.[21]

South African church groups, especially the South African Council of Churches and the Catholics, have strongly opposed the military buildup of the South African government. Like their counterparts in Europe, many churchmen are pacifist and nonviolent and oppose what they see as the growth of a military solution. A part of this reaction was the celebrated statement of the South African Council of Churches in July 1974, which held there was no automatic obligation of Christians to serve the warfare of the state. Despite pressure, the council refused to recant. One of the more progressive groups, the Christian Institute, was later declared "an affected organization" and deprived of funds from abroad, because of its activities including the SPROCAS studies. The Christian Institute has been both a courageous critic of militarism and an advocate of radical change in South Africa.

Even the moderate Bantustan leaders see South Africa's military power as a danger to them. They are fearful that retaliation might be taken against an African state for assisting the guerrilla armies and that they will be caught in the middle of any conflict that ensues.

There is a tremendous sympathy in Botswana for the international campaign against selling arms to South Africa and the often-expressed wish that it could be made compulsory. Botswana has consistently supported the arms embargo while Lesotho and Swaziland generally abstain, but do not vote against it. During the early 1970s, the brief renaissance of African and nonwhite opinion known as the Black Consciousness Movement (SASO, the Black Peoples Convention, and workers' groups like the Black Allied Workers Union) spoke for a large and silent black population which favors the arms embargo. Many of these leaders are now under detention or banned: Steve Biko, former president of SASO, Strini Moodley, Drake Koka and Aubrey Bokonena of the BPC, and dozens of others were listed by the Programme for Social Change in Braamfontein in December 1974. I happened to visit South Africa just at the time this black consciousness was beginning to get underway and spoke with several of its leaders. At that time, they expressed strong support for the international arms embargo and sanctions against South Africa. Their attitude regarding the arms buildup was that South Africa intends to use these weapons in the repression of rebellion at home as well as against invading liberation movements. South Africa has not hesitated to use weapons against African states which give support to guerrilla armies, justifying the action as "hot pursuit." The Black Peoples Convention condemned foreign support for the military strength of their oppressors: "Foreign investors by strengthening the economy of the Fascist regime make it possible for the minority regime of South Africa to strengthen its military force which is designed for perpetual oppression of Black people."[22]

The liberation leaders in exile have been foremost in pressing for a full and compulsory arms embargo against South Africa, since they regard it as both a propaganda and practical weapon in their struggle. Thus it is possible to conclude that there is a wide basis of support within South Africa and among South Africans in exile for a compulsory universal arms ban against their government. This ranges from the moderate liberal church opinion of the whites to the black peoples and nationalist movements. The support given this arms embargo by transnational movements is a source of much hope to these various groups. Only a part of the white minority in South Africa opposes it. The vast majority of South Africans could be said, without stretching the facts, to be strongly in favor of the arms embargo.

The most sophisticated reaction to the question of the arms embargo is South African psychological warfare, which reveals that the South African military does not really believe that the crucial battles will be fought by armies, but that their counterinsurgency campaign must take into account public opinion, morale, and the long-term attrition and economic measures employed by revolutionary groups. Taking a lesson from Vietnam, General Fraser stated:

Revolutionary war differs fundamentally from conventional wars of the past in that victory does not come from the clash of two armies in the field of battle. . . . Instead these wars are conducted by the revolutionaries (and the government in power—if they have learned how) as a carefully orchestrated dialectic consisting of a series of actions, political, administrative, economic, psychological, supported by military action. (The government has the added advantage of police and believe me they play an enormously important role, both their uniformed and particularly their security branches. They get involved before soldiers do and remain on long after our task is done.)[23]

Both the revolutionaries and the reactionaries realize that the arms-embargo issue is primarily a battle for public opinion. As dangerous as they are, most of the arms which South Africa is currently stockpiling can never be brought to bear in the decisive struggles for the sympathy and support of various groups not only in South Africa but throughout the Western world. And in this struggle, the revolutionaries, through the transnational anti-apartheid movement and their support at the United Nations, are far ahead.

The South Africans however, have a major ploy regarding their strategic position in the Indian Ocean arms race. An article in the *Africa Institute Bulletin* summarized their sense of indispensable role:

Apart from the fact that South Africa is the guardian of the Cape Sea Route, her strategic situation on the waterway and her economic development means that the Republic provides important facilities to vessels plying the Route. She is, for instance, an important supplier of oil for bunkering purposes and also provides the only major repair and rescue facilities available in a wide arc of the Indian and South Atlantic Oceans.[24]

While the decision of the British Labour government to end the Simonstown Agreement upset this conception of their role, the South African government continues to argue they are vital in the transit of peaceful commerce around the Cape and essential in an emergency confrontation between the Great Powers.

The South African government has correctly perceived the sense of a new threat in the United Kingdom and the United States to their energy supplies from the Persian Gulf states, which transit by large tanker, even after the opening of the Suez Canal, around the Cape. They have played upon the fears of strategists that somehow these supply lines might be cut by a major naval power, such as the Soviet Union. The Russian entry into the region raised "the threat level" for the American Congress and the British military.

The South African Foreign Minister, Cornelius Mulder, visited the United States in 1974 and again in 1975 and convinced a number of Administration and Congressional officials that South Africa could play a larger role. Since that visit, there has been an attempt by the American Secretary of Defense to establish a major monitoring installation on Russian ship movements in South Africa. At the May 1975 NATO meeting, the Dutch, Norwegian, and Danish ministers objected, and the Dutch even threatened to exclude NATO from Rotterdam if the step were taken.[25]

The South African argument that they alone can guarantee the safety of shipping around the Cape influenced defense strategy in the Ford Administration. Melvin Laird said in South Africa that the United States might favor the repeal of the arms embargo. This was pure propaganda for the benefit of South African whites, but it showed the sympathy for their views in high circles in Washington.

In England, the military has long been persuaded of the force of the Cape route argument discussed in Chapter 5. The British decision to allow the Simonstown Agreement to lapse does not change their basic agreement to use South African facilities.

If the American and British governments became fully convinced that their oil supplies depended in some measure on South Africa, this could could be used to develop a pro-South African sentiment in Congress and Parliament comparable to the Rhodesian chrome issue (which was strategic in its initial form). It could provide a major backfire to the arms-embargo pressures from the anti-apartheid forces. This is the goal of the more subtle South African strategists, who recognize that the real threat to them is not the Russian navy but the sympathy the liberation movements are gaining in important official and nonofficial circles in the West.

Some South African whites argue that South Africa is being forced into a nuclear capability by the arms embargo. Others believe that South Africa must develop these weapons because of her position and responsible role in preserving the Western outpost, since she now has the capability to develop these ultimate weapons. Others would agree with Jack Spence that she has remained nonnuclear out of deference to the attitudes of her Great Power friends. But this is more a public stance than an actuality. Indeed, the limited success of the arms-embargo campaign has increased the internal white pressure for nuclear arms.

The South Africans would probably be reluctant to use tactical nuclear weapons, which are very clumsy antiguerrilla devices because they affect civilian populations and those who use them, but the anti-apartheid movement does not underestimate the ferocity and final ruthlessness that an Afrikaner regime is likely to show if it believes the war and civilization are being lost. The threat to use ultimate force, if they have their backs to the wall is probably supported by most white South Africans.

The Liberation Support Campaign

Among the whites in South Africa, this has probably aroused the greatest opposition, since it constitutes in part the direct use of force and revolution. The African view on liberation movements is clearly mixed and very guarded on the part of those who support liberation—or "the terrorists" as they are called in South Africa.

It should be noted that a significant number of liberal, socialist, and Christian whites in South Africa have supported the liberation movements, both before and after they became revolutionary in the early sixties. These whites are the core of the abolitionists among the South Africans, and most have paid a heavy price for their convictions and activities. Many, such as Leslie Rubin, Joel Carlson, and Ronald Segal, have been forced into exile, and are participating abroad in anti-apartheid activity. Joel Carlson, after defending Winnie Mandela, was persecuted by the right wing, who bombed his home and shot up his car. He left one jump ahead of the security police. Others like Ruth First left after a term of prison, and a few chose to remain in prison, among them Bram Fischer. After his arrest in 1964, Fischer, a lawyer, left South Africa on bail to try a case before the Privy Council and then, after an agonizing decision, returned not to face trial but into the underground of the ANC revolutionaries. After a year, he was caught and imprisoned for life.[26] Other young South African whites formed their own underground sabotage groups. Hugh Lewin spent five years in prison before he was allowed to go into exile, and a less fortunate colleague, John Harris, went to his death in the Central Prison in Pretoria, singing hymns with his fellow prisoners.

These white abolitionists paid an immense price to oppose apartheid tyranny. Most of the white revolutionaries were either intimidated or eliminated by the police by the end of the sixties. However, they still exist, especially among the young. In 1975, after the FRELIMO demonstration, several young whites were among those arrested and tried.[27]

The gradualist whites in the anti-apartheid movement are allowed casionally arrested or banned. They often pay dearly for this opposition; their livelihood may be taken away or a threat made against their families, and they may be put on trial. External criticism of their conformity, when made from the security of relatively democratic societies, is often unfair. They lead precarious and quietly courageous lives, working in close association with African, Coloured, and Indian groups, within a police state which can turn on them at any moment.

Many South Africans, especially Anglican priests, while not supporting violence, have risked a great deal in providing assistance to the families of the victims of police repression and imprisonment. Dignitaries of the Anglican Church in South Africa have been prosecuted for cooperating with the banned organization Defence and Aid, for distributing assistance of this kind is considered subversive. The Reverend Gonville Ffrench-Beytagh, who was Dean of Johannesburg, was arrested under South Africa's terrorism act, tried, and convicted. He left, after the conviction was quashed, though he denied all the charges. The Dean stated after his departure: "To the end of my life, I shall probably be in doubt as to whether or not I was right to leave South Africa. The fact remains that I must do what I can from outside the country which I love and which I still feel is my home, in bringing about change within it."[28]

There are a great many unsung anti-apartheid heroes among the whites, such as the ladies of the Black Sash League, some of whom have paid heavy penalties under the banning orders of the government. Their lives have been disrupted, vocations lost, and friends gone, because they would not compromise with what French-Beytagh called "utterly irrational and utterly evil" policies.

However, the anti-apartheid movement left within South Africa among the whites is, on the whole, hostile to the support given to the ANC and the PAC by the movement abroad. The response of several Christian groups to the WCC actions of support for liberation movements was one of dismay. Laurance Gandar, who was a former editor of the *Rand Daily Mail,* summed up the reaction of the reformers, in discussing strategy: "Calls for boycotts and blockades and sending aid for the guerrilla movements may help to relieve pent-up indignation of well wishers at the manifest injustices of apartheid; but they seem destined to remain fruitless gestures."[29]

There are a number of African political leaders who agree with the white reformers and oppose the liberation solution. Some of these, like Chief Buthelezi, have become officials of the new Bantustans.[30] A few of these chiefs directly criticize the liberation movements. Such a person is Chief Lucas Mangope, Chief Minister of Bophuthatswana, with whom I spoke in London during a conference in 1970. I was startled to hear from the black chief the admission that he supported apartheid and that separation from the whites, whom he obviously detested, was the best solution for his people. Chief Buthelezi, on the other hand, has only indirectly criticized the ANC, of which he formerly was a leader. He modestly states that he believes his people must have a spokesman since they were without a voice after the banning of the ANC and the PAC. He is an advocate of a nonviolent approach to protest and lives in daily fear that he has transgressed the undefined boundary line and will be arrested. He described such a fear to me in December 1971, when he said the Minister of Native Affairs told him he had come very close to arrest. His power is intangible, resting on the South African government's awareness that his arrest would jeopardize their entire "outward policy" as well as the Bantustan schemes. Chief Buthelezi is one of the black leaders who participated in a multi-racial project calling for reform in South Africa, the Study Project on Christianity in Apartheid Society (SPROCAS), which included some of the most progressive intellectuals and reformers in the country.[31]

The ANC and PAC both claim extensive sympathy and support in South Africa for their activities. And they argue that they keep the hope alive for millions of their people that one day there will be an alternative.[32] Undoubtedly, there is immense latent support for people like Nelson Mandela who is in prison for life but still remains the leader of the ANC. The South African official denials that these people have any latent support within South Africa are, the revolutionaries believe, "the self-serving lies of tyrants." Because the leadership has been imprisoned or driven out of the country does not mean the loss of support. The Black Consciousness Movement among students and workers was one small reflection of this. The movement was based on a race consciousness. It was allowed to flourish because it fitted temporarily into the government's scheme of separate communities and of demonstrating reform. But like the Let a Hundred Flowers Bloom doctrine of Mao, the dissent was short-lived.[33]

The arrests began with a number of young people of all races, following the pro-FRELIMO rally at Currie Fountain in Durban in September 1974 and their detention without trial. Brutal treatment by police brought to an end an alleged new freedom for black political expression in South Africa. On 10 November 1974, a petition was delivered to the Prime Minister, signed by seven hundred persons, calling for the release of the detainees. *X-Ray* published a list of the detainees but no official charge had been made public against many of those held.[34] Presumably they were suspected of being supporters of the liberation movements, and the police, by brutal methods, attempted to find out who was involved. The security police are far more concerned than political leaders about the extent of potential support for the exiled and imprisoned leaders.

From September 1974 through 1975, subsequent waves of arrests took place, often of persons who had nothing to do with the rally at Currie Fountain. This indicated that the police were out to silence and end the entire Black Consciousness Movement and were tracing down leads obtained from earlier arrests. As of July 1975, only thirteen had been brought to trial, and at least another twenty-five were being held without trial.[35]

It is obviously impossible to measure accurately the degree of support for the liberation movements. One indicator widely used by liberation leaders and theorists is the spread of a class consciousness and a workers' strike movement, which they regard as closely associated with their own ends. The strikes of the seventies are part of a long history of working-class struggle, which is again part of the industrialization of South Africa, and an inevitably growing resistance movement, which will one day paralyze whole sections of industry and weaken the system of white dominance so that the revolution can take place.[36]

Repression of the Black Consciousness Movement contributed to the student and workers' strikes of 1976 in Soweto, Capetown, and other urban centers. On several days the strikes were 75-80 percent effective.[37] Parents were radicalized by their children, who braved police guns to protest against the hated separation-of-races policy. Moderate spokesmen warned that the actions of the youth expressed the bitter hostility of the African majority.[38] The ANC and the PAC assisted the strikes with pamphlets and demonstrations. However, the radicalized youth seemed to be more influenced by their own resentments against white rule than outside political stimulation. Nothing short of drastic change in racial laws could alter African antagonism and resistance, the moderate spokesmen stated. Police killed scores of schoolchildren, arrested thousands, and incited African tribesmen (Zulus) to attack demonstrators. Inevitably, these unorganized uprisings were crushed. Yet, they clearly showed the depth of passionate opposition, even among the so-called Westernized elite, whom many observers had assumed had been assimilated. The widely circulated belief that African nationalists no longer believed in the objectives of the liberation movements was clearly repudiated by the militant behavior of the demonstrators, who shouted slogans and used tactics long advocated by the exiled leaders. Demands for the release of imprisoned liberation leaders like Nelson Mandela intensified. An entire generation of African youth, despite their "Bantu education" and the intimidation of the total system, had grown up committed to the objectives of the liberation movements. Obviously, neither force by the police nor the mild reforms offered were going to change their admiration for the achievements of MPLA, FRELIMO, and the Zimbabwe freedom fighters.

Détente

The South African "détente," meaning accommodation with black African states, is a policy devised to counter anti-apartheid pressures. Détente is a shrewd deception—impressive but without substance. There has been a concerted attempt to show the world that reformism is working, that change is taking place, and therefore the outside world should not yield to the pressures of the terrorists but give South Africa "time." From the so-called reform of "petty apartheid" to the passports for Bantustan leaders, the contacts policy with the West, to the dialogue and détente campaigns with the African states, there has been a well-planned attempt to sell a new image of a South Africa changing and moving away from apartheid to separate development and multinationalism.

This effort began with the outward policy in 1970 when Vorster and Muehler attempted to make diplomatic contact with black Africa.[39] The independent African states of Botswana, Lesotho, and Swaziland were created and diplomatic ties set up with Malawi. From this they moved to dialogue over Namibia, which was shot down by the opposition of African states at the United Nations as we have observed. Now détente has made heavy inroads with official and reformist nongovernment opinion in Western countries.[40] The Black Consciousness Movement, which was clearly only tolerated in South Africa as long as it did not become a serious center of opposition, was widely lauded in the Western world. Then the elimination of "petty apartheid" was employed to show tangible and beneficial reforms were being instituted, which would lead on to greater changes if South Africa was given time and the reformers were respected abroad. The new Bantustan African leaders were selected to play a key role in this strategy. It was their function to talk to Africans and to blacks and to persuade them that peaceful change was taking place. The Buthelezis and Sebes undoubtedly realized what the whites were attempting to do but chose to play their roles in order to express their grievances more freely and to reach a wider audience inside and outside. Their role became glaringly apparent as détente turned to repression at home and direct aggression in Angola and Namibia.

Following the collapse of the Portuguese empire, South Africa's Prime Minister, in his famous Parliamentary détente speech, asked for time: "Give us six months and you will be amazed at what South Africa can do." The South African policy did shift to one of accepting "westernized" African rule in Rhodesia and Namibia, as buffer states in which African moderates, together with whites, were to hold off "the extremists and communists."[4] This was called the "voice of reason" initially by Kaunda and Nyerere, who responded in a conciliatory manner in order to facilitate negotiations with South Africa over Zimbabwe and Namibia.

However, the South African ANC strongly opposed any moderation of the total ostracism of South African policy. The OAU Council of Ministers, meeting in Dar es Salaam, sought to reassure them. They made it clear that there would be no compromise with racism, and that this, as Vorster himself had earlier put it, was not negotiable. Dialogue could only be initiated by changes such as the release of Nelson Mandela.[42]

The progressive chiefs in South Africa, especially Sebe and Buthelezi, have tried to turn Vorster's détente on himself by arguing no accommodation with the black African states was possible unless apartheid and the wrongs of separate development were abolished. They pointed to this as the repeated message they received in African capitals. As Sebe put it:

The challenge of getting South Africa accepted in Africa lies in the pro-Western climate of Nigeria and Zaire. Towards this end, South Africa's own people are her most effective ambassadors in Black Africa. They hold the key. . . . South Africa will have to succeed in her internal white-black relations if the door to Africa is to be opened. . . . If whites are not prepared to share South Africa will land itself in bloody confrontation and anarchy.[43]

South African détente has aimed also at bringing a settlement in Rhodesia and Namibia, and an African acceptance of the Transkei. The policy has produced negotiations over Zimbabwe and Namibia, but the fundamentals of separate development and racial privilege in South Africa are still nonnegotiable. And the prospect that Vorster will concede more to the liberation pressure is limited drastically by the hard right wing Verkrampte opposition.

The Sanctions Response

The split in South African opinion over the sanctions campaign has paralleled closely the liberation issue with the whites. Reformist whites, generally, have opposed economic disengagement and a large and ambiguous nonwhite opinion favors disinvestment pressures on South Africa.

The whites have taken the sanctions campaign very seriously, especially the government and the business community.[44] The reason is probably that the issue strikes at the heart of the question of reform and change. The government and most whites believe very emphatically that change is taking place, slowly and correctly. Some of the more liberal have seized on the opportunity to show that change was not taking place rapidly enough and urged that the pace be stepped up.[45] The more liberal businessmen have pressed the cause of wage-and-employment reforms on behalf of the nonwhites as a demonstration of the importance of growth and improved race relations. This has resulted in a number of improvements for blacks in industry, but just how significant these improvements are has become the issue.

The old debate of the standard-of-living gap between Africans and whites has been opened within South Africa, but with far fewer experts ready to state publicly the reasons why the gap is widening, since the subject has become dangerously sensitive politically.[46]

There are almost no white South Africans who are prepared to maintain publicly that economic disengagement would be a good way of pressuring for change in the situation in South Africa. The reason is undoubtedly that most of those left in South Africa are genuine reformists, who see gradual change as the only alternative that makes any sense, as put to me by the director of the Institute on Race Relations, who courageously hosted my visit to South Africa in 1971: "We want economic change, and political change will follow." Those like Don Morton, a United Methodist Minister who opposed the investment thesis, were forced out of the country. Morton simply could not remain and stay out of prison.[47] The government has banned investigatory research of businesses in this area.

There have been warnings, however, from numerous sensitive areas of research in South Africa. The SPROCAS study was very pessimistic about the growing alienation of urban Africans and the conditions of life for migratory workers. The breakdown of African family life in urban areas, fostering high rates of crime, was noted years ago by one of the centers of Afrikaner thought in the Dutch Reformed Church.[48]

The studies of the conditions in the reserves, where African workers are frequently dumped by authorities in order to lessen the pressures in the cities, have also been a strong storm signal. Such studies indicate that, because some progress has been made by a privileged elite in the manufacturing areas, this should not be taken to mean that the basic adverse trends of population growth and poverty were being offset. The banning of Cosmas Desmond for publishing *The Discarded People*[49] exemplified the way the South African government attempted to avoid the issues leading to the Soweto explosion and other urban uprisings in mid-1976. The initial issue of protest against the compulsory study by secondary students of Afrikaans rather than English was only the match which lighted the kindling. Laurence Schlemmer's findings about the psychological alienation of black youths, first published in 1968, have not been banned but ignored.[50]

Surprising support for the gradualists came from several Bantustan leaders. Buthelezi, in particular, lent himself to the propaganda campaign of the South African government, in their expensive overseas advertisements. He also has debated with disinvestors overseas and actively sought to convince the anti-apartheid movement that it should expand investments especially in the Bantustans and pressure corporations to reform, rather than force them out. Together with other chiefs, he has actively sought investment funds abroad for the Bantustans in what Buthelezi called "problem free labour resources." He is clearly convinced that the benefits to his people of economic growth in jobs, income, and influence through workers' organizations and strikes, which he had supported, outweigh the benefits of pressure from abroad for disengagement.[51] This view is widely held among the business and professional elite of Africans, Coloured, and Indians.

While the Bantustan chiefs have sought for government and private overseas aid for their own areas, they are also insistent that any such aid should be accepted only on the basis of African homeland control over development and taxation, which the government still has refused to grant them.

There are also many Africans within South Africa who welcome the prospect of economic sanctions against South Africa. Again, the accurate assessment of this simply cannot be made, and statements by the U.S. State Department and other sources that a majority are opposed to disinvestment are only speculative at best. But it is clear that the Black Consciousness Movement of the Black Peoples Convention SASO and the workers' movement favored the idea of economic sanctions and disinvestment pressures of all kinds. The Black Peoples Convention stated in 1973 at its Congress:

That this Congress noting:
  1) The vital role played by foreign investors in maintaining and supporting the economic system of South Africa.
  2) That this system is designed for maximum exploitation of Black people;
  3) That the riches and resources of this country belong to Blacks as their birthright.
  4) That foreign investors claim that their presence in this country contributes towards the development of the Black community.
  5) That this claim is disputed by the reality of the Black experience in their country.

Therefore, it resolves:
  1) To reject the involvement of foreign investors in this exploitative economic system;
  2) To call upon foreign investors to disengage themselves from their White controlled exploitative system.[52]

This view has contributed to the pressures brought to bear and the arrests without trial of many of their members. South African authorities regard such beliefs as subversive, because they contribute to revolutionary sentiments and conditions.

From a reformist or gradualist anti-apartheid view, the issue of pressure on the corporations has been very productive within South Africa. Together with the workers' strikes, it has put pressure on employers for improvements in occupations and salaries for a working elite. However, there is no convincing evidence that the gap is being closed. The contrary seems to be the case, and apartheid as a system has grown under industrialism rather than declined.[53] The public debate over the issue of disinvestment or disengagement in South Africa has been very limited indeed. The major discussion has taken place abroad. And as the outcome does influence the investment climate for South Africa, it has importance. An additional effect has been, as was suggested to me in South Africa by Africans and a few whites, that the disinvestment campaign against Western corporations gave hope to the powerless through the recognition that important outside humanitarian support groups had not forgotten them. This, in the end, was thought to be very significant in terms of keeping alive a revolutionary spirit.

Conclusions on the Transnational Revolution

The general impact of external links with the South African internal racial complex has generated immense pressures for change. The basic conclusion is that official policy has made attempts at adaptation through limited changes in "petty apartheid." A Black Consciousness and trade-union movement has been allowed to bloom briefly, followed by even more severe repression. Détente and dialogue have been tried to win African friends abroad, and the homelands policy has been presented as a nonracial solution to the needs of different ethnic groups. None of these has altered the basic stratification, the racial class system of South Africa.

The long-term-conflict forces appear well underway, and the transnational pattern of revolution has developed with a heightened black revolutionary consciousness in South Africa, i.e., Soweto rebellions and the urban strikes, an increased liberation activity abroad, and the improvement of the guerrilla geopolitical position on the Angola, Mozambique, and Zimbabwe borders.

The revolutionary option is real and is being facilitated by the abolitionist movement abroad. It is time that more people saw clearly the conflicts between the abolitionists and the gradualists and began to make some hard choices. It is not a question of whether Western citizens should be involved or not. We *are* involved, and the question is "Where do we want to place our influence as transnational persons and organizations?" Even though we may not change our government's policy, in the end the forces working for change and revolution go far beyond anything the United States or the United Kingdom can control. The racists of South Africa are an anachronism. They have shown no real capacity to adjust to the fundamental changes that are obviously accepted as the wave of the future by a vast majority of South Africans as well as the outside world.

To attempt to predict the future is like playing a dice game in the dark, as Alan Paton once put it. No one can say exactly how the end of apartheid will come, but we can only be certain that apartheid will lapse into history one day as slavery has done before it, as an evil and utterly uncondonable way of life.

One of the agonies that Americans and British have to bear is the knowledge that our own governments have failed to join in the abolition of apartheid and, in fact, aid and abet its continuance. However, as white men or black men, business men or professors, modern communciations make it possible to act as human beings across the barriers of state and culture to give assistance to those who struggle and die. This solidarity is not a vain venting of conscience but live human acts of great importance to the final outcome. We know that all freedom is relative and that when this great liberation comes, it will be only one step in the historical emancipation of the black man and ourselves. Yet it will be one of the great days of the human race.

That day will come much sooner if we understand that there is nothing to be gained by continuing the illusion of permanent power for the white men in South Africa. The choice of freedom and justice is in favor of maximizing pressure through ostracism and sanctions. This will lead to a breakdown of the social order and a new framework in which reconciliation of extremes and a new society can be built.

It is to be hoped that the United States and the United Kingdom will find their way to official support of this program. But this has been demonstrated to be unlikely. In fact, they may both become more involved, as they have elsewhere, in direct and open counterrevolution because of the immense economic interests and security illusions.

The task of the abolitionists for some period of time will probably be to cut back and limit the amounts of official and unofficial assistance that are supplied to the South African racists. The supply of arms and paramilitary technical assistance must be persistently exposed and opposed. As long as there are attractive profits to be had, it will be difficult to prevent the multinationals, from several points in the world, from supplying investment funds. But as the economic position of South Africa changes and weakens in the world economy, the investment of capital will be slowed, deprived of subsidy, and restricted against certain practices.

As the struggle deepens, it will be important for NGOs to interpret the liberation goals to the public, who will be subjected to increasing pressures from the South African whites and their sympathizers.

The wider result of this study is the demonstration that the nongovernmental actor plays a major role, with more significant results in influencing conflict situations and international systems than has generally been understood.

In the case of South Africa, NGOs have been indispensable in developing alternative ideas, facts, and policies at the national and international level. They have played active roles themselves in bringing new resources and ideas into various conflicts. The objectives of these groups are sometimes in conflict as in the case of the gradualists who advocate investment in South Africa and the abolitionist movements who want to disengage all Western activities from the country. However, they do not cancel each other out. The controversy and dialogue has led to a reconsideration of their role by many actors, a raising of the level of the issue, and the prospect of more extensive NGO involvement.

The transnational actor has played a revolutionary role and a conciliatory one within the internal-external system, in the case of South Africa. Some are reformist and believe that South African society can be transformed in time to make a transition to peaceful coexistence if not multiracial cooperation. The gradualists have had an important part in persuading many groups, including some high government officials, that reform is imperative if they are to stay afloat in the stormy seas around the Cape. The revolutionaries are convinced that only the overthrow of the Afrikaners by pressure and force will bring the kind of condition in which conciliation can then be implemented.

In the long run, in some conflict situations the transnational actors for change can actually be more influential and effective than the super powers, because they are not encumbered by the system. The immense impact of a Great Power's policy is frequently overestimated, because of the undue weight given to violence and force in international conciliation, which in revolutionary situations is at most limited.

The long run has to be weighed against the short run. This case of South Africa especially shows how the incremental influence of humanitarian-assistance groups can be of great importance in the growth of forces which might otherwise be defeated or take many more years to achieve their objectives. Over the years, the abolitionist idea has grown irresistibly, gathering consciousness and force among a broad global coalition. Western governments may well continue to support the apartheid superstructure. But its collapse has already begun and will continue until the persistent nongovernmental actors, along with the liberation movements, secure fundamental change.

Western analysis has been especially inaccurate in predicting and assessing this process, because of its bias in favor of stability, and its empathy for the status quo. We have now to revise our notions of the wisdom of the elites, the supremacy of Western states, and the nature of power itself. If we are interested in both understanding the course of events, especially in the Third World, and playing an active role ourselves, research on the nongovernmental actors is as indispensable as knowledge of the role of the governmental actors. This is more the case in the Third World, where the structures of official policy are less pervasively fused with the unofficial. The small and inconspicuous activities of some NGOs has yielded results of immense international significance. Sorting out the significant from the insignificant and showing its relationship to changing events and major policies are difficult tasks and much of them remains to be done. Often the significance of major events and movements of history remain unknown to their contemporary observers, like members of the crowd who watched Jesus on the cross. The official policies of the United States and other Western powers may well be bypassed by events Westerners neither understand nor control. Nevertheless, the American and British democracies have been major contributors to the human-rights movement. This anti-apartheid victory, when it comes, will be a step forward for all humanity, proving again that ideals can transcend the transitory lives of men and the dangerous pride of those who lead nations.

Notes

1. See Ralph Horowitz, "South Africa: the Background to Sanctions," *Political Quarterly,* April-June 1971, pp. 165-76. He opposes economic sanctions while accepting sport and cultural boycotts.

2. The author was refused entry in 1973, after a two-month delay. Others have been permitted limited access, restricted to certain places and times.

3. Lawrence Schlemmer, *Social Change and Political Policy in South Africa,* Institute of Social Research (Durban: University of Natal, 1970), has provided useful data but no clear guide to black South African attitudes. Other useful surveys of black opinion have been made by the Institute of Race Relations and SPROCAS.

4. David de Villiers, *The Case for South Africa* (London: Stacey, 1970), Ralph Horowitz, "South Africa: the Background to Sanctions," and *The Political Economy of South Africa* (London: Widenfeld-Nicolson, 1961).

5. Interview with Dennis Brutus, Denver, 7 May 1975. His viewpoint was substantiated by a statement from the Black Peoples Convention (BPC) and the South African Student Organization (SASO). See *The New York Times,* 8 October 1976.

6. The South African Committee for Fairness in Sport launched a campaign of international advertising to demonstrate this new multi-racialism, *African News,* Durham, N.C., November 1974.

7. Dennis Brutus, in a comment on a panel at the ASA,San Francisco, 1975, criticized Arthur Ashe and his Black Tennis Foundation for cooperating with the system. He used the example of a promising black tennis player who was forced to accept inferior coaching within the separate sports program.

8. By a vote of 227 to 145, the International Amateur Athletic Federation expelled the Amateur Athletic Union of South Africa, making permanent the year-to-year suspensions, *The New York Times,* 23 July 1976.

9. ASA Bulletin, September-October 1975.

10. During my visit to South Africa, this theme of exchange was constantly raised by spokesmen for Verlichte, liberals, and race-relations specialists.

11. John Matshikiza, "Intensify the Cultural Boycott," *Sechaba,* June-July 1975.

12. Interview with Oliver Tambo, president ANC. July 1973.

13. SASO is opposed to whites filling positions which might otherwise be filled by blacks: SASO press release, 5 March 1973.

14. Ibid.

15. Interviews in South Africa with military and business representatives confirmed this outward display of self-confidence and even ridicule of the United Nations and its bans.

16. *Report,* 1974, South African Institute of Race Relations, p. 37.

17. David Hirschmann, "Southern African Voting Patterns in the UN Assembly," 1971-72, South African Institute of International Affairs, occasional papers, August 1973, Braamfontein, Johannesburg.

18. Interview with Dr. Fourie, University of South Africa, December 1973.

19. Dr. Muller in *The Guardian,* 21 October 1970. Larry Bowman reports on these in *United States Policy for Africa,* edited by A. Arkhurst (New York: Praeger, 1975), p. 148. The association of NATO with the Advocaat installation in Silvermine has been discussed.

20. In a return visit, Congressman Bob Wilson, leading a group of American Congressmen, praised South Africa as a fortress of civilization. *Anti-Apartheid News,* 20 November 1975.

21. Lieutenant General C. A. Fraser, "The Strategy of the Revolutionary." The South African Institute of International Affairs, occasion papers, 11 December 1969, Braamfontein, Johannesburg.

22. Black Peoples Convention, Resolutions of the National Congress of the BPC, at St. Peters Seminary, mimeographed. Haminanskvaal, 16-17 December 1972.

23. Fraser, op. cit.

24. *Bulletin of the African Institute of South Africa,* No. 2, 1975.

25. *Star,* Johannesburg, 24 May 1975.

26. See the report of Fischer's death in *Anti-Apartheid News,* June 1975.

27. *X-Ray,* March-April 1975 and "Program for Social Justice Reports," 18 April 1975, Jorissen Saint Braamfontein, South Africa. Reprinted by IUEF Geneva. Mimeographed.

28. *The Observer,* 22 April 1973.

29. *The Guardian,* March 1973.

30. "South Africa—the Black Man's View," *The Times* (London), 26 May 1973.

31. See Peter Randall, *A Taste of Power,* SPROCAS Publication (Johannesburg: Raven Press, 1973).

32. Based on several interviews with ANC leaders Oliver Tambo and Alfred Nzo in London and Lusaka, and PAC of Azania leaders David Sibeko and Nana Mahone in London and New York, in 1971, 1972, and 1973.

33. Their leadership was decimated by arrest and imprisonment without trial in 1974 and again following the Soweto riots in 1976.

34. Letter from IUEF, 30 September 1975.

35. "Third Report on Arrests, Detentions and Trials." Mimeographed. Program for Social Justice, 80 Jorissen Street, Braamfontein, 1976. Reprinted IUEF, Geneva. Also see *Southern Africa,* July 1975.

36. Bernard Magubane, "The Continuing Class Struggle in South Africa," CIRR *Studies on Race and Nations,* Vol. VI, No. 4 (Denver: University of Denver, 1976).

37. *The New York Times,* John F. Burns, 24 June 1976.

38. On 21 August 1976, seven spokesmen of the homelands issued a combined statement which said in part:

Although some changes have taken place in South Africa, such as the opening of some hotels, libraries, parks and the loosening of sport policies, these are not seen by most blacks as representing fundamental changes but are seen as mere window dressing for show.

The statement blamed government failures for the violence and called for several reforms, elimination of Bantu administration boards, full human rights, permanence in urban areas, and rejection of independence through Bantustans. *Africa Report,* September-October 1976, p. 23.

In a later meeting, Prime Minister Vorster rejected all their major demands. *The New York Times,* October 9, 1976.

39. Colin Legum, *A Republic in Trouble: South Africa, 1972-73* (London: Rex Collings, 1973). Also, G. W. Shepherd, "The New South Africa," *World View,* June 1971.

40. NSSM 39, Option 2, was based on this program of communications, reform, and expanding rule for South Africa in Africa. See *The Kissinger Study of Southern Africa* (Nottingham: Spokesman Books, 1975).

41. *Bulletin,* Africa Institute, Vol. XIII (1975).

42. The OAU statement is printed in full in *Sechaba,* June-July 1975. The statement reaffirms ostracism of South Africa by the OAU, despite indications that negotiations with Vorster could take place on the basis of a real change in South African policy.

43. Chief minister of the Ciskei, L. E. Sebe, "The Key to the Door of Black Africa," *Race Relations,* Vol. 37, No. 3 (March 1975).

44. South African firms have taken advertisements in several American papers to put forward their view of the benefits of investment.

45. See Bernard Friedman, president of the South African Institute on Race Relations, speech to the 45th Council of the IRR, *Race Relations,* Vol. 37, No. 2 (February 1975).

46. *X-Ray,* March-April 1976, publishes figures showing a widening gap between blacks and whites in terms of absolute income. South Afri-

cans have undertaken extensive research on this matter, under the auspices of the Institute on Race Relations.

47. Morton, *Partners in Apartheid, A Christian Assessment* (New York: CCSA United Church of Christ, 1973).

48. Papers No. 6a and 7 of Special Commission on Race Relations, Cape Synod, Dutch Reformed Church.

49. Cosmas Desmond, a Franciscan priest, wrote *The Discarded People: An Account of the Settlement in South Africa* (London: Penguin, 1971), after several years of experience in "the homelands," witnessing the tragedy of human life under such conditions. The government banned him as a Communist and restricted his movements.

50. Lawrence Schlemmer, "The Negro Ghetto Riots and South African Cities," Johannesburg, South African Institute of Race Relations, 1968. Also see his "Employment Opportunity and Race in South Africa," CIRR, *Studies in Race and Nations,* Vol. IV, No. 3 (Denver: University of Denver, 1973).

51. Chief Buthelezi exchanged views with Dennis Brutus on this subject before the General Assembly of the United Church of Christ, U.S.A., in St. Louis, July 1972. See Morton, op. cit.

52. Resolution, Black Peoples Convention 1972, op. cit.

53. Francis Wilson, a University of Capetown economist, concludes some gains have been made among the elite, but he is not sanguine about the abolition of the color bar. See "The Political Implications for Blacks of Economic Changes Now Taking Place in South Africa," *Change in Contemporary South Africa,* edited by Leonard Thompson and Jeffry Butler (Berkeley: University of California Press, 1975), pp. 168-200.

SUBJECT INDEX

AUTHOR INDEX

About the Author

George W. Shepherd, Jr., is Professor of International and African Studies at the University of Denver's Graduate School of International Studies, as well as coeditor of *Africa Today*, and the author of many books and articles on foreign policy and African politics.

Professor Shepherd is Series Editor for the Greenwood Press series *Studies in Human Rights,* of which *Anti-Apartheid* is the third volume.